FEDERAL JUDGES
REVEALED

FEDERAL JUDGES
REVEALED

WILLIAM DOMNARSKI

OXFORD
UNIVERSITY PRESS

OXFORD
UNIVERSITY PRESS

Oxford University Press, Inc., publishes works that further Oxford University's objective of excellence in research, scholarship, and education.

Oxford New York
Auckland   Cape Town   Dar es Salaam   Hong Kong   Karachi   Kuala Lumpur   Madrid
Melbourne   Mexico City   Nairobi   New Delhi   Shanghai   Taipei   Toronto

With offices in
Argentina   Austria   Brazil   Chile   Czech Republic   France   Greece   Guatemala
Hungary   Italy   Japan   Poland   Portugal   Singapore   South Korea   Switzerland
Thailand   Turkey   Ukraine   Vietnam

Library of Congress Cataloging-in-Publication Data
Domnarski, William, 1953-
Federal judges revealed/by William Domnarski.
   p. cm.
Includes bibliographical references and index.
ISBN 978-0-19-537459-9 ((hardback) : alk. paper)
1. Judges—United States—Biography.
2. Lawyers—United States—Biography. I. Title.
KF372.D66 2008
347.73'140922—dc22
[B]
                                    2008030602

1 2 3 4 5 6 7 8 9
Printed in the United States of America on acid-free paper

Note to Readers
This publication is designed to provide accurate and authoritative information in regard to the subject matter covered. It is based upon sources believed to be accurate and reliable and is intended to be current as of the time it was written. It is sold with the understanding that the publisher is not engaged in rendering legal, accounting, or other professional services. If legal advice or other expert assistance is required, the services of a competent professional person should be sought. Also, to confirm that the information has not been affected or changed by recent developments, traditional legal research techniques should be used, including checking primary sources where appropriate.

(Based on the Declaration of Principles jointly adopted by a Committee of the American Bar Association and a Committee of Publishers and Associations.)

As before, and as always, for Kathleen, my wife, and for Colleen and Erin, our daughters

CONTENTS

INTRODUCTION

Where to go to learn about lower federal court judges, that is, about judges appointed under Article III of the United States Constitution serving on the United States courts of appeal and the United States district courts? If we want statistics, we can turn to the website of the Federal Judicial Center, where in twenty-six files, from A to Z, we find pages devoted not just to the 841 active judges (674 district court, 167 court of appeals) and 490 senior-status judges but to each of the nearly 3,500 we have had in our history. To open one file is to learn about a particular judge; to open all the files and tabulate the information therein is to learn, statistically at least, about the whole of the federal judiciary on topics such as dates and courts of service, legal education, gender, and ethnicity.

But while statistical facts tell us much, we do not learn anything about the two most important questions relating to the federal judiciary: who the judges are and what they do. Perhaps inexplicably, the sources we would ordinarily expect to turn to have not produced anything resembling a critical mass of information to allow us to begin making judgments about the performance of the federal judiciary, either on an individualized basis or on the judiciary as a branch of government. Judicial biographies have been perhaps the most useful source of information, but there have only been a handful of solid biographies of lower court judges.[1]

---

[1] Gerald Gunther, *Learned Hand: The Man and the Judge* (Knopf 1994). Other studies of lower court federal judges include Daniel Hawthorne, *Judge Medina: A Biography* (W. Funk 1952); Jeanette Tuve, *First Lady of the Law, Florence Ellinwood Allen* (University Press of America 1984); Frank R. Kemerer, *William Wayne Justice: A Judicial Biography* (University of Texas 1991); Robert Glennon, *The Iconoclast as Reformer: Jerome Frank's Impact on American Law* (Cornell 1985); Christian Fritz, *Federal Justice in California: The Court of Ogden Hoffman, 1851–1891* (Nebraska 1991); Arthur Selwyn, *A "Capacity for*

The basic approach in studying the federal court system has not been to study the judges but to look at the circuit and district courts as institutions.[2] Even when the appointment of judges has been studied, the focus has not been on the judges themselves. Sheldon Goldman's seminal study, for example, looked at the appointment process from the point of view of the executive branch.[3]

For answers to the questions of who the judges are and what they do, we need to turn to oral histories, which a significant number of the Article III judges have given and which I report on in this book. I read more than 100 oral histories of Article III judges—documents I found scattered around the country—totaling some 20,000 pages. The oral histories are not comprehensively indexed; finding them required contacting the various courts of appeal as well as consulting both the list prepared in 1992 by the Federal Judicial Center and the individual entries (all 3,293 of them) in the biographical database of the Federal Judicial Center to find references to oral histories.[4]

If we consider the histories by circuit, then two circuits dominate. The Ninth Circuit, not surprisingly given its preeminent size, leads with thirty-nine histories. In giving these numbers, I am jumping past the distinction between restricted and unrestricted histories and reporting on those I was able to work with. The Seventh Circuit, in second place, has twenty-two histories. Some circuits, such as the First Circuit, had none, while others had only a few. Some of the circuit executives took it upon themselves to compile oral histories of judges in their circuit. This was the case with Collins Fitzpatrick of the Seventh Circuit. In other instances, circuit historical societies, such as the Ninth Circuit Historical Society, established oral history programs.

Outrage": The Judicial Odyssey of J. Skelly Wright (Greenwood 1984); Gilbert Ware, William Hastie: Grace Under Pressure (Oxford 1984); and William Edward Nelson, In Pursuit of Right and Justice: Edward Weinfeld as Lawyer and Judge (New York University 2004).

[2] A good example is David E. Klein, Making Law in the United States Courts of Appeal (Cambridge 2002).

[3] Sheldon Goldman, Picking Federal Judges: Lower Court Selection From Roosevelt Through Reagan (Yale 1997). For another study that looks at the appointment process from something other than the perspective of the judges being appointed, see Nancy Scherer, Politicians, Activists, and the Lower Federal Court Appointments Process (Stanford 2005) and Lee Epstein and Jeffrey A. Segal, Advice and Consent: The Politics of Judicial Appointments (Oxford 2005).

[4] A Directory of Oral History Interviews Related to the Federal Courts (Federal Judicial Center 1992).

My oral histories feature federal judges who were appointed in the 1960s, 1970s, and 1980s, though there are a few with earlier appointments. Roosevelt appointed two, for example, Truman one, and Eisenhower five. Most of the judges I feature in this book have achieved senior status. In many cases, the interviews took place near the end of their lives. Putting the issue of reading law in an office aside, because, for this generation of judges, only law school educations counted, their statistical profile varies only a bit from the statistical profile of the entire population of Article III judges.

While the histories vary somewhat because the interviewers take slightly different approaches in their questioning, the oral histories share the goal of getting the Article III judges to discuss the major events of their lives and to respond to questions about their judicial work. The interviewers begin with questions about the judge's family tree before moving on to childhood, youth, college, and law school. Questions about law practice then follow before questions about the judicial appointment. Having gotten the judges onto the bench, so to speak, the interviewers ask questions about judicial philosophy and what makes a good judge and, for good measure, what makes a good lawyer. To set the oral histories in context, the interviewers also usually ask about the judge's responses to the major events of the day, most notably, the Great Depression and World War II.

Interviewer experience and qualifications vary. Only some are trained historians. Often a former law clerk is asked to conduct the interview, having been given an outline of what to cover. Interviewers were selected, it seems, because they have not only some prior history with the judge but because they get along with their subject. The goal is to make the oral history interview a relaxed session in which the judge brings up subjects and offers information as well as responds to established questions. Only two judges wanted to take out the intermediary and treat their oral history as an autobiographical statement. Those judges might have tried to follow an outline but only insofar as it let them tell their well-rehearsed stories. This method might well take them out of the category of oral history, but I am using them here nonetheless.

The rapport between the interviewer and subject is key. Collins Fitzpatrick conducted interviews that invariably leave the reader with the belief that he had gotten to know the subject as a person. Because the judges had long worked with Fitzpatrick and developed an impressive level of familiarity, they were their true selves with him. In part, they were reliving a shared past in the interviews, which, for the reader, produced candid and often revealing commentary. In contrast, when there is no rapport between interviewer and subject—which happens only a handful of times—the judges tend to give shorter answers and rarely go beyond the scope of the question at hand. There are, as an example, two ways judges can answer the all-important question of how they were appointed. They can give the known facts or they can describe what happened behind the scenes. The judges who feel comfortable with their interviewers are far more likely to be expansive than the judges who resist the interviewer at every turn.

The interviews sometimes yield stunning admissions. In the case of one judge telling the story of his appointment, we learn that the judge had, as part of his appointment, agreed in turn to make appointments for bankruptcy judge and clerk of the court that the sponsoring senator wanted, effectively becoming a patronage tool of the senator. After describing this event, the judge goes on to explain that he later resigned his position because his senator wanted him to leave so that the senator could appoint another judge. The judge, in his role as facilitator, gladly left.

Another judge, in recounting his years of private practice, describes giving a bribe on his client's behalf to an important California official to get access to President Kennedy's administration so that he could then make a pitch to the right official. Yet another judge, describing how he came to marry his second wife, explains that his first wife was having an affair with the husband of the woman who later became his second wife. The judge and woman both knew of their spouses' affair and met to commiserate. This became their spark of romance, and, after respective divorces from their adulterous spouses, they began a relationship and then married. And then there is the district judge pulling back the curtain, perhaps, and telling the truth about law clerks. "They are so good," a judge from the Central District of California says, "I think a dummy could probably do the job here if he knew cleverly how to use law clerks. I had better stop here and say that I don't think on this court that there are any that do that, maybe on the circuit they do."[5]

While the interviewer is important to the oral history, the nature of the final product turns primarily on the judges themselves. They might be moved a bit one way or the other because of the interviewer, but generally

---

[5] Robert Joseph Kelleher, "Oral History Interview with Judge Robert J. Kelleher," Ninth Judicial Circuit Historical Society (1990), p. 35.

the judges come to the interview knowing what they want to reveal and just how much they want to engage the interviewer. It is to the credit of the judges that, on balance, they want to talk about their lives and their roles on the bench, believing in some sort of accountability to the public. Of course, some judges have different motives. Some come to the interviewer with scores to settle and careers to promote. Surprisingly, those judges somehow think that their motives will not be betrayed in the interview.

It is not a natural thing for federal judges to talk about themselves to outsiders. After all, they answer to no one. These are people who have for years exercised substantial Article III power and who have been beyond the reach of others—the only restraint on an Article III judge is good behavior. It is a statement of the obvious that the temptation for Article III judges is to become imperial in their duties and in the way they see themselves. The imperial judges cannot hide this sense of self—they proclaim rather than describe themselves. Their proclamations rarely contain candid or even personal revelations. In contrast, those not taking the imperial path accept the unaccustomed role of interviewee and, with the right environment and prompting, show themselves in a way that is unique to our understanding of Article III judges.

The histories lead readers to make their own judgments about the subjects. The first judgment is the extent to which the reader likes the judge. This likeability factor is a function of any number of variables, ranging from the subject's politeness to his or her honest and candid responses. The result is that the very nature of the judges' personalities comes out. Readers respond, for example, to whether the judges are imperious, down to earth, modest, funny, witty, self-absorbed, dismissive, boastfully arrogant, or entitled. We read the oral histories as we read anything else, which is to say that we make judgments about characters and people in fiction and nonfiction alike. Judges might be able to control lawyers before them, but they cannot control readers.

Federal judges are, without question, enormously powerful. For this reason, federal judicial appointments are often a president's most important contribution to the present and most enduring contribution to the future. The judges serve long after the appointing president is gone. They decide issues and cases, taking the application of facts to law that have no predetermined result and shaping a result that, at some level, represents their own background and personality. Only impeachment can stop them. This is a succinct way of saying that it matters who sits on our benches.

Decisions are not preordained by either case law or facts. They are driven by the human element.[6]

The oral histories present the life stories of Article III judges. Better put, they detail the lives of the judges and present these judges as people. Some have simply remarkable stories. Some are impressive figures who will strike us as people we would like to know, to choose for our team, because we admire them so much. On occasion, having been caught up in the lives of these judges, the reminder that they have passed on saddens us.

Although readers can discern the organizing principles that the interviewers often use, my intention here is not to recreate the outline that can be sketched from these principles. I want to go further and follow the topics that come up and propel the conversation. Sometimes, organizing around the topic as found in the outline, such as the topic of a judge's appointment, works well, but often the best material is not material the interviewer was seeking but which is offered nonetheless. To give a sampling of the topics that helped shape the lives presented, I follow the judges along the usual path of youth, to high school and college, and then on to law school. But I want to use, for example, their impressions of law school days to present the legal education of the period, as described by the ones who were there. Also, some judges speak in detail and with great consideration and insight about law firms, providing an almost sociological view of the subject of how organizations start, transform, and sometimes die.

It is always the case that no matter how successful or happy a judge was as a practitioner, the appointment to the bench is the seminal event of his or her professional life. Invariably, the event has often been long in the making, and, to their great credit, the judges give the background and describe how they succeeded. Their accounts often confirm what we suspect, but the stories often present different interpretations of the key event. And what we know from the histories is that, for the most part, the judges are telling the whole story. In telling these stories, the judges often see themselves as stars of a sort—not legal stars, as in the best lawyer in the county, for example—but stars because they know the top politician in their area or state. It is an elitism that pervades and that prompts, I think, the judges to relate the stories of the appointment as success stories. Most of the judges know they are not particularly talented in the law and would not have received the appointment if it were based solely on

---

[6] For a remarkable account of this phenomenon, see Richard A. Posner, *How Judges Think* (Harvard 2008).

merit—which makes the appearance of real talent in this group so striking—but they know they are connected and believe this connection to be a function of some great personal quality that permits them to assert themselves over others.

The oral histories give us a new way to understand the behavior of judges. We find that, when in an environment lending itself to talk among friends, the judges frequently talk about other judges, and this talk is far more valuable than commentary coming from the lawyers. The descriptions judges give of other judges, of course, reveals qualities about themselves, but what they really do is give us insider information that cannot be found elsewhere. The judges talk about the judges they like and dislike, the tyrannical ones and the decent ones. They talk about ambition and about how some of the judges just did not get along with others. The histories raise the question—not easily answered otherwise—why there should ever be rudeness from the federal bench. The conclusion is all but unavoidable when we hear federal judges complain about other federal judges they have known and the awful things they did to lawyers. It would be one thing if all the judges were laughing at the stories as part of a us/them approach to the world, but the judges who describe the brutality and petty tyrannies of their brethren are critics, not boosters.

The histories also provide extensive information about how judges work in their courtrooms, their chambers, and during oral arguments. The most interesting information is about the way the judges handle their opinion-writing duties, which are important, given that so much of what a judge does is write (or at least that should be the case). The judges seem to be telling the truth in describing their work habits because they willingly admit to the massive extent that they rely on their law clerks to do their opinion-writing work. They talk about the relationship between the opinion, as a product of the judge's work, and the ruling itself, which is also a product of the judge's work. We learn that most judges have come to terms about that relationship and are able to divorce the decision-making function from the opinion-writing function.

There are more topics, to be sure. We learn what judges think about good judges and good lawyers. We learn about their understanding of the role of the judge and very nature of justice. We hear their views on the important subject of sentencing guidelines; through their responses, we can declare, from the judicial point of view at least, that the guidelines were ill conceived and a major mistake, leaving open the question of how long we as a nation will tolerate the damage that the guidelines have done to the nation. Again, as with judicial appointments, we did not have this information before, and with it we can make much stronger assertions about key issues in the judicial branch.

We also learn about personal issues for the first time. We learn how the judges feel about the money they make and the demands they face in their jobs. We hear how satisfying their judicial careers have been, sometime from judges who have resigned their commissions—a rare event for federal judges. We hear judges talk about how they respond to obstructionist and obstreperous lawyers and about the personalities that are better suited for the judicial life in the face of these challenges. And, from one judge who did not go onto the bench until he was sixty, we hear extensive thoughts, refreshing in their own way, on how he keeps himself awake during trial when the impulse is to nod off, as it was for Homer.

We hear about the judges' ways of life as they grew up. We hear them talk about how their lives changed, sometimes going from indifferent student to committed student. Their childhoods and student days appear removed from us today, but those lives are completely mainstream, or, better put, they define what it is to be an American. In telling their stories, the judges are telling the American story. They represent an educated, highly literate class. We are better off knowing what they know.

For all that the oral histories tell us, we need to keep in mind what they do *not* tell us. In these oral histories, federal judges describe their lives and careers, which might prompt us to think that lives before the bench and lives on the bench are more directly connected than they actually are. There is no causal relationship between a judge's life and the way he or she decides particular issues in particular cases. There is a relationship between the person before the bench and the person on the bench in all sorts of ways that the judges make wonderfully clear, but that is all we can say. No claim can be made about the relationship between personal lives and judicial performance. What the oral histories make clear, in contrast, is that a judge is a person with a personal history. This point is made nowhere else as well and commends the oral histories to us, at a minimum, for this contribution.

The descriptions that the judges give of their lives before the bench and their work on the bench will likely appeal in some ways to different audiences. Lawyers and judges, as a more specialized audience, will more appreciate what the judges say about the way they run their courtrooms and how they generally go about the business of judging, while the general audience might be drawn more to a judge's description of life before the bench. In as much as the oral histories serve the dual purpose of covering both topics, an account of them cannot be limited to one audience or the other. This does not mean, however, that there are essentially two books contained herein addressed to two different audiences. Both audiences profit from the recognition that the judge's life has its components. Both audiences profit from recognizing the integrity of a judge's personhood. General audiences follow the judge's life into the highly specialized world of judging, while specialized audiences such as lawyers can work back from the complexities of judging to the judges as they have been shaped by other influences. The whole of the judge's life commands consideration by each audience.

In practice, of course, not much separates the general and specialized audiences. The general leans toward the specialized and the specialized leans toward the general. It's not as though different languages are spoken for each. One of the most notable features of the oral histories, in fact, is the way in which judges make their work on the bench understandable to nonspecialists.

The oral histories, then, remain as stories of individual lives. Discussions of the judicial life tend, perhaps understandably so, to concentrate on a judge's life on the bench. With these oral histories, we recognize that the judicial life should be more properly understood as a life that led to work on the bench and then continues once there.

CHAPTER ONE

LIFE BEFORE ADMISSION TO THE BAR

Life proceeding to admission to the bar moved in a series of steps. The early ones are common to us all, while the later steps reflect a particular professional choice. In writing about childhood, school, and early jobs, the judges present reflections of their America. Childhoods affected by the Depression, for example, reflect the hardships that many experienced across the nation. Later, when the judges had gone off to war, they report on experiences common to many, though the ones recounted here are particularly striking. We get, for example, an account of D-day from a soldier who stormed the Normandy beaches. Once the judges had reached law school, we get a different sort of American portrait. Here we learn about legal education at the greatest schools and at some other very fine ones. Recollections of judicial clerkships by some are also important as presentations of the judicial function as seen by those who themselves became judges. One clerkship story, that of Abner Mikva (C.A.D.C. 1979–94), is especially important as an insider's account of the Supreme Court in the tumultuous early 1950s. Law school and clerkship stories are followed by bar examination stories. We recognize from them that states once gave bar examinations strikingly different from the bar examinations they give today.

Childhood, School, Jobs

The childhoods of the Article III judges contain no real surprises and represent a national socioeconomic cross-section. The Great Depression was the defining event for many of the judges. This was, after all, the period in which many of them came of age. What matters more than the relative affluence of the families, though, is that none of the judges recounts having a bad childhood.

There were certainly hard times for some. It is tempting to suggest that the hard times that Abner Mikva (C.A.D.C. 1979–94) describes, when his father was out of work for five years during the Depression, helped make him the liberal Democrat he became who served five terms in Congress before going on to the appellate bench. There certainly could be a causal connection, but what matters more for oral history purposes is the description of hard times and the sense of personal aggrievement that was a product of the system in place at the time. In this sense, his account contributes to a description of the time.

> We were on welfare, we were on relief. It was very painful. Milwaukee, socialist town that it was, did not look kindly on people who did not work and so it was not made easy. We got no cash. Everything was in-kind. . . . Our books were stamped "Property of the Milwaukee County Outdoor Relief Society," so I would never leave my books lying loose in school because I didn't want the kids to know. But there were other ways to tell. We had all our clothing from relief. Everyone knew that if you wore a black wool cap and these big black shoes that they were relief shoes and a relief cap. We had to pick up food in a wagon, and I would go help my father pick it up a few blocks from the house and my mother would give us a cloth to cover the wagon. My mother would throw out the lard and the bacon because while she didn't keep a completely kosher house, lard and bacon were not staples of our household. I kept thinking as I grew older how sad it was that we really never did have enough food in the house and always good staples were being thrown out. The authorities did not take into account that some of the recipients were Jewish. That was probably the most searing experience of my growing up. Feeling that we were outcasts because we were so poor. I remember the excitement when my father got this WPA job. I don't remember what he was doing. He didn't know how to type. I think they gave him a job typing anyway, and I seem to remember that it had something to do with scripts for the WPA Theater. I'm sure it was hunt and peck because he didn't know how to type. But it was very exciting that he finally had a job again. Every month or week there was a paycheck.[7]

---

[7] Abner J. Mikva, "Honorable Abner J. Mikva Oral History," Historical Society of the District of Columbia (1996, 1999), p. 4.

Most recall their childhood with delight. Harold Ryan (D. Id. 1981–95) describes a classic childhood in the West, in Weiser, Idaho.

Well, like I said, it was a town that did have sidewalks and curbs, but it was dirt streets everywhere, and so we played marbles in the street and we played football in the streets and anything else that occurred to us to do it in the streets. There wasn't all that much traffic, and so our playgrounds were in the streets and there was a lot of vacant lots around town and we would rig up our own baseball fields. In those days recreation programs were unheard of; we created our own and just had a marvelous time doing it, and there was always a bunch of neat kids that I played with in the neighborhood. We had a lot of projects and as we got a little older, we started going down to the river fishing, and as our fathers gave us guns, we started— we'd go from our houses and walk out of town and start hunting at the edge of town, and that might be jackrabbits to start with or whatever there was there. Then later on I was into hunting birds, and Weiser was a great pheasant and Hungarian partridge and all kinds of bird hunting, so I did a lot of bird hunting all my life. As a kid I got my first dog, who was my close buddy, and she and I just went hunting constantly and she was—wherever I went, she went, and so I guess she was one of my best friends, was that little springer spaniel I had. But I had a scad of friends that were around and my mother was a great cook and she always liked to hand doughnuts out the back kitchen door that she'd just baked or cookies or whatever was going on.[8]

Hubert Will (N.D. Ill. 1961–95) of Wisconsin delights in describing growing up above a drugstore. "It was fun living above the drugstore. I would say to my mom that it was always interesting, never a dull moment living above the drugstore. We lived above half a dozen different flavors of ice creams, all kinds of chocolate, all kinds of medicines, or if we needed something, it was sort of like living in a small supermarket."[9]

He put the special ingredient into Will's Cough Syrup, which was

one of our very profitable and very special items. It was my responsibility to see that it was unique. It got to be unique by the addition

---

[8] Harold L. Ryan, "District Judge Harold Ryan," Ninth Circuit Library, Boise, Idaho (1990), p. 8.
[9] Hubert L. Will, "The Unfinished Oral History of Judge Hubert L. Will," Circuit Library, U.S. Court of Appeals for the Seventh Circuit (2001), p. 5.

of maybe three or four drops of tincture of capsicum. Tincture of capsicum was a pepper—red. The cough syrup itself was a white pine tar-based sugar syrup. But the tincture of capsicum was red. The color would disappear the minute you put it in the white pine and tar, which was dark. But the zing that would sharpen it—the pepper—stayed. And you got a tingling feeling in your throat. In the winter time, we would display bottles of cough syrup stacked up and a sign behind it would say, "Head off your cough or cough off your head. Use Will's Cough Syrup." And I was the one who made Will's Cough Syrup effective and special. You couldn't buy Will's Cough Syrup any place else, because I had put drops of capsicum in there.[10]

And as a by-product of working in a drugstore, he became an ice cream aficionado.

We had some interesting rules. No candy, no ice cream until 10:30 p.m., which was closing; then you could have anything you wanted. So I had almost every conceivable combination of ice cream and syrup. And there are some exotic ones that you can't buy for love or money. I have always thought that hot caramel on peach ice cream was sensational. You try to buy it some place. One of my favorites of course is one you can buy, which is hot fudge on butter pecan. I love that. Marshmallow on peppermint is very good, delicious.[11]

While Will worked in his father's drugstore, others had backbreaking manual labor jobs. Robert Grant (N.D. Ind. 1957–98) wonderfully describes picking onions in Indiana.

But back in those days that I speak of, they were growing onions, different types of onions, beets, and carrots. These were tremendous fields. Imagine a field of ten acres of just onions, crawling on your hands and knees for a quarter of a mile, maybe, and then back and up and back, all day long, all summer. They paid us fifty cents a row; that meant $1.50 a day for me. I took three rows and I made $9.00 for six full days, if we weren't rained out. It was a great source of income from which I used to stock up most of my winter clothing

---

[10] *Ibid.* at 9–10.
[11] *Ibid.* at 11.

for the new school year upon which I was about to enter. Anyhow, out in those onion fields, we used to weed onions—crawl on our hands and knees all day long. When you were a beginner you would take one row, and if you were farther along you could take two, but when you got real advanced you could take three rows. You would straddle one, do one with each hand. All day long. We would assemble downtown in Hamlet at 6:00 a.m., be on the onion field at 6:30 and work to 12:00 and be back at 1:00 and at 5:30 we would quit and be back in town at 6:00 p.m.[12]

Samuel Dillin (S.D. Ind. 1961–2006), who grew up on an Indiana farm, records for us the days of the old McCormick reaper and bringing in the wheat harvest. He describes the relationship between mechanical power and human power and etches a portrait of a town communally mobilized to bring in the harvest. He begins with a description of life on the farm and then moves to the wheat harvest itself.

Well, just like any other farm kid, you got up early, and you would pick up the eggs, throw down a little hay for the horses—we didn't have a tractor or anything like that. We had horses. We went out and picked the potato bugs off the potatoes. That was a chore that I didn't appreciate very much but I did it. And we didn't have a lot of chemicals either. Things were a lot different. When wheat harvest time came, I was privileged to drive a team out *in* the field. In those days when the wheat was reasonably ripe, the farmers went out and cut it with a binder, which cut the wheat and actually bound it into sheaves. That was the old McCormick reaper. Then you went along and picked up these sheaves and put them into a shock or bundle or whatever you want to call it. We called them shocks. Then there would be a threshing machine go through the neighborhood, and that consisted of a steam engine fired by coal and the threshing machine itself, which was a great big thing. Nobody owned his *own* threshing machine, like people own combines today. This was a custom operation. And when it came to a given community, all of the men in the community would band together and clean out a field and go on to the next one. It was a communal operation. And of course, the women would all bring food to the place where the

[12] Robert A. Grant, "The Oral History of Judge Robert A. Grant," Circuit Library, U.S. Court of Appeals for the Seventh Circuit (1988), pp. 8–9.

threshing was going to be that day and have a big meal. So I thought I was pretty important when I got to drive a team out in the field for the men to pile on those shocks of wheat.[13]

There was, of course, school for all. Those in the rural areas were sometimes taught in one-room schoolhouses. Richard Mills (C.D. Ill. 1985–present) recalls,

In those years, the 1930s and coming up to the beginning of World War II in 1941 were just informative years. They were the elementary and secondary, the elementary and middle school age where you just had more fun and enjoyed life. We lived at the edge of Jacksonville just outside the city limits, and I went to a one-room country schoolhouse. We had moved from further inside the city to out there, and I had gone to the first grade in town and then the second all the way through the seventh grade I went to Mound School. It was a one-room country school just a little further out from the edge of town. I think that was probably one of the best educational experiences in my life because we had seven different grades, one through seven, and we were all in one large room in rows, and you had to study while others were reciting in different classes. I think that is probably the best experience in concentration that helped me in the future. There were somewhere in the neighborhood of 45 students in the school, with one teacher, Mrs. Howard, a wonderful woman. I remember one time I was— and this was another wonderful lesson in life—in the third grade and we were having a spelling test. I looked over the shoulder of a new girl in front of me and I copied down her spelling of that one word, and all of a sudden Mrs. Howard was standing right at my shoulder. She said, "Come with me," and I followed her down to the basement. She had an eighteen-inch ruler. "Hold out your hands, palms up," and she gave me one tremendous whack right across the hand. I never cheated again my whole life.[14]

---

[13] S. Hugh Dillin, "The Oral History of Judge S. Hugh Dillin," Circuit Library, U.S. Court of Appeals for the Seventh Circuit (1994), pp. 14–15.
[14] Richard Henry Mills, "The Oral History of Judge Richard H. Mills," Circuit Library, U.S. Court of Appeals for the Seventh Circuit (2000), pp. 20–21.

In many ways, his school years remained with him throughout his life. Looking back, he says,

I made some lasting friendships. My best friend all through school and high school and continues to this day, we were in the same grade out there at the country school. But it was a very good experience when we came into town, of course, for eighth grade and high school. It was a wonderful, wonderful town to grow up in. Jacksonville was ideal. A town between 23,000 and 25,000 people. It has never varied. You could get on your bike and go anyplace in town and back without any exertion or worry. You'd throw your swimming trunks and a towel into your bike basket, go out to Nickels Park, go swimming, get back home in plenty of time for dinner. It was a wonderful, wonderful place to grow up. There were a lot of kids in the neighborhood, all the same age. We just had a wonderful life.[15]

Andrew Hauk (C.D. Cal. 1966–2004) of Los Angeles had a Catholic school education.

We had a lot of the usual, you know, mathematics, trigonometry, a little bit of calculus, not much, and history and languages, geometry of course was part of the class, which I hated. I hated geometry and I did it because it was required. So there we had Latin, lots of Latin, one year of Greek, and so I think I had three years of Latin in high school and three years in college, one year of Greek in high school and two years of Greek in college, so I got so I could read the original of Virgil and Homer and various Latin and Greek authors, Cicero. Remember Cato's famous words, *Carthagemum de lindum est*. He made speeches when Carthage was threatening Rome. He would wind up every speech *Carthagemum de lindum est*. Carthage must be destroyed. And finally it was.[16]

June Green (D.D.C. 1968–2001) of Maryland had an unusual high school language experience. "I had English teachers who were English persons. The French teachers were French. I had four years of Latin, I had four years of French, and I had four years of English."[17]

---

[15] *Ibid.* at 22.

[16] A. Andrew Hauk, "Oral History Interview with Hon. A. Andrew Hauk," Ninth Judicial Circuit Historical Society (1990), pp. 7–8.

[17] June L. Green, "Honorable June L. Green Oral History," Historical Society of the District of Columbia (1998, 1999), p. 4.

Mary Lou Robinson (N.D. Tex. 1979–present) of Texas remembers when she first thought about the legal profession. She was in the seventh grade, and "one of our little projects was to make a career notebook. And in the career notebook, I said that I was going to be a lawyer and wrote the book based on that. And that was not what girls ordinarily did then. In fact, they just didn't do that then."[18]

Joyce Hens Green (D.D.C. 1979–present) describes her painful shyness and breaking out of it, achieving peace and self-confidence.

> This adolescent period saw me particularly shy: 13, 14, 15, and 16 were difficult growing years. I had many friends, but due to the shyness, I didn't have the full kind of social life I wanted in high school. I was always prepared when I'd be called upon to stand up and recite in class, but, nonetheless, I would blush and gulp and find it difficult to express myself in front of everyone. Finally, in my senior year—17—in high school, as I was looking forward to college, the time came when I decided that for the rest of my life I was going to carry [that] with me (including shyness) unless I made the change. And so I forced myself to meet people, I forced myself to laugh uproariously at jokes that I didn't think were funny, even feeling the stretch marks on my face when I came home at the end of a day. But, remarkably, after a few weeks of this, I discovered that the jokes were really funny, I enjoyed the people who welcomed me into the circle and I absolutely glowed in that regard. While I still have minor shyness on occasion, by and large that has been conquered; I'm very proud I met this challenge myself. As a psychiatrist's daughter, I did not go to my dad and say, "Help me here." I knew I was the one to conquer the problem.[19]

Abner Mikva (C.A.D.C. 1979–94) recounts his own story of blossoming.

> High school was when things started to change for me. First of all, I did develop some friends. I started up with a couple of them in junior high school but then [we] became good friends in high school and the circle widened a little bit. I began to develop a little self-confidence. Still, the key things in high school, my high school,

---

[18] Mary Lou Robinson, "The Oral History of Judge Mary Lou Robinson," Circuit Library, U.S. Court of Appeals for the Fifth Circuit (2006), p. 4.

[19] Joyce Hens Green, "Honorable Joyce Hens Green Oral History," Historical Society of the District of Columbia (1999, 2001), pp. 16–17.

were sports and girls. I wasn't very good at either of those. I didn't know how to dance, or didn't know how to dance very well, and I didn't dress well. That was an important measuring stick of how poised you were, how "cool" you were, to dress well. One, I didn't have the money for clothes and, two, I didn't have very good taste in clothes. I still don't, I think. I remember my first reason for getting a job was to go out and buy some clothes and at least think I looked like the other kids in high school. But in other ways I began to feel a little bit more comfortable with myself. First of all, I think doing well in school became a little less objectionable. I began to handle it a little better. There were some recognitions of some of the scholastic things that I did, like the honor society and the honor roll and the newspaper.[20]

Alfred Goodwin (D. Or. 1969–71, C.A.9 1971–present), who had lived on a ranch and could have taken to the twentieth-century version of the cowboy life, saw the future one day and got the advice to choose college over horses.

I was watching the old broken-down cowboys limping around Prineville, men in their fifties who looked like they were seventy, dragging their crippled leg after having a horse buck them against a corral and break their leg in two or three places and not heal up right. I'd see those old men, and then the boss's wife on the ranch where I spent the most time was a well-educated woman, a former schoolteacher who had married this rancher. And she said, "Teddy, you don't want to end up like old so-and-so down there at the Paulina Store. You'd better go down to the university as soon as school starts." I was wanting to put it off, in fact I kind of wanted to put it off a year, and she'd say, "Don't put it off. Go now."[21]

Joyce Hens Green (D.D.C. 1979–present) learned a profound life lesson at a summer job.

I had my first full-time job the summer before I went to college just after my high school graduation. The company, Butler Brothers, in Baltimore, was a merchandising house, something similar to Sears

---

[20] Abner Mikva, "Honorable Abner J. Mikva Oral History," Historical Society of the District of Columbia (1996, 1999), pp. 17–18.

[21] Alfred T. Goodwin, "Oral History Interview with Alfred T. Goodwin," U.S. District Court Collection, Oregon Historical Society (1986), pp. 47–48.

Roebuck and Montgomery Ward, and the work that we did was piecework. One hundred women, the proverbial 100 women sitting in a room, each at her typewriter (here's where typing came in handy) and hitting a steel blade, which was the tab on the type-writer, so it would deeply crease the hands; and there was a small meter in back of the typewriter that noted the starting and ending point daily to reflect productivity. There was but one man. His full duties were to walk around the room ceaselessly, loading each person with paperwork when it began to look as if the employee was going to run out of work. I had a supervisor who was an abso-lute tyrant, who, when I recklessly told her one month after I started, and two months before I was to complete, that I was going to be leaving at the end of the summer, refused to talk to me until my last day of work. . . . That summer I earned a total of $219.08, from which $22.10 was withheld for federal income taxes. I learned that the 99 other women were going to have to support themselves and their families for the rest of their lives. I was going to escape to col-lege at the end of the summer and so my life was, even then, recog-nized as tremendously better. I learned that these wonderful women were remarkable and they took good care of me because I was the youngest there; they could not have been more caring. I learned that you have to leave people with dignity and hope, something I have tried to teach my children and all my law clerks and something I've tried to put into effect as I pass through life. There was a day when I, not challenged by this boring work, decided there had to be a more stimulating way to do it; I was going to be the fastest in the room just one time. I worked breathlessly and as fast as I could. I got down to the last piece of paper on my desk as I glimpsed the man with his load of papers. I typed faster and faster, but I didn't make it. I was still on the last two lines on that last piece of paper when he piled perhaps a hundred pieces of paper on top of it. At that point I didn't care if I did any more or not. It took away all hope. And these are the things that you learn and carry with you in life. I have thought of that innumerable times. A great lesson. People need encouragement, need to be left with dignity, need to have hope, however tiny.[22]

---

[22] Joyce Hens Green, "Honorable Joyce Hens Green Oral History," Historical Society of the District of Columbia (1999, 2001), pp. 23–25.

College

We see the full range of collegiate experiences when the future judges head off to college. James Moran (N.D. Ill. 1979–present) had a classic big state university experience. "I just had a wonderful time in college. I loved it. I joined a fraternity. I missed the triple crown. I was Phi Beta Kappa. I was Michigama, which is sort of Michigan's equivalent of Skull and Bones, but I missed the Stein Club by one vote (how much beer you could drink)."[23]

Thomas Fairchild (C.A.7 1966–present) took the route of an experimental college. Deep Springs College, set in the vast desert wasteland in southeast California, was one hour from the nearest town—Bishop, California, near Death Valley. The two-year school had a student population of about twenty-five when Fairchild attended and now thrives on its geographical isolation. The school focuses on three essential themes: academics, labor, and self-governance.

> The whole approach at Deep Springs was on the importance of being a responsible citizen, making a contribution, public service and that sort of thing. Mr. L.L. Nunn [the school's founder] would write letters to the student body when he was still alive, and we were exposed to those letters. One letter, I think, starts out, "Young men, why came ye into the wilderness?" And he was definitely interested in people thinking about themselves and their life, and what they were going to do with it, etc. etc. Well, you basically studied in very small classes with faculty. There were people capable of teaching college-level subjects. And you studied half time, and you were supposed to work half time, and you'd work whatever kinds of jobs that were passed around—the dairy, which meant milking the cows; garage mechanic; office person; student laundry; general farm work, which meant whatever kind of work, or hauling, or anything of that nature that had to be done at that time; and chicken man— somebody who fed the chickens, and so forth. And that was all part of the program. The other part of the program was that the student body should be a very responsible, self-governing institution, which

---

[23] James B. Moran, "The Oral History of James B. Moran, Senior District Court Judge of the United States District Court for the Northern District of Illinois," Circuit Library, U.S. Court of Appeals for the Seventh Circuit (1994), p. 11.

it always was and still is. And, the student body was permitted to elect one of the eight trustees of the institution.[24]

Following his two years at Deep Springs, Fairchild moved to Cornell, which had a long-standing relationship with the experimental school and accepted the credits he had earned there.

Sometimes these future judges struggled with either performance or direction in college. David Williams (C.D. Cal. 1969–2000) explains that when he came out of high school he had terrible grades.

> I got some ambition to get into college, and I went to junior college and I got into their makeup course to eventually qualify me for UCLA, and I stuck with the studies there, the pre-legal studies, political science, and history and English. I managed to get pretty average grades. I don't think I ever got an A in my life. I may have gotten B's and C's, that was about it. I never thought of myself as a bright person, but I thought of myself as a plugger who was going to make it, so help me. And it was just that initiative that brought me through. I never failed a course in my life. I took courses in Latin and kind of mastered that pretty well, and I took courses in Spanish and mastered that pretty well, and courses in political science. I loved that, about governments. But I never considered myself an intellectual or the brightest guy in the class. But I held my own, and that was about it.[25]

Raul Ramirez (E.D. Cal. 1979–89) had a similar but even more striking story. He spent two years at Glendale Community College, where he says he was lost.

> I was really lost. I wouldn't say I was a disturbed young man or anything like that, but I was wild. I thought that playing football and drinking beer and racing cars—my wife's not listening—chasing young ladies, was the only way to enjoy life, and I did; almost flunked out. I managed to graduate, though. I think it took me two and a half years in junior college. I'd like to say something happened—a light went on, I got struck by lightning—something. But I suddenly realized after I had decided to quit school to become a policeman;

---

[24] Thomas E. Fairchild, "The Oral History of Judge Thomas E. Fairchild," Circuit Library, U.S. Court of Appeals for the Seventh Circuit (1999), p. 7.
[25] David W. Williams, "Oral History Interview with Hon. David W. Williams," Ninth Judicial Circuit Historical Society (1998), p. 27.

to become a fireman; to become an air traffic controller; animal controller, whatever that means. I mean there were ten occupations that I'm sure I wanted to be. Anything that didn't entail additional schooling. Someone said, "Why don't you become a lawyer?" and after I stopped laughing I looked around and I discovered that L.A. State was the only school in Southern California, be it a private or public, that offered a degree in pre-law. It was part of the government major with a pre-law emphasis. It says Bachelor of Arts Pre-law. And, I decided okay, why not, got nothing better to do; take a shot at it. All of a sudden, I got straight A's.[26]

Harold Ryan (D. Id. 1981–95) tells an absorbing story of his college struggles.

It's Depression times and I mentioned earlier I didn't want my parents to have to pay for any of my education. I had $640 saved up from all the jobs I'd had here and there and the other place, plus caddying on the golf course at McCall, and so I had that in a savings account and I was going to see if I could make that do for my first year at the university. Dad says, well, he'd back me if I got into need, which was really a wonderful thing to know that if I ran out of the last $25, he'd see that I was taken care of. I had a kind of sense of pride in those days, but I did manage to get through the first year at the University of Idaho on $640. I had that much when I went up and when I left I was dead broke. I went down to McCall and started working in the sawmill to immediately get some change back in my pockets and get some money together for the next year at the school. In fact, I passed this one five-hour credit math course—I don't think I was doing very well going into it, and I practically memorized the math book and took the final exam and I got a perfect paper off it, and the old professor I had that always wore a vest because he had to have his Phi Beta Kappa key showing, looked at me and with a Prussian accent said, "Uhh, Mr. Ryan," he says, "I got your grade here." He says, "At first I thought you cheated, but then I remember you were over in the corner and there was nobody to cheat from." So he says, "Therefore, I passed you in the course. You deserved to flunk. I don't believe you learned it, but somehow

---

26 Raul Ramirez, "Oral History Interview with Hon. Raul Ramirez," Ninth Judicial Circuit Historical Society (1990), p. 3.

you wrote a perfect paper." And I went out of there—gah, I was never so happy in my life. You know, I was just clear out of my element in this area. Somehow in the Weiser school system I didn't get a real solid foundation in algebra and geometry and that sort of thing, and that being the building subject, I got up there into this analytical geometry and talking about parabolas and hyperbolas and figuring out the mathematical equations to get there was just, just boggled my mind, and always has and always will.[27]

Military Service

The oral histories are distinguished in part by the high percentage of subjects who served in the military during World War II or the Korean War and the stories they tell of what they did. A few accounts from World War II veterans sketch a range of involvement and life-altering experiences.

Alfred Goodwin (D. Or. 1969–71, C.A.9 1971–present) speaks for many when he reflects on his military service and the opportunities he saw ahead.

The main thing I remember about that whole experience was the extreme sense of gratitude of being alive at the end of the war. I mean, the war was over in Europe and I was still alive; and I thought, wow, this is it. You know, from now on life is going to be pretty good because the big problem that had been in the back of all of our minds was are we going to survive. Now here the war was over and we were still alive, so that felt pretty good. I think I have been kind of optimistic ever since as a result of that sense of having been spared.[28]

John Reynolds (E.D. Wis. 1965–2002) left college for the army and went south for training. What he saw there had as profound an effect on his life as the experiences of others abroad.

Then I went to Mississippi. And I knew the train was going south. I could tell by where the sun was. And we got off the train at Shelby and that very night a black kid was lynched. Right there. I didn't see it, but everybody was talking about it. He was hung from a trestle,

---

[27] Harold L. Ryan, "District Judge Harold Ryan," Ninth Circuit Library, Boise, Idaho (1990), pp. 16, 18.
[28] Alfred T. Goodwin, "Oral History Interview with Alfred T. Goodwin," U.S. District Court Collection, Oregon Historical Society (1986), p. 56.

railroad trestle. And that was my introduction to what I considered the most foreign place at the time that I had ever been and that was southern Mississippi. It was so different than anything I had experienced that later on when I got around the world, it didn't shock me nearly as much as what I found there. When I was there, I was assigned—I wound up as an enlisted man in Third Army Headquarters. We had troops, black troops, and the sheriff in Centreville, Mississippi, one day saw a black guy, black soldier holding down a white MP, which in Mississippi at that time was a capital offense. He walked over and put a bullet through the black soldier's head. Our troops revolted. It was the 364th Infantry regiment. They were all black. They were brought to Mississippi so that the black soldiers could have lady friends. That's what they said anyway. They revolted. They wanted to get their weapons to march on Centreville. It was a traumatic experience for me. For everybody, I guess.[29]

Laughlin Waters (C.D. Cal. 1976–2002) was at D-day assaulting a Normandy beach. His is a riveting account of just how the landing occurred and what he did.

D-day right off. We were on a landing craft infantry. You'll recall it was the aborting of the initial landing plans, and then they set it up for June 6, and we went over. The navy was supposed to put us in about three feet of water and so on, but the craft hit a sandbar which, as I now recall, was 150 yards off from the beach itself, and that's as far as the captain would take it. So we piled off of that boat into about fifteen or eighteen feet of water. And the instructions and orders were that if you sank, why, you get rid of your weapons. And I was the first one off the boat. I debated with myself whether or not I should show leadership and go off first or be the last one off and make sure I kicked everybody off the boat that had to go. But in any event, these fellows came off in rapid fashion, went down, dropped their rifles, their radios, their machine guns, their mortars, their ammunition, and then they floated to the top.

Well, when my company finally reached the beach, I was the only one who had a weapon of any kind. I hung on to mine. We had

---

[29] John W. Reynolds, "The Oral History of Judge John W. Reynolds," Circuit Library, U.S. Court of Appeals for the Seventh Circuit (1997), p. 10.

these waist inflatable things with copper dioxide tubes. You'd squeeze something that would puncture the tube, it would inflate and you'd come back up. But the GIs and the other officers followed instructions, so when we landed we were virtually an unarmed unit. So then we had to rearm, and we began picking up German weapons. And that created problems, because the German weapons had a very distinctive sound compared to the American weapons; it was a sharper crack. And other GIs in adjacent units were, as we were, trigger-happy, and when they heard this different sound. . . . [chuckling]. So we took a little bit of fire from our flanks there.

I remember leaving the boat, sinking, operating my life belt, and then swimming into shore, and my lungs were bursting. I could not have taken another step as I stood up in about three feet of water. And it was at that point that I heard my first .88 shell come in, and I made a dive that would have won me a medal in Olympic diving history getting out of the way of that thing.

In any event, Roosevelt did observe that the navy had put us ashore at the wrong place, and so he did, as you said, decide that the war ought to start there, and it did. And we moved in. Now there had been other troops ahead of us, but we came upon them and then we began to see the real wreckage of war, dead personnel lying around, tanks that had been destroyed, and so on. I was wounded on D-plus-nine, so we had around nine days of brisk activity there prior to the time that I was hit. The first time I was wounded, it was an American artillery shell that fell short.[30]

Military service changed and influenced the lives of those who served. Alfred Goodwin (D. Or. 1969–71 and C.A.9 1971–present) recalls a lighter side of personal change.

I didn't really discover much about girls until I was a soldier at basic training. I did finish the junior year and then I went to Camp Roberts. And I met a guy, alphabetically you know how you're arranged in boot camp. I don't know if I'm getting ahead of the story, but reproductive behavior is part of life, and I was essentially still a teenager. In 1943 I was turning twenty. And I was still virtually I guess, if one

---

[30] Laughlin E. Waters, "Oral History Interview with Judge Laughlin E. Waters," Ninth Judicial Circuit Historical Society (1989), pp. 14–18.

can be virtually a virgin, at age twenty. You know these fumbling affairs in high school or college never really amounted to anything.

But I met this friend and we became friends in boot camp in Camp Roberts. His name was, I think to protect the guilty I'll just not, he's still around. Anyway he was a professor at Berkeley who had gotten drafted. He was about seven or eight years older than I was. He felt sorry for me. He told me, "Ted, you're sexually retarded. You haven't had any experience." He said, "I've got a couple of single women friends in Berkeley that you ought to get acquainted with." And so he'd take me home with him on weekend passes from Camp Roberts, which was 100 miles south of San Francisco, during the summer of 1943, and he'd fix me up with a date. And that was a wonderful summer, courtesy of the Berkeley professor. So from then on I decided that there was a whole lot more to it than just howdying and shaking [hands].[31]

Law School

Getting into law school was not always an easy task for some of the future judges. Prentice Marshall (N.D. Ill. 1973–96), who later became a law school professor, found that he had to take summer courses to improve his grades. He had been, as he puts it, a screw-up in high school, flunking Latin and French, cutting classes, and doing no homework, and he was a mediocre college student after navy service in World War II. He went to the admissions office at the University of Illinois law school and was told that the school accepted the top 150 applicants and that he needed better grades. He took and aced twelve hours of summer school and went back to the admissions office. This time he got in. He had the highest grades in his first-year class and went on to an important Seventh Circuit clerkship, all after having almost missed out on getting in.[32]

Jesse Curtis (C.D. Cal. 1962–90) had a nerve-wracking admission ordeal. He had done his undergraduate work at the University of Redlands,

[31] Alfred T. Goodwin, "Oral History Interview with Alfred T. Goodwin," U.S. District Court Collection, Oregon Historical Society (1986), pp. 45.
[32] Prentice H. Marshall, "The Oral History of Retired Judge Prentice H. Marshall," Circuit Library, U.S. Court of Appeals for the Seventh Circuit (1999), p. 3.

which had, in 1928 at least, a special arrangement with the Harvard Law School that allowed Redlands graduates to enter with an examination. It had this arrangement because one of its alumni had gone to Harvard and returned to teach at Redlands, before moving back to teach at Harvard. Admission was not, however, quite so simple, as Curtis explains.

> I went back and got all adjusted in my apartment [in Cambridge] and got my books and went up to register and the registrar said, "I don't see anything in your file to indicate that you were in the upper fourth of your class." I said I didn't know anything about that. They said, "That's one of our requirements for admission—the upper fourth of your class." I said I was never told about that. I said you mean I've come all the way back here and given up an opportunity to go to some other school and all set to go and I can't get in because I'm not in the upper fourth of the class? Well, she said the only thing I can say is see if you can get a certificate that you were. That shook me a little, and I wrote back to Redlands and finally got a certificate that I was in the upper fourth of the class, but I also got a private note from the registrar saying, "Dear Jesse, you will never know how hard we had to push to get you this."[33]

Bruce Thompson's (D. Nev. 1963–92) path to Stanford Law School, unlike Curtis's, did amount to just showing up. He had graduated from the University of Nevada in 1932 with a major in philosophy and English and a minor in Latin.

> That was in the depths of the depression, and there weren't jobs available and I always had a inclination toward trying to be a lawyer, and my father was willing and able to send me to law school, so that's why I went. In those days it was interesting, compared to today where you have to get within the top ten percentile on the LSAT and have an outstanding undergraduate academic record to be admitted to Stanford Law School. All I had to do was knock on the door and present my credentials as a graduate of the University of Nevada and pay $135 for the first quarter's tuition.[34]

---

[33] Jesse William Curtis Jr., "Oral History Interview with Hon. Jesse Curtis," Ninth Judicial Circuit Historical Society (1989), pp. 8–9.

[34] Bruce Rutherford Thompson, "Oral History Interview with Hon. Bruce R. Thompson," Ninth Judicial Circuit Historical Society (1988), p. 9.

Alfred Goodwin (D. Or. 1969–71 and C.A.9 1971–present) remembers when it all came together for him in law, making it a great time in his life. He had worked for three years before starting law school as a reporter on an Oregon daily and had learned some skills that later applied to law. He learned, for example, to set type and read upside down. "Incidentally," he notes, "as a lawyer it's good to read upside down because you can look across at the other guy's documents and see what he's pulling on you before he's ready for you—another good application of journalistic thinking." He put his writing and typing skills to good use at examination time.

At the University of Oregon Law School, and most law schools today, they allow the students who want to, to type their exams. I'd read the exam question, I'd sit down at the typewriter and I'd answer in simple declarative sentences which were easy to read. Apparently the professors enjoyed reading my papers because they'd see I didn't waste a lot of time chasing rabbits. I'd get to the heart of the issue and put down the reasons for the decision and answer the question.

I remember that habit I developed of reading the cases that the professor mentioned in his lecture. I'd go and read them in the library and put notes in my notebook. Well a couple of days before each exam, we'd have exams once every term, I'd go back through my notes and I'd read these little one-line or two-line or short paragraph summaries of these cases that the teachers had mentioned in their lectures. It was amazing how many of those showed up in the exam questions. So I'd get an exam question and I'd say well this point is covered by such and such a case and name the case, and it was a case that the teacher had mentioned in one of his lectures and I'd gone and read it. Well, the average student didn't do that. So I'd get an A because my paper would have that stuff in it that the teacher was surprised to find in a paper.

Later on, I did a little teaching myself so I know, even though I didn't know it at the time, how valuable those kind of lucky intuitions were. I knew that I ought to pay attention, that these lectures weren't just for the amusement of the faculty and I ought to be paying attention and taking notes, so I did. I typed up my notes. About once a week I'd type up all my class notes, so I'd have my little typewritten notes so they'd be easy to read. And then the night before the exam I could go through and read all that stuff. The exercise of typing it up, thinking about it again, putting it in my notebook, put it in my head. Then the night before the exam I could flip through it and read it in an hour, the whole course. Then the exam would come up and I'd have that recent memory of these elusive points that the professor had mentioned during the lecture. So I was getting a lot out of the casebooks and also matching it up with the lectures. And for me from then on law school was a joy.

I really enjoyed it. I had fun. I enjoyed being the top dog. I was kind of a cocky bastard. I was smoking cigars and swaggering around a little bit. There are probably not many lawyers who can look back on their law school days and say it was one of the happiest times in their life. But for me it was a totally happy life. I had lived through a war which I hadn't expected to live through. I had found out that I didn't really want to be a newspaperman all my life, and so I was doing something that I really thought I wanted to do. I wanted to be a lawyer. So it was a happy time of my life. I was being successful in an area where it all depended entirely on my own work. I wasn't being successful because of who my father was or how much money I had inherited or anything. I was being success-ful in my own right in a field of my own choosing. I was happily married, and I was doing things that were interesting. I had the GI Bill paying a good part of the bills. So it was really a happy time and it did a lot for my self-confidence and for my self-image and for my own mental health. I just began to feel good about who I was and what I was doing.

And that's useful to a young person. A lot of what's happened to me since then I think, the foundation was being laid with these early successes in law school, and it wasn't because I was super bright. I think my IQ is unremarkable. I qualified for all the different things that one had to qualify for, but I wasn't nearly as bright as a lot of people I know. In terms of taking law school aptitude tests today, I doubt that I would have an LSAT that could get me into Yale or Harvard. I might, but I don't know. I've never taken one.[35]

For those a bit older than someone such as Bruce Thompson (D. Nev. 1963–92), World War II affected their law school educations. Some, like

---

[35] Alfred T. Goodwin, "Oral History Interview with Alfred T. Goodwin," U.S. District Court Collection, Oregon Historical Society (1986), pp. 141–143.

Joseph Sneed (C.A.9 1973–2008), had their educations interrupted. For him, though, the interruption became something of a bonus.

> One of the interesting things appeared out of that was that I made much better grades after I came back. Didn't make bad grades when I was there before, but I made much better grades. Part of that was not because I was any better, it was because the curve had expanded to accommodate the increased numbers. If you work a curve and you've got a lot of people, it's kind of hard to cram them all into eighty-five. If you've got a few people, you can sort of cram them in at eighty-five, just to use that number arbitrarily. But then you have to begin to stretch it out. So grades in the ninetiess began to appear.[36]

For Aubrey Robinson (D.D.C. 1966–2000) and many others who began law school after the war, the years lost in service made them eager to get through with school and get on with things.

> I was in a bigger hurry to get things done. We felt we had lost things and just buckled right down. As a matter of fact, I went, once I got back out of the service I went right straight through summer, and I came back in March is my recollection. I went through that semester, went through, studied through the summer until I got my, finished my work and got my degree. There was no fooling. When I came back out of the service and came back to law school, it was an entirely different atmosphere throughout the entire law school. I was joined by dozens of others who, coming back at various stages of completing their education, and all of us were a much more mature group in approaching our studies. We had no time to waste. We felt we had to catch up. We felt we were lucky to be able to complete our military service and get on with what we wanted to do. The classes were larger but it worked out because with a more mature student body you had less foolishness. Everybody was pretty much in the same boat.[37]

---

[36] Joseph T. Sneed III, "Oral History Interview with Hon. Joseph T. Sneed III," Ninth Judicial Circuit Historical Society (1994), p. 9.

[37] Aubrey E. Robinson, "Honorable Aubrey E. Robinson, Jr. Oral History," Historical Society of the District of Columbia (1992), p. 15.

Harvard

Harvard Law School figures prominently in the oral histories. Several judges went to school there and, luckily for us, detailed their years there, giving us a fuller picture of that school's particular take on legal education. In some ways, it was no place for a woman and no place for any one not a wealthy WASP. It was, to be sure, a hard-driving place.

James Moran (N.D. Ill. 1979–present) says that he thoroughly enjoyed his three years at Cambridge: "I had some wonderful professors. I particularly liked Henry Hart and Al Sacks, but I had a lot of good ones. It was intellectually challenging. It was fun. Some things I had to endure, like estate planning, which I had absolutely no interest in whatsoever, but other than that it was fun."[38]

William Gray (C.D. Cal. 1966–92) describes his experience this way:

> I worked. I knew that I had some brilliant classmates, really brilliant. I never thought that I was brilliant and I still don't, but I knew if I was going to keep up with them I would have to work a little bit harder. And having been out of college for two years I knew what I wanted and I did work. I got up at 6:00 in the morning and would walk down to Harvard Square to have breakfast at one of those restaurants and come back and work from say 7:30 until 10:00 when class began and I worked at night too. The only interruption was to play a game of squash. I think I played squash each day; it pulled me through. But I worked hard.
>
> I had Dean Roscoe Pound for Criminal Law the first half of the year and Livingston Hall the second half. And Pound of course was a great man with a great memory. He laid out a lecture about as well as anybody I've ever seen. And we had Edmund Morgan, Eddie Morgan, whom we all loved. We had him for Procedure. And he probably knew more about procedure and evidence than anyone else in the country—at least his book on evidence was a bible, I guess. We had George Gardner for Contracts. Williston was right across the hall—you've heard of Williston. Well, Williston was right

---

[38] James B. Moran, "The Oral History of James B. Moran, Senior District Court Judge of the United States District Court for the Northern District of Illinois," Circuit Library, U.S. Court of Appeals for the Seventh Circuit (1994), p. 24.

across the hall, but I'm glad I had Gardner. I think that was probably the best of all the courses because where Williston laid out the law, Gardner would, by his Socratic questioning, cause a person to recognize the issues and the distinction between points of law. He never told us anything, but he caused us to be able to figure things out for ourselves. I liked that course. We had Bull Warren, who was colorful. There are all kinds of stories about Bull Warren. And we had Seavy for Torts, who was—well here again he probably was the master of—he was the peer of Torts, I believe.

Yes, we had some fine professors. I was a year or two older than my classmates because as you'll recall I was out a year between high school and college and two years after college, so I was a year or two, sometimes three, older than my classmates. We had no women. There was only one black fellow in my class that I can remember. Otherwise it was pretty much a cross-section. It was certainly a cross-section countrywide. That's one of the great things about it. I developed friends from all sections of the country, perhaps almost all the states.[39]

Herbert Choy (C.A.9 1971–2004) remembers,

I did not have any class with Professor Edward H. Warren, "The Bull," whose reputation as the most colorful law professor was copied by the movie and television character, Professor Kingsfield [in *The Paper Chase*]. But I did sit in on a couple of Professor Warren's classes and found that he lived up to his billing. His Friday classes were often attended by visitors, including girlfriends of students who wanted to see the professor perform. One day, however, he was not in the mood for feminine spectators, and seeing a girl in the class, he interrupted his sentence by walking up to where she sat, extended the crook of his arm to her, which she took, escorted her to the door, opened it for her, bowed, and closed it behind her, then finished the sentence. During my time, and prior thereto, Harvard Law School was strictly a men's-only school.[40]

[39] William Percival Gray, "Oral History Interview with Hon. William P. Gray," Ninth Judicial Circuit Historical Society (1994), pp. 10–14.
[40] Herbert Young Cho Choy, "Oral History Interview with Hon. Herbert Y.C. Choy," Ninth Judicial Circuit Historical Society (1990), p. 20.

Jesse Curtis (C.D. Cal. 1962–90), with the admissions ordeal behind him, remembers,

> The thing that got me was, as I say I came from a small school, it was a religious school of sorts to some extent. Smoking was absolutely forbidden and anybody that drank would be severely punished, and when I got back to Harvard the professors themselves would be as drunk as anybody on the weekends and they would all be tapping a cigarette about the last fifteen minutes of their lecture getting ready for their recess and almost everybody I ran into was different.... One fellow was a millionaire, he made a million dollars on the stock market and he had his own apartment, and a secretary and mistress and a driver and a Rolls Royce. It was not a social place at all.
>
> I sat next to a fellow from Princeton. We'd get in class and immediately open your book to sort of refresh your memory on what you've been reading in order to be prepared in the event you're called on, so you don't pay any attention to anybody. After about six months I met this fellow on the street one day and I spoke to him and he looked at me as if, Where did you come from?
>
> Yes, in that year, one fellow brought his girlfriend one day and she sat in the back of the class and the professor just sat there. Sat there for twenty minutes and nothing happened. Finally, I don't know how it came about, I guess he indicated to some extent that he wasn't going to proceed as long as there was a girl in the classroom. Another professor, if a girl ever came to his classroom he would start telling her dirty stories and it would be the expectation of embarrassing them, which it did, and he would pick out some case apparently unsuitable for discussing.
>
> Once in a while there would be somebody in class who wanted to answer a question. Usually didn't know what he was talking about and the class, if he got to talking too long and became really obnoxious, the class would began to stamp and stamp their feet and the whole class would stamp until he would shut up. A lot of fellows got stamped out.
>
> A lot of fellows from New York had gone to New York University, and at New York University the last two years they took some law, which meant that if you continued on at New York you could have graduated in two years from law school. Harvard would not accept

any of those credentials so a lot of those fellows would come over to Harvard. Well, they had two years' experience and we just thought they were brilliant at first. It was funny the next year hardly any of them came back. They all got flunked out.[41]

Other Schools

We get glimpses of other law schools in the oral histories. At UCLA, Dorothy Nelson (C.A.9 1979–present) struggled at first but had the good fortune of having the famous Roscoe Pound encourage her.

I did not do well my first semester, and, indeed, when I got my first semester's grades, which were just practice exams (days of old Common Law Actions and Contracts), I walked down the hall to resign from law school, thinking, "I'm going to take a year off and I probably will come back. Maybe I'll go into teaching for a while." I was met in the hall by the wonderful Roscoe Pound, who had left the Harvard Law School to come out and be associated with the UCLA Law School for a few years, and I had taken his Common Law Actions exam. And as I walked down the hall he held up my paper in Common Law Actions and said, "Brilliant, Mrs. Nelson, brilliant!" And it was the one grade that hadn't come in. My Contracts grade was terrible, my Torts grade was terrible, my Property grade was terrible. I had been used to getting very good grades, and it was the first time in my life where I really felt depressed over grades.

But that one little statement in front of my classmates who knew my terrible grades, sort of caused me to pause and say "Well, maybe I'll go in and talk to Dean Pound." He was not the real dean but was dean emeritus. He was given this title. And I sat down to talk to him about my exams. Now, his exam had been a short answer exam, the sort of exams I had been used to in undergraduate school. The other exams he looked at for me, and he read a couple of my answers, and he said, "Mrs. Nelson, you didn't answer the question. You told them everything you knew, but you didn't answer the question."

---

[41] Jesse William Curtis Jr., "Oral History Interview with Hon. Jesse Curtis," Ninth Judicial Circuit Historical Society (1989), pp. 9–12.

And that was one of the most startling revelations to me in my first year of law school. It caused me to remain in law school, and once I caught on to the system I was all right.[42]

Milton Schwartz (E.D. Cal. 1979–2005) went to Boalt Hall, the University of California at Berkeley's law school.

First of all, we had two brand-new ones who were called instructors, which was the lowest level. And they were very—they were very little older than we were. Maybe four years older. But they had gotten through just before 1941 and had graduated. They were brand new and they related far better to the students than they did to the professors, who were much older. And so they joined our groups of things and they'd come to parties of ours and that kind of stuff. And they were really nice guys.

Of the professors, Ballantine, was everybody's favorite. A real nice, gentle guy. You could write a law review article under him and he was the most knowledgeable and the nicest and the most accomplished. He didn't expect anywhere near as much from you as the younger guys, who were Grrrr, and go get 'em, and fight. And then, of course, the great character was the one they called Captain Kidd, Alexander Marsden Kidd, who was just a wild man. A nice guy off—outside the classroom. Once he told me that he thought my brains had turned to mayonnaise. I never quite understood that.

But, we liked our—most of our professors and related to some of them very well. There was a guy named Bill Laube who was very laid back. Really laid back. You almost had to have a couch for him to carry around. He didn't really expect hardly anything. He was so kind of nice and gentle and all that sort of thing. I don't think we really liked very many of the professors, except for few of them. We kind of worshiped people like Ballantine.[43]

Joseph Sneed (C.A.9 1973–2008), who was a professor at Texas and Stanford before becoming dean at Duke prior to going onto the Ninth

---

[42] Dorothy Wright Nelson, "Oral History Interview with Hon. Dorothy W. Nelson," Ninth Judicial Circuit Historical Society (1988), pp. 10–11.

[43] Milton L. Schwartz, "Hon. Milton L. Schwartz Oral History," Historical Society for the United States District Court for Eastern District of California (n.d.), pp. 30–31.

Circuit, brings a special insight into legal education when he describes his years at the University of Texas Law School. After learning how hard the students worked and the conditions they learned in, we learn from him about the casebook method and about the way the Legal Realists taught law.

Well, I'd had the advantage of going to the very small college for four years, and that gave me some socialization, you might say. And it had been an easy course of study—had not been taxing at all. Too easy, as a matter of fact, and I had lots of time to work and lots of time to play, always had a girl and this, that, and the other. So really, when I went to law school it was putting all this behind me more or less—and going to work.

And it was work; it was a hot summer. I shared a room with a fellow from west Texas about a block from law school with no air-conditioning at all. So we worked up in the library in the afternoons with these big airplane fans to keep the air moving. Anyway, when we got home at night we might go back to the library for the rest of the evening or we turned on the fan in our room and worked there. It was a fairly fast program in the summer. We'd meet two hours a day on Contracts I and then on Torts and do that every day and on one day a week, twice a day. We had two different types of teachers entirely. One was an old man who'd been around since 1900 almost and had been dean of the school, but he had been dean for many, many years. His name was Hildebrand—Ira P. Hildebrand. He taught Contracts, and he had taken Contracts at Harvard under Williston and thought Williston was the greatest thing that ever happened. So everything he asked, you knew Williston had the answer in his book somewhere. And, of course, the casebook was the Williston casebook.

The casebooks in those days were truly casebooks. They did not have any notes. It was case after case. Every once in a while they'd have a little note citing another case that bore some relationship to it, but nothing else—just pure cases. And that, of course, was the Langdellian notion that you take the cases and figure out what the principles are and nobody would help you. Then you get into class and begin to bat it around, refine what people think are the principles in the cases. That's not a bad educational technique, actually. I took to it, but not immediately. It seemed fairly foreign at first

The other teacher was a young man at that time—not just right out of law school—he'd been in law school in the '20s. He was a football player, was bald headed, rather rotund, and could snarl more naturally than anybody I'd ever seen in my life. A snarl was just about his natural facial configuration. He just had a talent for it. He was a good dresser. I remember him coming in with a pair of white linen pants—remember, this is all very hot country—a blue shirt monogrammed, and a huge Windsor knot at his neck, which was a bold neck. He was a disciple of the Realists, who, of course, were beginning to dominate legal education, having had their formative period in the '20s and '30s. And he taught Torts from that point of view, and he had a very rigid structure in teaching Torts. He would tell you know the functional reason for this rule is "blah, blah, blah, blah." But what he meant by that was the purpose of this rule is "such and such." And we would, you know, go round and round in class about what the functional reason was and somebody would give it, but not quite the way he wanted it. So he'd go to somebody else, then you'd be thrown off the track. We'd think, "He didn't want that—so what is he after?" so then he'd wander around. Finally, somebody would say it the right way, and he would be delighted and pounce on it—"That's it, that's it, that's it!" But, you know, he was a good trainer, but it was kind of frustrating because, my gosh, we're wasting an awful lot of time on phrasing here. But that wasn't bad because phrasing is very important.

I was fairly quiet in class. When I thought I really knew something, I would pop up. I didn't sally forth on some half-baked notion about which I was uncertain. And some students were quicker than I was in guessing what the proper answers to the questions really ought to be. But I got better at it as we went along. It was essentially a very foreign form of instruction to me. I'd never seen anything quite like it. Nothing in my college came anywhere close to it. But I was more at home than I am to this good day in contracts than in torts. I understand bargains, I don't understand torts. To this very day. You get me beyond fault, I think it all becomes very murky.[44]

---

[44] Joseph T. Sneed III, "Oral History Interview with Hon. Joseph T. Sneed III," Ninth Judicial Circuit Historical Society (1994), pp. 33–36.

Bruce Thompson (D. Nev. 1963–92) at Stanford describes one of the greatest teachers he ever had, George Osborne, who taught a first-year class called Remedies and Personal Property.

It was about early English forms of action and development of the actions of trespass and trespass on the case and assumpsit and so forth. All the formalities that were involved. Then we got into the questions of possession of personal property and wild animals and all sorts of things like that. Then he taught Securities. He was highly skilled in the Socratic method and he asked very searching questions and didn't hesitate to have fun with the students if they didn't appear to be as bright as he expected them to be. His lectures were, I thought, quite logical and understandable and I really enjoyed him as a teacher.

Then addressing an issue that has continued, he notes,

I think it was at Stanford Law School I learned not to believe in the maxim "publish or perish" for professors and teachers because the best professors I had in law school, like George Osborne and Clarke B. Whittier and Dean Kirkwood, had the least national reputation from having published things. Arthur Cathcart was another one. The professor there who was supposed to be the great genius, Walter Bingham, who taught Trusts and Water Law, I thought was one of the worst teachers that I ever had. It was basically the Socratic method. The professors had different approaches. Some of them spent almost the whole class in questions and answers and discussion of particular cases while some of them, like Dean Kirkwood, who taught real property and future interests, spent most of the class period lecturing. I think it's a personal thing with the particular professor.[45]

Procter Hug (C.A.9 1977–present) also remembers Osborne from his time at Stanford and further describes the use of the Socratic method in class and how that approach—laced as it is with the fear element—helped him later in his career.

Well, one thing that stands out is the first day of class there was a professor there by the name of George Osborne who had a very

---

[45] Bruce Rutherford Thompson, "Oral History Interview with Hon. Bruce R. Thompson," Ninth Judicial Circuit Historical Society (1988), p. 9.

deep, commanding voice. On the first day he began asking these questions using the Socratic method and making us realize that we had to be very careful in our thoughts and expressions because he was a brilliant man. It was a little bit like *The Paper Chase* where he just could scare the very dickens out of all of us and he eventually during the year, went around the class and got everyone. It took him a little longer with some of us than others to realize we are complete fools. But eventually he got us all. Even though he scared us so much, it was a very valuable thing in my mind. It made us realize that we had to do some very critical thinking and we couldn't just sort of coast along like sometimes we do in some of our social science classes where you just talk on and on.

Speaking more generally, Hug notes,

It's funny the way that works out sometimes. The ones that you may think you're the best in you don't necessarily get the best grade in. I liked a number of subjects. I liked Contracts and Torts and Constitutional Law and I liked Trusts very much, too, and I thought I was a real star in Trusts during the summer. We had a visiting professor and it turned out that I got a C+. That's the only C I ever got in college or law school. It also kept me from getting on Order of the Coif. It was a subject I thought I was really good in [laughter].[46]

Abner Mikva (C.A.D.C. 1979–94), University of Chicago Law School, class of 1952, remembers what an exciting place it was for him.

Law school was the most important intellectual experience I have ever had in my life. First, as I said, I came in very awed by the company. But I was determined to do well. Over half the class had gone to undergraduate school at the University of Chicago, and I had some very bright people in the class. Bob Bork was a classmate. He and I became friends early on. He'd gone to the University of Chicago and was very bright and showed it in class. One of my other famous classmates was Patsy Mink, then Patsy Takemoto, who was very bright, like most women had to be. We only had three women in the class. We had three women, three blacks in a class of 153.

46 Procter Ralph Hug Jr., "Oral History Interview with Hon. Procter Hug, Jr.," Ninth Judicial Circuit Historical Society (1995), pp. 45–46.

The faculty was outstanding. Edward Levi was then a young professor at the law school. He became dean in my second year. Harry Kalven was a young professor at the law school. Bernie Meltzer had just returned to the faculty. Walter Blum was there as a tax professor. They were all in their early thirtiess, late twenties, and just full of enthusiasm and full of excitement about the law. The old guard that were there were good. Charles Gregory who taught Labor Law and Torts was a good professor. He was older, but he was pleased at the new faces that were coming on. William W. Crosskey, a controversial Constitutional Law professor, was there. He liked the idea of all this ferment going on. Sheldon Tefft taught Property. He was an old guard, but he tolerated these young whippersnappers. Others of the old guard sort of began to fade into the woodwork as these young and bright educators took over. It was exciting.

Of course, all the professors used the Socratic method and so nothing was ever given to you in black and white. It was always, "What do you think?" The really good professors had this marvelous way of teasing out all variations. It occurred to me when I took the bar exam with the incredibly good education I had that, even though I did not learn a lot of black letter law at law school, when it came to taking the bar exam, I knew how to think about these questions. With the smattering of black letter law that I picked up in bar review, I was able to analyze the questions and get back enough of an answer that I think I passed. I remember feeling, when people were coming out, saying, well, I did terrible on the bar exam, how awful it was, I didn't feel at all uncomfortable about it. I felt I had done well on it. I would have been shocked if I hadn't passed.[47]

Gerhard Gessell (D.D.C. 1967–93) at Yale had the good fortune of having been taught by Thurman Arnold.

Arnold had courses called Procedure I, II, and III—we called them Thurman Arnold I, II, and III. He covered much more than procedure, often very practical matters. He was a fascinating man. At that time he was writing those two famous books of his, *The Symbols of Government* and *The Folklore of Capitalism*. Arnold had been a trial lawyer.

[47] Abner J. Mikva, "Honorable Abner J. Mikva Oral History," Historical Society of the District of Columbia (1996, 1999), pp. 41–45, 51.

He had been a mayor of a town. And when he began to talk about procedural matters, he was talking about actual use of procedural rules to defend or to take advantage. And he made you think.

I learned a valuable lesson in his first class the first year. He came in and drew a jackass on the blackboard. It had three legs. He then went down row after row getting different students to say what was wrong with the picture—only three legs; two-dimensional; eyes disproportionately large; ears bad—you know, all the different things students could think of. Then he ended the class by saying, "Well, that shows how many different ways you can look at a subject."[48]

Leon Higginbotham (E.D. Pa. 1964–77 and C.A.3 1977–93) had a Yale experience—and life—different from most others at the prestigious school. There was the initial decision to attend the school. Higginbotham could have gone to nearby Rutgers, which would have paid for his tuition, books, and incidentals. Yale would pay for nothing, but nonetheless Higginbotham insisted on going there, a brave choice for a poor black young man. Yale was an altogether different world from the world of his hometown, Trenton, New Jersey. To be sure, no one from Trenton went to Yale. But for him the choice was simple.

That was a real dramatic moment for me in my life, because people who I knew and who I liked, and who I respected just thought that going to Yale was almost a frivolous choice because they saw the cost. And after I talked it over with my parents, I said—and my mother was present—I said, "You know, I think the world is bigger than Trenton and I'm going to take it." And I think that my going to Yale made a big difference. I think I would have been a good lawyer if I'd gone to Rutgers, but going to Yale just gave me a passport which I would not have had, in all probability, if I had not gone there.[49]

That his background was different from the backgrounds of most of the others students was made clear to Higginbotham when he compares

[48] Gerhardt Alden Gessell, "Honorable Gerhardt A. Gessell," Historical Society of the District of Columbia (1999, 2001), p. 8.

[49] Aloyisus Leon Higginbotham Jr., "Interview with the Honorable A. Leon Higginbotham," Historical Society of the United States Court of Appeals for the Third Circuit (n.d.), pp. 19–20.

himself to his friend Alice Gilbert and her experience in a Torts class taught by Harry Shulman.

> Harry Shulman was just superb Socratic teacher. The first day in class he called on Alice Gilbert, and she gave an answer which was just parsed perfectly. It just seemed so logical. There just seemed to be something wrong. I had read the same case, and I saw none of those issues. And then the second day, he called on her, and she again was spectacular. And the third day, I believe he called on her. And so, since at that time, you were listed alphabetically—her name was Gilbert; mine was Higginbotham—I think I was next to her— and as we walked out of class, I said, "Alice, what's your full name?" Now, to this day, I do not know any reason why I would have asked such a stupid question. But my mother has a concept, that God moves in mysterious ways. And she says, "Alice Brandeis Gilbert." And when she said that, I clued in on the fact that her father was— her grandfather had been justice of the Supreme Court, her father, a lawyer, I believe her mother, a lawyer and also a Ph.D.

As Higginbotham puts it, "I found the first semester a serious question as to whether I had made the right decision. And I, coming up to Yale in a cardboard suitcase."[50]

Clerkship

A fair number of judges had themselves been law clerks in the federal courts, either as law clerks to a district judge, to a court of appeals judge, or, as in one instance, a law clerk to a Supreme Court justice. They have different stories as to how they got their clerkships. For Abner Mikva (C. A.D.C. 1979–94), who clerked for Justice Sherman Minton, his dean at the University of Chicago Law School was keen to gain attention for his school by getting a Supreme Court clerkship for one of the students. As he explains,

> Edward Levi had become dean of the law school, and he was deter- mined to bring Chicago back to its earlier glory as far as being a national law school. He thought one of the ways of doing this was

---

[50] *Ibid.* at 23.

to get the students back into the clerk stream again. He literally camped on Justice Minton's doorstep until Minton agreed to take a clerk from Chicago, and it was me.[51]

Prentice Marshall's (N.D. Ill. 1973–96) Seventh Circuit clerkship appointment had a certain casualness to it. The dean had picked Marshall as the best candidate and arranged for an interview with Judge Walter Lindley. The judge, in a rather odd interview, asked Marshall why he wasn't a Phi Beta Kappa man, and after getting a satisfactory explanation said, "The dean says you are a good fellow, good person. Get in touch with [current clerk] Ted Scott and make arrangements for when you start. I will see you in Chicago."

According to Marshall, "That was it. That was the interview, no résumé, no writing sample. Then he stood up again and shook my hand as I walked out. 'Well, I suppose I will be seeing you in Chicago.' And the next time I saw him was up at 1212 Lake Shore Drive."[52]

James Moran (N.D. Ill. 1979–present), who clerked for Joseph Lumbard (C.A.2 1955–99) on the Second Circuit, remembers that "one day I was sitting in evidence class and the instructor, Dean Cavers, came up and said, 'How would you like to clerk for Judge Lumbard in the Second Circuit?' I thought about it briefly and thought it was a good idea."[53]

Once on the job, Moran had an experience that makes for the best clerkship story.

> Learned Hand was right across the hall, so I got to know him very well. Learned Hand, who gave me what I've always thought of as my most treasured compliment, came into the office one day with a draft opinion which I drafted—he knew I drafted it—with para-graphs circled—and he threw it on my desk and said, "Who wrote this? Law clerks don't write this well," and left, which I treasured.[54]

[51] Abner J. Mikva, "Honorable Abner J. Mikva Oral History," Historical Society of the District of Columbia (1996, 1999), p. 57.

[52] Prentice H. Marshall, "The Oral History of Retired Judge Prentice H. Marshall," Circuit Library, U.S. Court of Appeals for the Seventh Circuit (1999), p. 22.

[53] James B. Moran, "The Oral History of James B. Moran, Senior District Court Judge of the United States District Court for the Northern District of Illinois," Circuit Library, U.S. Court of Appeals for the Seventh Circuit (1994), p. 27.

[54] *Ibid.* at 27–28.

Harold Greene (D.D.C. 1978–2000) remembers that he was quite involved in the work of his judge, Bennett Champ of the D.C. court of appeals.

> Judge Champ wasn't that well. He died the year after I was with him. He wasn't that well, and frequently let me handle a lot of things—the writing particularly. The decision-making was never mine because the judges would sit together and make a decision. But as to the writing of the opinions, he left me a pretty free hand because he wasn't that well and went home.[55]

Stephen Reinhardt (C.A.9 1979–present) clerked for Luther Youngdahl, a U.S. district judge for the District of Columbia (and former governor of Minnesota) and had a different experience. Youngdahl was a very decent man, Reinhardt explains. He was goodhearted and well meaning, but he was also not very sophisticated.

> In those days in the District of Columbia, for instance, the federal court was the state court also. So they did all kinds of things. Once he had an annulment case and the wife came in and asked for an annulment because the man had wanted to have oral–genital sex with her and [Judge Youngdahl] wanted to grant the annulment because the man had asked her to do that. And I told him that I thought that was a little excessive, and he said, "You don't understand what it is he wanted her to do. It's like animals," he told me. That's what I mean by being a little naive.[56]

Abner Mikva (C.A.D.C. 1979–94) had a clerkship on the Supreme Court and has recollections that any Supreme Court historian should consult. When Mikva came out of law school in 1952, the place to be (as it is for any law school graduate today) was the Supreme Court. It was the promise of meritocracy fulfilled.

> It was an exciting clerkship. Just being there was exciting. You felt like you were the center of the universe and, especially for somebody who led as insular a life as I had, this was incredibly exciting, to be involved with all these important cases and to be in Washington.

55 Harold H. Greene, "Honorable Harold H. Greene," Historical Society of the District of Columbia (1992), p. 44.
56 Stephen Roy Reinhardt, "Oral History Interview with Judge Stephen Reinhardt," Ninth Judicial Circuit Historical Society (1993), p. 9.

Washington was and is an exciting place to be. The clerks were absolutely, I think, person for person, it was the most brilliant group of people I had ever been around at any given time. If there is a meritocracy in this country, it has to be the way clerks are chosen. Nobody, no matter how political their background or how unusual their management style, no judge will take anyone but the very best clerks he or she can get. The result is you just bring out these really bright people.

Mikva's explanation of the working procedure of his justice, Sherman Minton, tells us something about Minton and the Supreme Court. The clerks read petitions for certiorari and wrote bench memoranda. They also wielded influence.

Justice Minton made it clear that he wanted cert memos to be as brief as they could be and give him everything he needed to know. So we would try to boil them down to reasonable length. He always wanted a recommendation from us as to whether we thought cert should be granted or cert should be denied. I can't ever recall his disagreeing with us when we said cert should be denied, but he frequently disagreed with us if we thought cert should be granted. He had many disagreements with us on the merits.

Saturday at the Court was the big day—conference day.

On Saturday mornings, the conferences, and Monday mornings were opinion days. And that was rigid. Occasionally, they had extra opinion days, maybe, occasionally, extra conferences; but traditionally, Saturday morning was conference day. We'd be there at 9:00 and the Court would work till noon, sometimes later, in identifying cases that they were going to grant cert. on, and the cases that had been heard would be decided and assigned. There were only the nine justices in the conference. I think that's still the way it is. Minton, as the junior justice, which he was then, would be the one who answered the door. Our standing instructions were that we were never to knock at the door unless somebody in his family said it was an emergency or unless he had asked for us to give him something. Other than that, we should never be responsible for the knock at the door.

But it was very exciting because the clerks would all hang around. We didn't have a lot to do. We were kind of waiting for what was going to come out of conference, and we'd speculate about what they were going to do on this case or that case, if they were going to grant cert or affirm or reverse. Then the conference would break up. Sometimes right after the conference, but usually on the following Monday, he would go over, not in any detail, the results of conference. . . . All he said was what was going to be the *ratio decidendi* of the case. He would usually do it, as I recall, on Mondays. He would tell us what he thought we needed to know. He would say the chief assigned the opinion on so and so and on so and so. I think we got everybody but Hugo [Black] and Bill [Douglas], but this is the way I want the opinion to look. Then he would go into some detail on what he'd want.

The clerks were the engine for opinion writing, so long as they wrote imbued with Minton's conservatism. Mikva recalls one case involving teacher loyalty oaths.

Usually, we would do the first draft. Very occasionally, he would do the first draft. I never had any problem about whose opinion it was because you knew damn sure by the time it was through that it was his. There were occasions where he was very unhappy with our drafts; this was the height of the McCarthy era, and both clerks tried to carry out his wishes but sometimes he was just so determined to get to a particular result.

I remember on one opinion—it was a teacher's oath case—*Feiner v. New York*. I wrote the first draft. Clearly he was going to uphold the oath and the teacher remained fired. I wrote it the way I thought he told me to write it, and he looked at it and came back in the room and said, "God damn left-wing University of Chicago, I don't know what they teach you there." And he handed it to my co-clerk who was way to the left of me. I was a moderate compared to Ray. And so Ray took a stab at it and later the judge said, "I don't know what the hell is going on at the law schools these days. I don't know what they teach you." And he sat down with his secretary and they wrote the opinion. It was pretty rough. Frankfurter's clerks were mimicking the judge, saying unpleasant things about it and other judges were saying it just didn't hold together. And it got worked over some by other judges. He didn't want us working on it any more. It finally came down, I think it was five to four or six to three. It was not one of the clearest expositions.

Mikva sketches for us portraits of the best-known justices that, on average, reflect the standard take on the subject. On iconoclastic William O. Douglas, who cannot be assessed without looking to his fellow liberal colleague, Hugo Black, we find that

Douglas was this very shy professor who literally just could not relate to people the way Black did. Douglas's chambers were right next to Minton's chambers; and every morning on the way in, I would pass Justice Douglas going to his chambers—we were on the same time sync. So I would say, "Good morning, Mr. Justice," and he would look straight ahead and never even say hello. I thought about that many years later when I was trying to fight back Gerald Ford's efforts to impeach Justice Douglas, and my effort sure wasn't based on any personal relationship because there wasn't one. He was just a very cold cookie.

Mikva provides a second example.

There is a story that happened a year before I was there, maybe the year I was there, but it's a story that is often told. There was a practice of inviting one of the justices down to the clerks' dining room to talk to them about matters. The clerks had their own dining room, so they were free to talk about the cases without somebody overhearing them. The practice is that the clerks go through the regular cafeteria, get their trays, and take them to the clerks' dining room. The justices normally eat in an upstairs dining room, where they're served by their messengers.

Well, one time, whoever was inviting the justices invited both Black and Douglas to come down the same week. Black frequently ate in the cafeteria with his clerks, and so, when it came time for this lunch where he was supposed to talk to the clerks, he went through the cafeteria with his clerks and came into the clerks' dining room with all these clerks around chattering like magpies. And there was Justice Douglas sitting there, being served by his messenger, who had brought his tray, his lunch, down from the upstairs dining room. Black looked at him and called out, "Well, Bill, how's the man of the people today?"

As for other justices, Mikva says,

Justice Reed was probably the least known of the justices. Everyone respected him but he was getting on in years. Justice Clark was very pleasant, very nice, but no one could really quite figure out where he came from. He had not been known as a great legal scholar; he clearly had some loyalty to President Truman, but that was not always visible in the way he voted; and his reign as attorney general had not been that outstanding. Justice Jackson was admired by a lot of people but, again, people didn't quite know how to figure out where he would land on the ideological landscape. His writing was always brilliant. I thought Jackson was the best writer on the bench of all the justices when I was there.

And then there's Felix Frankfurter, perhaps the most controversial of the group of justices serving in 1952. Mikva confirms that Frankfurter moved about the Court with mischief.

Well, I think I learned some things not to do from Justice Frankfurter. For instance, he was always writing memos to judges about what they should do in their opinions and then not joining them. I remember my boss complained several times and other justices' clerks complained at how Frankfurter would encourage judges to make changes in their opinions and then wouldn't join in the opinion anyway. I realized that if you're not going to play the game, don't try and make the rules. I took that very seriously when I got on the court. If I wasn't prepared to join in an opinion, I would not make comments on what I thought about the opinion and what changes I thought it needed. If I was going to join in, then I would suggest changes. In fact, we developed a phrase on my court called, "Take it or leave it," which meant I would go with the opinion anyway, but I would like you to think about such and such a change, which you could leave alone if you want to.[57]

Bar Exam

With law school done and a clerkship for some finished, only the bar examination remained. We learn from the oral histories that bar examinations were handled differently in earlier decades.

---

[57] Abner J. Mikva, "Honorable Abner J. Mikva Oral History," Historical Society of the District of Columbia (1996, 1999), pp. 64–66, 77–80.

Luther Swygert (N.D. Ind. 1943–61 and C.A.7 1961–88), who came to the bar in 1928 in Indiana, thinks that "the bar exam at Michigan City was sort of a charade." Both Swygert and one other lawyer were actually practicing for six months or so when "the bar finally decided to give us an examination. There were two opposing firms who had a lawsuit involving suretyship. So the bar thought they would give us some questions on suretyship. They turned us loose at the court library and we started looking up some of the answers."[58]

Bruce Thompson (D. Nev. 1963–92), who passed his Nevada bar examination in 1936, explains that the examination lasted for a week.

> The first day they did something that I think they ought to reinstitute in the bar examination process. They gave you a statement of facts, turned you loose in the law library, and asked you to identify the legal problems that were involved in the statement of facts and to write a memorandum of points and authorities with respect to those. That was the first day of the examination, which I think is important because over the years I have found that quite a lot of lawyers don't have much of a conception of how to find the law and what to do with the reference books that are available. Then we had four solid days, eight hours a day of essay questions. That took us through Friday. Then on Saturday morning, the members of the bar examination committee would meet with us and ask us questions on Nevada history and legal ethics. All of the examinees were together. There were fourteen candidates for the entire state.[59]

Alfred Goodwin's (D. Or. 1969–71 and C.A.9 1971–present) typing skills helped him when he took his bar examination.

> We had a record in those days that practically everybody who graduated from the University of Oregon Law School passed the bar exam anyway. We didn't have bar review courses in those days. We just went back over our case notes of our courses that we'd taken. We took special effort to look at the subjects that were listed that we would be examined upon. Mostly I think we spent the time between commencement and the bar examination, which was roughly a

---

[58] Luther Merritt Swygert, "The Oral History of Judge Luther M. Swygert," Circuit Library, U.S. Court of Appeals for the Seventh Circuit (1985), pp. 24–25.

[59] Bruce Rutherford Thompson, "Oral History Interview with Hon. Bruce R. Thompson," Ninth Judicial Circuit Historical Society (1988), pp. 35–36.

month, maybe five or six weeks, we all spent that time just reviewing our notebooks that we'd save from each of the courses that we took. Sometimes we'd seminar together, four or five of us would sit and ask each other test questions and sound out how quick our memories were on some of the points that we were reviewing. But nobody seemed to be particularly worried about it. If they did, they didn't talk about it. My wife and I probably shared some concerns about what would happen if I didn't pass. But I don't think I ever seriously thought I wouldn't pass.

Dewey Wilson and I took a room in the old Senator Hotel in Salem and shared the expenses. The bar exam at that time was a two-day examination, all essay questions. It's different now, but at that time it was a two-day essay exam. And Dewey and I were both typing our exams, which we were permitted to do. Those who typed their exams used the House chamber and those who wrote their exams in longhand used the Senate chamber, or vice versa, I forgot, one or the other. The bar examination was just as rough as we thought it would be, but at the end of the first day, Dewey Wilson and I both went to a movie. We decided to purge our brains of worrying about the bar examination. We went to a movie, and then the next day we came back and took the rest of it. We both passed.[60]

Harold Ryan (D. Id. 1981–95) passed his Idaho bar examination in 1950. "That building's still up there, but I think it's a library now, the city library for Lewiston. So I took it sitting in the chief judge's chair in the supreme courtroom in Lewiston, banging on my typewriter. I figured that would be a good omen if I went up and sat in the chief justice's chair and set down my little portable typewriter and started banging away."[61]

---

[60] Alfred T. Goodwin, "Oral History Interview with Alfred T. Goodwin," U.S. District Court Collection, Oregon Historical Society (1986), pp. 141–142.
[61] Harold L. Ryan, "District Judge Harold Ryan," Ninth Circuit Library, Boise, Idaho (1990), p. 31.

CHAPTER TWO

WHEN THEY WERE LAWYERS

They were lawyers before they were judges. Their oral histories portray the practice of law in the decades of the 1940s, 1950s, 1960s, and 1970s and present a sharp image of young lawyers—before large firms and online research tools—struggling and then succeeding at the practice of law.

As lawyers, they tended to work in smaller firms—sometimes by themselves. Although some evolved toward various specialties, such as litigation, most worked in the general practice of law. There were, for many of them, surprisingly modest beginnings.

Harlington Wood (S.D. Ill. 1973–76 and C.A.7 1976–present), whose father was on the bench when he began his practice but later joined his son when he left the bench, tells us,

> I rented one room in the Reisch Building on the west side of the square in Springfield, one little room and no secretary. I had some of Dad's old furniture, a desk and a swivel chair. He had some *Illinois Reports* that were outdated, but they looked all right up against the wall. I started getting business right away, I think largely because they connected me with him. After a while I was able to hire a secretary, but we had to share the same office. She typed in there, but when I had a client, I had to ask her to wait out in the hall because you couldn't interview somebody about a private matter with a secretary sitting there. Then Dad quit the bench, and we got a better office.[62]

---

[62] Harlington Wood Jr., "The Oral History of Judge Harlington Wood, Jr.," Circuit Library, U.S. Court of Appeals for the Seventh Circuit (1997), p. 27.

Fred Taylor (D. Id. 1954–88) "had the statutes of course, the *Idaho Reports*, the *Pacific Reporters*, and the *Pacific Digest*. I didn't really have any texts except Bancroft *Pleading and Practice*. My opponent had *Corpus Juris*. Sometimes I'd get a case and go down and borrow one of his *Corpus Juris*. But we just had a small working library, but nothing on the federal side because we didn't have any federal cases."[63]

All had their own take on it, though. What many of them shared is that, in the beginning at least, they took whatever came through the door.

Milton Schwartz (E.D. Cal. 1979–2005), for example, started out by himself and took "anything that walked in the door. I thought I was going to be selective, but when you sit there in the office, any warm body that walks down the hall you'll grab him. So I took virtually anything that came in that had any possible credibility, and I'd figure out a way to collect the fee later."[64]

Paul Rosenblatt (D. Ariz. 1984–present) "opened up an office and just started practicing law." He explains,

> In a rather idealistic concept, I was going to represent the cause of anybody that came in the front door, whether they had any money or not. I rented space in an historic office building and my practice really took off. I was pleasantly surprised. Sole practitioner. And it's still the best practice, if you can cope with it. But it's pretty hard as the practice grows. You can never get away. But I got some excellent clients right off the bat and a couple of high-profile cases.[65]

Mary Lou Robinson (N.D. Tex. 1979–present) tells us,

> We started out in an office in what's called the Johnson Building, and then we moved—to what was then called the Barfield Building. That building is not an office building any more. And we just practiced there together. We took anything that walked in the door, and that was not too unusual at that time. Even the large law firms took a wide variety of activities. They were not as specialized as law firms are now, particularly the boutique law firms. We had clients

---

[63] Frederick Monroe Taylor, "Oral History Interview with Hon. Frederick Monroe Taylor," Ninth Circuit Library, Boise, Idaho (1987), p. 11.

[64] Milton L. Schwartz., "Hon. Milton L. Schwartz Oral History," Historical Society for the United States District Court for Eastern District of California (n.d.), p. 24.

[65] Paul G. Rosenblatt, "Oral History Interview with Judge Paul G. Rosenblatt," Ninth Judicial Circuit Historical Society (1998), p. 79.

wanting contracts drawn. People wanting divorces. An occasional criminal case, although we didn't really set out to practice criminal law. Real estate transactions. One of my clients was a person that had a real estate business here, and I ended up examining lots of abstracts over time and writing opinions on them.[66]

Gene Brooks (S.D. Ind. 1979–96) describes himself as a general practitioner, explaining, "I did a lot of title work. I examined a lot of titles and worked for a couple of banks. I did have some bankruptcy practice, but not a lot."[67]

Samuel Dillin (S.D. Ind. 1961–2006) began work with his father in a general practice firm.

Of course when you start out, you do plaintiff's personal injury work because you are not known by the insurance companies and they already have a lawyer in your area anyway. But at the time I went on the bench I was about fifty–fifty. For a number of years I represented a major interstate gas pipeline company, doing condemnations and putting together three underground gas storage fields. In other words, my practice was more extensive and varied than the typical small-town practice of real estate, probate, and divorce matters (although we did our fair share of those, too.) I enjoyed every minute of it[68]

Harlington Wood (S.D. Ill. 1973–76 and C.A.7 1976–present) had a very general practice.

I was a specialist in anything that a client needed to have done, whether it was a divorce or anything else. For example, I had a client in rural Illinois named Marie Birch. She and her brother didn't get along very well. They raised pigs, and for some reason or other they got into odds about who owned a big sow. Marie had it in a pig pen on her farm. Her brother lived on the adjacent farm. He got mad and wanted the sow, so he brought a replevin suit. We had the trial about that sow in the justice of the peace court. In the middle of

66 Mary Lou Robinson, "The Oral History of Judge Mary Lou Robinson," Circuit Library, U.S. Court of Appeals for the Fifth Circuit (2006), p. 13.
67 Gene E. Brooks, "The Oral History of Retired Judge Gene E. Brooks," Circuit Library, U.S. Court of Appeals for the Seventh Circuit (1994), p. 16.
68 S. Hugh Dillin, "The Oral History of Judge S. Hugh Dillin," Circuit Library, U.S. Court of Appeals for the Seventh Circuit (1994), p. 16.

this suit before the justice of the peace, the sow had pigs. That made a very complicated legal question because we didn't know if we had to file a separate replevin suit for each piglet or whether they went with the sow. Anyway, it was almost too much for the justice of the peace. But then somebody killed that sow. I never knew what happened, but that ended that family lawsuit.[69]

Jesse Curtis (C.D. Cal. 1962–90) describes having a general practice.

I avoided mining law when I was in law school for the rather obvious reason that San Bernardino was full of old miners who always had a gold mine somewhere that they never could find, so I didn't want anything to do with mining. But as soon as I got back I found that the father of a close friend of mine was in the recorder's office, the County Recorder's Office, and he was interested in mining and he said that all of the old mining lawyers had died off and there was nobody in San Bernardino handling any mining. You had to go to San Francisco and there were a few mining lawyers in Los Angeles but not very many, so he said, "If you'll get in and study up I'll send you some cases." So he did, and I developed quite a mining practice in which I represented salt companies. I patented hundreds of mining claims for Southwest Cement Company. I was the only one in this area that could patent claims. They would send me work from San Francisco and Los Angeles. Then I did trial work for the Santa Fe Railroad. They had lots of crossing accidents, and also I did some divorce work, which I hated. That's one of the reasons why I went on to the superior court—so that I could get away from divorce court. I didn't like those clients.[70]

Thomas Tang (C.A.9 1977–95) was also a general practitioner.

Just general practice of the law. A little bit of everything, general practice, domestic relations, criminal defense once in a while, commercial practice, personal injury case, whatever came in the door and we felt confident to handle is the way it went. What always happens anytime when one goes back into practice, it takes time for your

---

[69] Harlington Wood Jr., "The Oral History of Judge Harlington Wood, Jr.," Circuit Library, U.S. Court of Appeals for the Seventh Circuit (1997), pp. 27–28.
[70] Jesse William Curtis Jr., "Oral History Interview with Hon. Jesse Curtis," Ninth Judicial Circuit Historical Society (1989), p. 14.

practice to build up. I don't care who you are unless you go in with a big firm. In order to build up your practice it usually takes about two years before you have any kind of a practice that will sustain itself.[71]

Procter Hug (C.A.9 1977–present) describes his practice:

It was quite a general practice. I think I still did some criminal defense because we were required to take appointments from the federal court. So I still did some of that for maybe the next couple of years, but I also did general business law, utility law, because I was involved with that phone company, and some other utility law, and represented some insurance events and also some plaintiffs' work. I tried a couple of cases for the Southern Pacific on crossing accidents. They were hard clients to represent because they didn't want to put those gates on some of the intersections, so when the crash would occur the suit was against the Southern Pacific for not having gates and relying on the whistle or engines. Tough cases. A typical day would be coming in to handle the cases that we had and, if it was a personal injury case, I would be working on researching the law or on developing the evidence. Or it could be a transaction, wills and contracts. Then we had some criminal cases that we were retained on.[72]

William Justice (E.D. Tex. 1968–present) practiced for many years with his father, a well-known criminal defense lawyer, in a small Texas town.

We very seldom had any scheduled appointments. People just dropped in if they needed legal advice. It was a very successful practice in the sense that we had a whole bunch of people coming in. I remember when I first started to practice law in 1946, air-conditioning had not become prevalent. I was in this rather small office adjoining my father's and we would raise the windows to get all the air that we could. Right next to my office was looking out over the rooftop of a building that had this rock and tar covering. We had to put paperweights on everything. We had a central fan, and everything would fly around if you didn't keep the papers covered, weighted down.

---

71 Thomas Tang, "Oral History Interview with Hon. Thomas Tang," Ninth Judicial Circuit Historical Society (1998), p. 18.
72 Procter Ralph Hug Jr., "Oral History Interview with Hon. Procter Hug, Jr.," Ninth Judicial Circuit Historical Society (1995), pp. 52–53.

As people would come in and sit there they all wanted to see Mr. Justice. That didn't mean me, that was my father [laughter]. I was just Wayne. We had a partner at that time by the name of Homer Moore, a very fine lawyer. They would wait until they got to see the lawyer they wanted. My father would assign me tasks from time to time. It helped me to realize that I had a master next door if I got into any legal difficulties. I could always call on him. That's the way it continued. Later on, of course, we got better offices with air-conditioning. It made a lot of difference.[73]

Others built what they describe as a civil practice, with some staying away from criminal work. David Williams (C.D. Cal. 1969–2000) explains,

[I] avoided criminal practice and tried to build up, and did successfully build up, a civil practice. Mostly anything that came in the door [chuckling]. I handled probate law, preparation of wills and probate of estates. I handled real estate law, domestic relations, divorces and adoptions and that sort of thing. Anything in the civil field I handled. But I did not like criminal practice because it put me in the company of people of the lowest caliber, and I was kind of a snoot [chuckling].[74]

Fred Taylor (D. Id. 1954–88) speaks of his practice:

[I] had quite a little civil business—the ordinary run of civil business, negligence cases, representing corporations, setting up corporations, probate, and office practice. And then I got somewhat into the I.C.C. trucking business through my good friend Maurice Greene. I didn't like it very well, so I didn't handle too much of it. But I would say, generally, it was a very comfortable practice. I was probably making more money then, than this job paid at that time. I did some work for the banks—one in particular—and quite a little real estate business. It was just a general practice.[75]

---

73 William Wayne Justice, "Oral History Interview with Judge William Wayne Justice," Fifth Circuit Court of Appeals Library, New Orleans, LA (2002), pp. 21–22.
74 David W. Williams, "Oral History Interview with Hon. David W. Williams," Ninth Judicial Circuit Historical Society (1998), p. 55.
75 Frederick Monroe Taylor, "Oral History Interview with Hon. Frederick Monroe Taylor," Ninth Circuit Library, Boise, Idaho (1987), p. 20.

For Aubrey Robinson (D.D.C. 1966–2000),

it was sort of a general, basically civil practice. We did a reasonable amount of court work. We had some small businesses that we represented. I was initially, just as most young people are, I guess, the "go for." I did all kinds of things. Drafted pleadings, filed pleadings, motions. Among the people we represented, we represented one of the local unions. It got involved in a series of confrontations as a result of which a lot of the union members had criminal charges filed against them and I helped in some of the defense of those cases. I tried some of those cases.

I was particularly interested in the area of probate law. And to the extent we represented small estates, I did a lot of that. I enjoyed that. And when I left Lawson's office [my first law firm] I hooked up with Charles T. Duncan and I then just decided to leave and establish our own little partnership. We then hooked up with Frank Reeves. The three of us practiced law for several years.[76]

Joyce Hens Green (D.D.C. 1979–present) practiced for many years by herself before sharing space with June Green (D.D.C. 1968–2001). Both became district court judges. Joyce Green recalls two phases to her career.

In the beginning, I was everything to the office. I did my own typing, my own legwork; I was the messenger; I answered the phone, except when the answering service performed that function for me in my absence. There was no one else. But after the first year, and during the second year, I was able to afford a part-time secretary. As I put it, I was able to afford half a carpet, then things improved substantially, and thereafter I was able to afford a secretary and other support services.

Then there was practice with her nominal counterpart.

When I joined forces with June Green, she had two offices, one for each of us, a common waiting room, and a secretary. We shared the cost and operation of the office and the secretary right down the middle and that worked remarkably well. Each of us bought as many books and supplies as we could afford. It's amazing to think back to

---

76 Aubrey E. Robinson, "Honorable Aubrey E. Robinson, Jr. Oral History," Historical Society of the District of Columbia (1992), p. 21.

the day when there was no computer, there was no LexisNexis, no Internet; we did not have research assistants, you did the research yourself, and that meant going down to the bar association library, available to members only, and spending a great deal of time there (located on the third floor of the U.S. courthouse), and doing whatever research was necessary. There were typewriters in the back of the library's large room, accessible for people who had need for them, which I used over and again.

My practice, essentially, was a civil litigation practice. I did a good deal of domestic relations work, probate, estate work, personal injury work, and only on rare occasions did I do criminal work. Primarily those latter cases resulted from court appointments. As an example of some of the cases that went to litigation, I recall representation of intervening petitioners, the grandparents, in a most acrimonious five-day divorce trial involving custody of two minor grandchildren. There was also representation of a mother who sought support from her deserting husband, who years later became a famous country musician.[77]

Before opening her own practice, Joyce Green spent a summer working at a law firm, where she learned an important lesson about the way women lawyers can be perceived.

I worked with a partner, Alvis Layne, an incredibly wonderful man, gentle and brilliant, and also with his young associate, a recent graduate of the University of Chicago. All of a sudden, at this wee hour of the morning, the associate had a brilliant idea: completely revamp the theory on which we had been proceeding for weeks. He asked me if I knew how to type. I sensed this as a moment of moments and told him, untruthfully, that I did not know how to type, even though I was happy to make a cup of coffee for all of us right then and there. I recognized that had I acknowledged my secretarial skills, I would be a typist for the remainder of my days with this firm, something I did not want to do. Years later I confessed what I had done; he had suspected it and his partner thought this dialogue was hilarious. The very next day Al and Chuck brought an evening secretary who stayed with us for the duration. We were a

77 Joyce Hens Green, "Honorable Joyce Hens Green Oral History," Historical Society of the District of Columbia (1999, 2001), pp. 70–71, 77–78.

wonderful team, working remarkably well together. I look upon that very short stint as momentum in my career.[78]

Three women judges interviewed for the Federal Judicial Center's oral history project on diversifying the judiciary describe different obstacles they encountered and overcame when they entered the job market in the 1940s, 1950s, and 1960s, respectively.

Coming out of Stanford in 1949, Shirley Hufstedler (C.A.9 1968–79) felt she did not have many options. She was offered a clerkship on the California Supreme Court, but because her husband, also right out of Stanford, had taken a job in Los Angeles, she did not want to stay in San Francisco for the clerkship. She wanted to litigate and lucked out when she found a job with a successful litigator. After a year, she struck up a relationship with another solo practitioner. She would do some work for him to pay her share of the expenses, but she built her own practice as well. She came to like being hired by other lawyers to participate in different phases of their litigation and became a lawyer's lawyer, work that included appellate litigation. This type of practice gave her the work she wanted but also the freedom she needed for her growing family.[79]

Rya Zobel (D. Mass. 1979–present), coming out of Harvard in 1956, did not even bother interviewing at the big Boston firms. It was well known that they would not hire women. She had the good fortune to clerk for the chief judge of the Massachusetts district for ten years, until the judge died. The first firm she went to had the reputation of giving the more tedious and routine work to its women lawyers, and it was no different for her.

"They had me doing pension plans. A man who had been my classmate in college was the guy who was overseeing it, and he was pretty arrogant. He would think nothing of sending me literally on a messenger run, to take a document to Providence or something like that."

Zobel began to develop divorce work as her specialty. She did well in the courtroom and was also able to attract clients. This prompted one of the big Boston firms to recruit her. She became the firm's first woman partner.[80]

---

[78] *Ibid.* at 55–56.

[79] Shirley Ann Mount Hufstedler, "Diversifying the Federal Judiciary: Interview with Judge Shirley A. Hufstedler," Federal Judicial Center, (1995), pp. 10–11.

[80] Rya Weickert Zobel, "Diversifying the Federal Judiciary: Interview with Judge Rya Zobel," Federal Judicial Center, (1995), pp. 24–25.

Barbara Rothstein (W.D. Wa.1979–present) of Harvard (1966) spent only two years in private practice before going west to Washington and working as an assistant attorney general and chief trial attorney in the Consumer Protection and Antitrust Division of the Washington State Attorney General's Office for ten years, from which she went onto the state court bench. She thrived in private practice once she got the chance, but it was on getting the chance that she had an interesting, amusing, and ultimately sad story to tell.

> I'll give you the best example, and I won't mention the firm because they may still be around. This guy came in, and he looked at my résumé—I didn't even know why—well, I guess I signed up. You see, they don't select. You just sign up and fill in a slot, and they do interviews every half-hour or so. I had filled my name in, so it wasn't like he could say, "Don't let her come in," you know; I was in. He looked at my résumé and he said, "I've known women like you all my life." He said, "They did better than I did in high school, they did better than I did in college, did better than I did in law school. I'll be damned if I'm going to let one of them come into my law firm." And believe it or not, I mean, it's hard to believe from where I'm sitting now, I went home, I told this to my roommates, and they said, "What did you say, what did you say?" thinking I told him—whatever. I said, "I didn't say anything." They said, "How could you not say anything?"
>
> You have to know what it's like. I mean, here you are, you're going through a whole battery of interviews, and they're all very discouraging. You've spent three years thinking of yourself as, "You know, I'm in the finest law school in the country, and I'm going to get a great job," and suddenly nobody wants to hire you. And now this guy is actually putting it into words. I didn't say anything. What could I say? Looking back on it, you know, it's one of those occasions where you think you missed a golden opportunity; and, of course, today, I think—well, today, he'd never say it. But that was probably the worst. But there were others.[81]

One judge as a practitioner specialized in hard-core criminal defense work. Raul Ramirez (E.D. Cal. 1979–89) in Sacramento explains.

---

[81] Barbara Jacobs Rothstein, "Diversifying the Federal Judiciary: Interview with Judge Barbara J. Rothstein," Federal Judicial Center, (1995), pp. 15–16.

[I] got appointed the most difficult, the most obnoxious, dangerous clientele that ever came down. I was involved in, I think my résumé says twenty to twenty-five first-degree murder cases, and I tried a lot of them. And some of the judges who spoke at my swearing in—my robing ceremony at both municipal court and when I came over to federal court—told the audience that "we used to appoint Raul because he was the only one that could control some of the clients." And I used to always say, "Thanks fellas, you're putting my life at stake here," because I remember my biggest clients literally and figuratively were "hit men" for the Mexican Mafia, the Black Gorillas, and the Aryan Brotherhood, which were prison gangs and you couldn't even sit at a table with them and not feel that they were gonna put a pencil through your ear—you never turned your back on them, etc., etc. So, I was flattered that I got appointed and I always had the best fees. I mean, I could put in a fee then for $5,000 or $6,000 where if someone else had the same type case, same issues, would get $3,000 or $4,000. They would never question me because nobody would represent these guys; they were afraid of them.[82]

Abner Mikva (C.A.D.C. 1979–94) was recruited by the great Arthur Goldberg, famous labor lawyer and future Supreme Court justice and ambassador to the United Nations, to work in his small Chicago office. Mikva had been a top student and had clerked for a Supreme Court justice, so the transition to private practice had some difficulties. He explains,

I was persuaded, charmed, cajoled by Arthur to come to work in the Chicago office; and I never had any regrets. Oh, I shouldn't say I never had any regrets. The early years of practice, and I guess it's not too different today than it was then, there were ups and downs. There were some days that were very exciting. There were other days that were as boring as all get out. Here I had been involved in all these important cases, all these exciting constitutional issues and the drama between the Executive Branch fighting the Legislative Branch and the drama of those loyalty oath cases and those criminal cases. My first chore at the firm was to find out where the municipal

---

[82] Raul Ramirez, "Oral History Interview with Hon. Raul Ramirez," Ninth Judicial Circuit Historical Society (1990), pp. 11–12.

court of Chicago was located and to file some silly pleadings to make some rich client richer. It was very troublesome to digest.[83]

Today, in an environment increasingly dominated by large firms, young lawyers are taught by others to do their jobs. Moreover, they can always rely on what lawyers in the firm working on similar problems had done, using their work as a template for their own. Our judges as lawyers worked in a time and place in which they usually had to struggle through on their own, relying when they could for instruction and direction.

James Foreman (N.D. Ill. 1972–present) explains his learning curve this way:

> Well, you fumble around with some of that. I did some income tax return work, for example, with which I was already familiar. And I remember the first divorce, I had to ask another lawyer what to do and he told me and gave me the forms. You'd hang around the courthouse and the circuit clerk's office and the older lawyers would help you out some. The circuit judges which we had at that time were tolerant and fairly helpful. I had no clinical experience at all because they don't have clinical experience or didn't have back in those days. It's a big thing today in law school. I had none of that. You learn by feel, touch, and smell. You just do it. Learn the hard way. You know, I had some tough lessons. Some older lawyers would teach you some pretty good lessons in the courtroom sometimes.

Samuel Dillin (S.D. Ind. 1961–2006) worked with his father and learned from him, later thankful for his father's generosity. Together, he explains, they did everything.

> I did most of the trial work. Not that my dad couldn't do it. He was one of the best students of evidence that I ever saw, but he wanted me to go forward and so he put me in the first chair when we were trying cases, which I appreciated. I appreciate it even more now because I think back on other father-and-son law firms where the senior member insisted on being the front man all of the time. But this left junior not a very good trial lawyer when the old man had to quit.[84]

[83] Abner Mikva, "Honorable Abner J. Mikva Oral History," Historical Society of the District of Columbia (1996, 1999), p. 87.

[84] S. Hugh Dillin, "The Oral History of Judge S. Hugh Dillin," Circuit Library, U.S. Court of Appeals for the Seventh Circuit (1994), p. 30.

Luther Swygert (N.D. Ind. 1943–61 and C.A.7 1961–88) has his own story about starting out and knowing nothing.

My first client was a German in Michigan City. He had a bad case to start with. He ran a hotel at the north end of Franklin Street, allegedly a little shady. The city commission decided to close the alley in back of his hotel. The owner came to my office. I was just sitting there with a typewriter, *Corpus Juris*, Indiana statutes, and a set of form books. I had no idea what to do. I didn't even know how to file a complaint. I had a hard time with that case, and I finally went to the meeting where the council was going to take up this matter. I asked for a continuance in a very frightened manner. They gave me a continuance. I had forgotten how it came out, but I think they withdrew the petition. I think I got a fee of $25—my first fee.[85]

For Procter Hug (C.A.9 1977–present), the learning came from the doing.

One of the nice things about our small firm practice was that we got into court a lot, so one of the things where I was really learning to try cases was at the criminal appointment process in the federal court and at the state court where they would appoint young attorneys to represent indigent defendants. At the federal court you'd do it for free; it was part of your responsibility as a lawyer and anyone who became a lawyer automatically got on the roll and they'd be called. The judge would call you over and you would represent people. I had several trials there that were really learning experiences for me and it worked out pretty well. It worked out for the defendants because you worked really hard for your clients to give them appropriate representations. There was one that I think contributed to my becoming a federal judge.[86]

Otto Skopil (D. Or. 1972–79 and C.A.9 1979–present) had problems with the ethics of representing murderers in his criminal practice and describes his struggle. His conclusion is that

it isn't the province of the attorneys to go ahead and enact the law. They're going to go ahead and represent their client and to call the

---

[85] Luther Merritt Swygert, "The Oral History of Judge Luther M. Swygert," Circuit Library, U.S. Court of Appeals for the Seventh Circuit (1985), p. 26.

[86] Procter Ralph Hug Jr., "Oral History Interview with Hon. Procter Hug, Jr.," Ninth Judicial Circuit Historical Society (1995), pp. 52–53.

attention of the court to the law. I think in those situations, and it's even more and more applicable as far as a criminal case is concerned—is that I think the person you represent is entitled to the best possible representation they can get. In the criminal cases it's even a little bit harder because in many situations, you know, there's a feeling maybe the guy's guilty, or the person's guilty. But you're not trying to prove his innocence. You're requiring the government to prove beyond a reasonable doubt that he's guilty of the charge. So your duty is to go ahead and establish the fact that the prosecution, the state or the federal government, has not proven this case beyond a reasonable doubt. That's your obligation. That's your responsibility.

But, as he explains, he had trouble with that concept on his first murder case. The insight that spurred his vigorous defense came from the Bible. He had asked himself what he was doing defending his first murder client and thinking, "Well you know, if this guy has done it, what am I doing up there defending him?" But then, he says, "I actually, through reading the Book of Romans in the Bible, found the reason I made my decision. That is, that we're subject to the government and the government is God-made. We should follow the law as it is established by our government. So that was really the thing, I think, that convinced me, at least gave me some peace of mind."[87]

Abner Mikva (C.A.D.C. 1979–94) learned a lesson in the beginning about oral arguments that he was able, as it turned out, to truly appreciate when he himself went to the appellate bench.

I never wrote out my oral arguments. I learned early on, I forget whether it was Goldberg who told me, "Don't write out an argument; make an outline and put down the things in the key cases. Don't write it out." We have a rule in the court of appeals in D.C. that prohibits the reading of arguments. I am amazed at the number of lawyers who, notwithstanding that rule and notwithstanding what a bad practice it is, literally get up there and start reading their arguments.[88]

[87] Otto Richard Skopil, "Oral History Interview with Judge Otto Skopil," U.S. District Court Collection, Oregon Historical Society (2006), pp. 9–10.
[88] Abner Mikva, "Honorable Abner J. Mikva Oral History," Historical Society of the District of Columbia (1996, 1999), p. 106.

Lawyers starting out not in private practice but as government lawyers have their own stories of struggling in the beginning. Gerhard Gessell (D.D.C. 1967–93), for example, started out at the Securities and Exchange Commission when he was called on to file a complaint.

> Early on, when I was just starting I found a note under my door from a colleague, saying, "My mother is ill. I've gone to New York. File a complaint tomorrow in federal court." I was on my own, but I had never drafted or filed a complaint in my life. I had met one of the U.S. district court judges. I wrote out a complaint and saw the judge in chambers, explaining my inexperience. He agreed to look it over. This saved my life for the moment because, with a twinkle in his eyes, he simply said, "It looks O.K. to me but don't you think it would be a good idea to say what ruling you want?" Talk about learning by doing![89]

James Parsons (N.D. Ill. 1961–93) was a young Assistant U.S. attorney who learned by observing others. In particular, he learned from Leo Tierney and Floyd Thompson, Assistant U.S. Attorneys in his office.

> I observed, for example, Thompson, who was very good, with this capacity at making that exhibit, that exhibit that he was having identified, so important in the minds of the jury and the judge that for the other side to get that exhibit held out would be to perform an impossible task. He would bring a document up to the witness and hand it to him and say, "I'm showing you this exhibit which carries the court number." He would read the number and he would just stand beside him, shoulder to shoulder, and look at it as he would hand it over and he would say, "Take a look at this, now look at it real good," and he would look at it and then he would let the witness have it and walk away. "By the way, let me *see* that once more," and he would go back over and get it and walk around with it. By that time, your appetite to see that exhibit if you are a juror or the judge is so whetted. By the time he would play with you with that exhibit, there isn't any way that anyone would hold it out of evidence. He was a master at that.

---

[89] Gerhardt Alden Gessell, "Honorable Gerhardt A. Gessell," Historical Society of the District of Columbia (1999, 2001), p. 17.

Floyd Thompson was a master at cross-examination, too. I watched him never ask a cross-examinee, never ask the witness for the other side, a direct examination question. Never let him say anything but yes or no or I don't know. Everything is placed in a declaratory statement punctuated with an interrogatory. "Isn't that right?" is the way he would finish off his question, and, "Didn't you?" "Then you did this, that or the other, did you not?" This was a great experience for me, a great opportunity. This nine-year stint that I had in the U.S. attorney's office helped me a great deal.[90]

Paul Rosenblatt (D. Ariz. 1984–present) had no time to consult with mentors. As he explains,

I got a job with the Arizona attorney general. Bob Pickerell was the attorney general at that time. And that was a great job because the first day I went to work the chief deputy handed me a file and said, "You're due in court in thirty minutes." And that's how they gave you your baptism by fire. It would never happen in a private law firm.[91]

Many of the judges had worked for at least some of their practice years as solo practitioners. Many started that way and then took one or more partners to form small firms. Some of those small firms then grew into larger and sometimes large firms. Only a few judges went to the bench from a solo practice.

William Gray (C.D. Cal. 1966–92) addressed some of the difficulties solo practitioners faced when he describes his decision to found a firm. He had, like many solo practitioners, been doing "whatever came down the street." He had been doing this for five years when he concluded that it would be better not to be practicing by himself.

As he explains, "I couldn't afford to take a vacation and I looked with longing to be able to go to a colleague and say, 'Well, now here's this situation. What do you think we should do with it?'" He then proceeded to sound out one good transaction lawyer and one good litigator and suggested they form a firm. From that humble beginning they grew

---

90 James Benton Parsons, "The Unfinished Oral History of District Judge James Benton Parsons," Circuit Library, U.S. Court of Appeals for the Seventh Circuit (1996), pp. 101–102.
91 Paul G. Rosenblatt, "Oral History Interview with Judge Paul G. Rosenblatt," Ninth Judicial Circuit Historical Society (1998), p. 49.

into a good-sized Los Angeles firm, with Gray leaving the firm to go onto the bench.

For Milton Schwartz (E.D. Cal. 1979–2005), his years as a solo practitioner right out of law school were a struggle he was glad to put behind him. This struggle in turn shaped his view on practice in a larger firm. For him, the firm became something that demanded unequivocal loyalty. He had been a founding member of what had started out as a small firm, and he was instrumental in increasing the firm's size. The lesson he had learned, that life in the firm was immeasurably better than life in solo practice, made him insist that associates in the firm have the same dedication to it that he had. He had no patience for those who complained that their hard work was not being sufficiently rewarded. He describes these lawyers as thinking more of themselves than the firm, and he was convinced that such lawyers were likely to create mischief. In a remarkable passage, he describes meeting with one of the self-centered, disgruntled lawyers.

One of those lawyers would come to me periodically and he would talk like this: "I am really getting had. I put in all these hours. I kill myself. And then I see somebody else, and I see the hours that he puts in, and I don't know why I'm not getting more money than he is, or as much," or whatever his status was at the time. And he said, "I come to you because your hours are always up high, and so I know how hard you work. But some of them don't."

And I remember saying to him, "I think you ought to quit." And he said, "I don't understand. Why?" And I said, "I do. Because as long as you think you're taking—you're putting more into this firm than you're taking out, one of these days you're going to screw all of us. Because you're not going to be able to stand the thought that you're getting screwed. Even if it may not be true."

And he said, "Don't you think you are? Look at your figures." And I said, "No. I'd starve to death. I never once believed that I'm giving more to this firm than I'm taking out of it. Because none of you people started solo practice and went through that awful period. And I've gone through that period, and then a very small firm, and then a growing firm, and then larger and larger. And throughout all those stages I have always honestly believed I get more out of this firm than I put in it because I know what it was like when I was in solo practice." And here I had all these things done for me, and I had lawyers who would associate with me to help me in a case and I would get credit. Because I was the lead lawyer. And I would be able to enunciate the principle in court and I would get the credit for all their work. And I would have quit years ago if I had thought—I'm not that neat a guy—if I had thought that I was putting more [in] than I'm taking out, I would have quit. If I'd had the courage to quit, I would have.

And, I said, "I think that you are going to stick it to us. One of these days you're gonna say, 'I don't understand why.'" And he said, "How am I gonna stick it to you?" And I said, "You'll steal from us. You'd steal from us by not reporting things, and charging them on the side to a particular client, or you'd take it easy on the client and you'd justify it in your own mind as okay because you're really just paying back to yourself what you are already entitled to."[92]

Stephen Reinhardt (C.A.9 1979–present) was an unhappy associate at Los Angeles's largest firm in the late 1950s and could not in his oral history cabin his derision and bitterness in describing his time there. As is often the case for young associates, he had worked for different people in the firm. One, the head of the litigation department, was also the admiral or commodore of the local yacht club. His chore for young Reinhardt was to research whether the excise tax on yacht clubs violated the equal protection clause. Reinhart recalls,

I said, "Violates the equal protection clause?" He said, "Oh, yes." He said it was really unfair to tax yacht clubs, private yacht clubs. He said, "They don't tax public yacht clubs." I didn't know there were public yacht clubs. I said, "Okay, you want me to research that I'll research it." So I went up to the library, and I found two Supreme Court cases on taxing private golf clubs as opposed to public golf clubs. Some other genius thought of this argument and the Supreme Court said it was not a violation of the equal protection clause to have an excise tax on private clubs. I came back up and I said, "Mr. Mitchell, I have got the answer. Here are two Supreme Court cases," and he said, "What are the names of those cases?" I told him the names and he said, "They don't count," and I said, "Why is that?" and he said,

---

92 Milton L. Schwartz, "Hon. Milton L. Schwartz Oral History," Historical Society for the United States District Court for Eastern District of California (n.d.), p. 68.

"Those are Jewish golf clubs." I said, "It didn't say that in the opinion, Mr. Mitchell." And he said, "Well I know, but the Supreme Court knows about Jews," he said. "That's because the Jews cheat on their taxes." That was the head of the litigation department.[93]

Eventually Reinhardt moved into the Entertainment Department, which was then very small.

There were only one or two there. I got sent to the Beverly Hills office where I spent two years. When you were a young associate, you didn't get interesting cases. You got to work on contracts, and I did agreements with the Crosby boys because Bing Crosby was one of the big clients. I got to do contracts with his sons. They were all failures. Red Skelton was another client so I got to do the leases for his apartment building. Mainly, we worked on production distribution agreements, where the issue was who got to pay the taxes. Which side. This side or the other side, who got stuck with the taxes. The entertainment business gets to be interesting when you get to be a partner, when you deal with clients and you have lackeys to draft the agreements.[94]

Reinhardt was unhappy at the large firm and moved to a small firm specializing in labor law. He had thought about a criminal practice, but he didn't think there was a living there.

So the next best thing seemed to be labor law, because it would be on the right side. We were representing unions. Labor law sounded interesting. I thought I would be involved in things that were kind of dynamic. And it was to a certain extent. And the litigation was much more immediate. In the event of a strike, there was a dispute that had to get resolved; you didn't have to wait fifteen years until somebody died to see whether somebody screwed up his will, or what happened to his tax planning, and it's not like a long-term, seven-year anti-trust litigation, spend two years in a warehouse looking at documents. Things happen or don't happen very quickly in labor law.[95]

---

93 Stephen Roy Reinhardt, "Oral History Interview with Judge Stephen Reinhardt," Ninth Judicial Circuit Historical Society (1993), pp. 11–12.
94 *Ibid.* at 12–13.
95 *Ibid.* at 13–14.

When asked what he disliked about practice, Reinhardt was candid.

Clients, billing, having to get clients, the business aspects of the firm, and then, if you could just practice law it wouldn't be too bad. But even then, there's a lot of drudgery. I can imagine some types of law, I don't know what kind I would have liked particularly—but, it still is not as good as making the decisions. I think there are some kinds of law that really would be very rewarding, if you were a civil liberties lawyer, or you were involved in some kinds of litigation, I think, but it's also so enervating and debilitating. I don't know how real trial lawyers survive. Most of them are a little nuts, real trial lawyers and the people I knew particularly who are the PI trial lawyers, they're all a little bit wacky, they don't lead normal lives. It's really an awfully high-pressure kind of life if you're in court a great deal. I really didn't have that kind of career. I think it's probably stimulating if you're reasonably young, a courtroom life is exciting. But after you reach your peak it's awfully tough to do that kind of thing. But I think that would be one of the types of practice that would be satisfying, if you felt you were on the right side of things, that you were accomplishing something.[96]

Gerhard Gessell (D.D.C. 1967–93) describes an interview for his first job, in 1935 after coming out of Yale Law School, that provides a look at an era long since past. Gessell, who apparently did not lack for self-esteem, quaintly writes,

I knew I had a vague promise from [SEC Commissioner] Landis that I was sure he had probably forgotten. My first thought was that I wanted eventually to be a senator from Connecticut. I thought I had better practice in Connecticut. Hartford seemed the best place to start, so I went to Hartford. It was not an easy time to get a job. It's difficult to realize that many in my law school class never practiced law. They became policemen. They became investigators for insurance companies. The only law jobs were jobs where your dad was a good client of the firm, or if your dad was a practicing lawyer, you could get yourself a job with him.

---

[96] *Ibid.* at 26.

But there were few jobs advertised. I went up to a firm, Robinson & Cole or something like that, and I talked to a senior partner and he hired me. I was surprised and excited. I thought, I was about to get married, although the same lady actually kept me waiting a year, and with a job I could go ahead. As I got up to leave I said, "By the way, what's the pay?" He was a very nice man but looked at me and said, "We don't pay anything." Since my father was a college professor, there wasn't a lot of money running around. In my egotistical way I said, "Well, supposing someone does an outstanding job the first year, what could he expect the second year?" Well, he looked out the window a long time and then said, "We have one person that we are paying $50 a month in his second year." And I said, "Well, I think you'd better give this job to a more deserving person." I walked out and went on down to the SEC.[97]

One judge, Prentice Marshall (N.D. Ill. 1973–96), left his law firm to teach law, but even there he continued in his specialty, litigation. Marshall had clerked for a Seventh Circuit judge, Walter Lindley, and had compiled a list while there of the best trial lawyers. When he finished his clerkship, he looked these lawyers up for his first job and landed with a fine Chicago firm known for litigation. But it was not as it is now, Marshall makes clear in his oral history. "Lawyering in those days, you did it almost all yourself. I do not think I was ever involved in a case that had more than two lawyers."[98]

He tried cases all over the country and was never home. This led him to move to the faculty of the University of Illinois Law School, but when famous Illinois judge Walter Schaefer advised him to always keep a foot in the courtroom, he tried some twenty-five cases while a professor. His best litigation story brings out what he values most in criminal trials. He was representing a defendant in federal court and had filed an appeal. In some cases the solicitor general would invite the lawyer to Washington to try to persuade the government to confess error. Marshall went and had an audience with then-solicitor general and future Supreme Court justice Thurgood Marshall. After he had made his pitch, Solicitor General Marshall said to an astonished Prentice Marshall that for him the issue was always guilt.

97 Gerhardt Alden Gessell, "Honorable Gerhardt A. Gessell," Historical Society of the District of Columbia (1999, 2001), p. 14.
98 Prentice H. Marshall, "The Oral History of Retired Judge Prentice H. Marshall," Circuit Library, U.S. Court of Appeals for the Seventh Circuit (1999), p. 54.

For Prentice Marshall, on the other hand, the issue in looking through the record was always whether there was error.[99]

Alfred Goodwin (D. Or. 1969–71 and C.A.9 1971–present) went to work for a two-partner firm and had the good fortune to be taught by the partners.

> They spent a lot of time helping me with my early work. And they never let me put out anything on my own unsupervised. They looked over everything I did for the first several months and made lots of suggestions, marked up changes on my copy and handed it back and said, "Do it over again this way." That was good. They spent more time on me, I think, than a lot of older lawyers would on a young lawyer. But they both had a kind of pedagogical bent and they both realized that it was probably a good investment of their time. If they taught me well then later on they could let me work on my own and they'd have more time for their own production.[100]
>
> One of the things they insisted was never going to court without being well prepared and have everything written down in a notebook, even the questions you were going to ask a witness, so that you didn't leave things to chance. They were very wary of lawyers who would go into court and wing it, just unprepared. I developed an early awareness of the importance of being well prepared. It helped because when I became a judge I knew the difference between lawyers who were well prepared and those who weren't.[101]

William Schwarzer (N.D. Cal. 1976–present) went to work at one of San Francisco's largest firms after law school at Harvard and thrived there. Oddly enough, though, he says that, even as a designated litigator in the firm, it took some time before he acquired any jury trial experience. This was the way it was at his firm in the 1950s. He explains,

> I had some limited experience sitting as a second chair in some minor matters. But I think that we as associates had very good training at on the paper side, that is, analysis and writing. Briefs didn't go out, for example, pleadings didn't go out, without very thorough

---

[99] *Ibid.* at 35.

[100] Alfred T. Goodwin, "Oral History Interview with Alfred T. Goodwin," U.S. District Court Collection, Oregon Historical Society (1986), p. 185.

[101] *Ibid.* at 186–187.

examination by the partners for whom you worked. But people did not have a lot of courtroom experience, and the reason why is that we didn't represent corporations that had a lot of small cases that you could give to young people to try. Lawyers had small cases from the phone company and Safeway and Standard Oil. We didn't get that sort of work. The closest thing to the small cases were these Greyhound route cases on which I worked, and so I got courtroom experience by doing those cases. I argued a lot of motions, but I didn't try a jury case until about three years after I became a partner. I really didn't have a full-blown trial until that time. . . . So I went in to try this jury case on relatively short notice, and I was held out to the client as an experienced trial lawyer. We didn't tell them I never tried a jury case before. That's pretty much the way things operated in our firm and in most corporate law firms—you didn't really get trial experience until you were pretty well along, when people assumed that you're already experienced. [102]

Harold Ryan (D. Id. 1981–95), who practiced in Weiser, Idaho, from 1950 to 1981, details in his oral history thoughtful analysis of a variety of issues relating to the beginning, middle, and end of his highly successful practice in Idaho. His practice and the lawyer's life come alive in his history. He was with his father in the beginning. As he explains,

I told my dad in very simple terms, "I've got my law degree now, believe it or not, and I'd like to, if you would like me to, come in with you here for a year and see how it goes, with a thorough understanding that if I walk out of here in a year you'll understand that this isn't what I want to do, that I may want to go do something else." That year just never ended, just went on and I got fascinated with the practice of law and with solving people's problems, and it just became the most interesting thing I ever did.[103]

There was then the problem of learning how to actually do things as a lawyer.

[102] William W. Schwarzer, "William W. Schwarzer, Litigator, Federal District Judge, Director of the Federal Judicial Center, and Professor, 1952–1997," Northern California U.S. District Court Oral History Series, Regional Oral History Office, The Bancroft Library, University of California, Berkeley (1997), pp. 122–123.
[103] Harold L. Ryan, "District Judge Harold Ryan," Ninth Circuit Library, Boise, Idaho (1990), pp. 29–30.

Well, there was—you know, I didn't know anything. You get out of law school and you start the practice of law, and the first thing you got to do, is you got to find out where the courthouse is, and things that, frankly, you don't learn in law school right off the bat is—you don't even know how to file a case up in the clerk's office. I can always remember the experience of getting around to the first case and getting the complaint ready and the summons ready, and now what do I do with it? Filing fees in those days were $5 or $10, wasn't much, but I just picked it up in hand and walked up to the clerk's office—her name was Naomi Black, a neat old gal that was there, and I walked in and I says, "Well, Naomi, you got another one to train." I says, "I came to file a lawsuit; what do I do now? Here it is." She got a kick out of it. There was a clerk over in Payette that was the same way, and the first time I walked in, she looked at me and she says, "Well, I got another young lawyer to train again." We took it with good humor and it was a lot of fun, and I got very close to those people. It was rich and rewarding.[104]

The first client experience, Ryan recalls, exposed how much he did not know.

Shortly after I went in there, my dad had a serious illness in his family; I don't know whether it was his brother or—I think maybe his sister died or something—he went back to Kansas and left me there alone with a secretary, and I'll never forget—it was the first client I had. He walked in and he wanted me to do an escrow contract of sale, and I didn't have the slightest idea how to do one. So I asked all the questions I could on it, got the description of the land, a lot of things that occurred to me to ask, and then I had the sagacity to tell him that, "I may have some more questions I'll need to call you about this, but I'll have it out here"—gave him a time when I'd have it out.

I had no idea how I was going to get this out, but I knew we had a secretary—so as soon as I got him out, I got her in and I said, "My god, I got an escrow contract of sale to do here; what's that?" And she says, "Oh, we do those all the time," you know. So she brings one in and I study one of those things through, work those up and using

---

[104] *Ibid.* at 31–33.

the bank as an escrow holder and the deed, and so between the two of us we got that thing out and in good shape.

But I'll tell you, I was scared to death at that point that I wouldn't do it right or something would be out of it, or something would be wrong. In those days [...] they didn't—there were no form books—about anything. There was no pleading form books, there was no contract form books, there was no—none of that was out. So I felt I had the most wonderful thing in the world—I had my father's files, which became my form books. So I'd go through the file drawers and come up with something that was similar to the problem I had, and figure out how to do it.[105]

Ryan, like many lawyers before him, looked to the information found in old files as a way of learning how to handle new files. Because he had not been there at their creation, Ryan set out to cull all that he could from the files.

Dad always could remember where everything was and he didn't need any index. And somehow the secretary didn't need an index. But I needed an index, by subject matter or something, to find things in these files. So I'd go down there nights and I started an index system, and then sometimes when my secretary wasn't all that busy, I had her working on it, and I told her what it was I was finding and interested in and put this here and that there, and so I got the whole thing pretty well organized. We had a little recipe box filled with cards of where everything was, and we actually didn't move anything. They were all in these very same file drawers that I found them in.

Well, dad heard about it, that I'd indexed all of this and that I could now find my way around through here, and one day, as he got a little older, his memory was just as good, but it was a little bit shorter and he got to ranting and raving around there one day and he says, "You know, I used to be able to find any damn thing I wanted around here. Ever since you changed this filing system and put in that index system, I can't find a damn thing." I said, "Well, from now on, ask Margery, she'll get it for you." But we both got a big kick out of that. Those files were so valuable to me because that

---

[105] *Ibid.*

was my source of forms and my idea books—I always thought forms were idea books.[106]

Then calamity struck. A fire threatened the books in the library and the filing system.

We went through a fire during that time, and the whole office didn't get burned up, but it surely got wet, and if you've ever tried to dry out a filing system with onionskin paper in most of the files, and dry out a library—that is a formidable task. I was months and months drying out our library books. I took them all home—I had a big home with a large basement in it, and I had an old pickup and I'd cart all of those up there, wet and soggy—*Pacific Reports*—and I set them in an upright position and spread the flyleaf on each side, set them on the floor, and then I set a ladder up there, and then I put a vacuum cleaner on the blow side on the tube, hanging over a rung of the ladder, and that thing just went night and day, and I'd go down and change books from time to time. I managed to dry them out so that when you opened them they didn't all stick together in one big solid mass, which is the only thing you have to do.[107]

The next big event was moving to a new building following the fire.

Then we roosted across the street for awhile, my dad and I. Then the Washington Hotel was purchased by a California group; we became their attorneys on this, that and the other thing there, and finally, they says, "Well, this fifth floor of the Washington Hotel"— which was a grand old building—was a dance hall at one time, up on the top floor, and he was wondering what to do with that. I says, "I know what you can do with it." I says, "If you'll make a law office out of it, partition it, I'll come up and lease it." So we went up there on the top of, the fifth floor of this five-story building in a two-story town, and it had an elevator and everything, and—a beautiful view—and they made these neat law offices up there. But dad only lived a year or so while we were up there, and then I got— my next partner came along in 1960, and we built an office down

---

[106] *Ibid.* at 32–33.
[107] *Ibid.* at 33.

over on another street, and that's the one I just sold last year, I sold that one.[108]

Technological changes affected the practice of law and Ryan wanted in his corner of Idaho to embrace change and makes the office more efficient.

Those were slower times. At that time everything was done on carbon copies, and when I first started, with manual typewriters. So if you needed a bunch of copies, it was a tough job for a secretary with a manual typewriter, to try to get, say, eight copies into a typewriter and get clear through it, because if there was a mistake made, they'd have to stop and do all the erasing that was necessary through that.

A very short time later we had electric typewriters, and then our biggest step was, they had wet copying machines called a Verafax, which was really messy to use and you kind of needed it off in a darker room. The first dry copier that came out was called a Thermafax and 3M put it out; it was a heat process machine. I know because I read about it in a magazine and I called 3M Company to see where I could look at one of these, and they sent an immediate response to me, and about two days later a salesman called on me. So I bought about the first dry copy machine that was sold in Idaho from Bob Brown of Finch-Brown here in Boise. That was a big step because before that, if you could imagine it, if you were probating an estate and you had a will, you had to attach copies of the will to the petition and one thing and another such as that, so that meant your secretary had to go and retype the will and many more, much more typing had to be done. So this way we could make a copy of that and attach it to it and it went off to court that way.[109]

There was more technological change:

Another big time waster we had in those days—every secretary had to know shorthand because there weren't any dictating machines. Finally, Dictaphone came out with a kind of a belt-driven dictating machine that I bought and a number of them bought over the years,

---

[108] *Ibid.* at 34.
[109] *Ibid.* at 38.

so that then we were able to do our dictating at nights and weekends and whenever and without our secretary having to sit right there and, it seems like every time you started to dictate to a secretary, the phone rang; so she was wasting her time while you were answering the phone. So those were slow practice days because we didn't have the equipment around to move paper like we do today. So I practiced through an era where we were just probably one step removed from the pin up to where it's now on computers and fast printers.[110]

As to the work itself, Ryan recalls,

We had a lot of cases—like I say, it was a slower time. I think most cases in those days—it was rare that you would ever have a case that would take a whole week to try. It seems like we could try pretty near any kind of a case in three to four days maximum, maybe five days; but those were in the days of co-pleading, before we even adopted the federal rules in Idaho where you had to plead your case, and discovery wasn't used at all, and so lawyers on each side went out and did their own investigation. Depositions were unheard of— we didn't do any of that—and you went in and tried your case. We could have a case come in the office and we could have it ready for trial and have it tried and over and done within six to eight months. That would be a very common time schedule in those days, the time frame to have a civil case tried from beginning to end. But again, the dollar went a long ways in those days and you'd go into court just as hard as you could and you got a $4,000 or $5,000 verdict out of it; you felt like you'd really hit the jackpot and that that was a whopper.

Legal fees were different then.

Cases dollarwise were not as we see them today—were very small in amounts. A $10,000 verdict would have been just an absolutely huge verdict on practically anything in civil cases in those times, which began to change rapidly, I'd say—didn't change rapidly would probably be a better way to say it—until probably the mid to late 60s, and then we began to notice a very rapid change in what was happening in verdicts and judgments and that sort of thing. But I think inflation was all a part of that and brought that on.

---

[110] *Ibid.*

I can recall the first Cadillac I bought. It was a 1966 Cadillac and you could still buy one of those with all the bells and whistles for $6300 or $6400. Things really, from the mid to late 60s on, started to go, but it went with inflation and it traveled from that time.[111]

The practice was hard work. Ryan says,

I worked long hours. I worked a lot of nights, a lot of weekends, to the point almost to a fault that I did that, and I had to take a hold of myself after about ten years of practice and readjust my whole thinking because I realized after a time that I was getting inefficient in that I would actually put things off in the daytime when I could have gotten them done if I'd approached it right, and come down at night and do this and that and the other thing, or weekends, and so then I learned to reorganize myself. It took me about ten years to figure that out so that I was working a lot less nights and a lot less weekends, although there is a certain amount of that always, even as a judge, you find yourself working at nights and weekends getting ready for cases. But it took me awhile to learn that I didn't have to spend sixteen hours a day, seven days a week practicing law, and I got it so I can do it in quite a bit less time than that and become proficient at it.[112]

Then a turning point came. Ryan had tried a case in Moscow and, as he was driving home, he assessed his position.

I had tried other cases up north in Lewiston and in Moscow, and it was an interesting time, but driving home after that case—I had spent probably the previous six months, including the trial, either preparing for or trying that case, and I decided life was too short to try any more criminal cases, so as of that time I got completely out of the criminal practice and didn't touch it again until I found myself on the bench fifteen years later or so.

---

[111] *Ibid.* at 39.
[112] *Ibid.* at 42.

CHAPTER THREE

JUDICIAL APPOINTMENTS RECOUNTED

The practice of law for these future judges was, of course, but a prelude to the most important step in their career paths—being appointed to the federal bench. Their accounts of this event, this political appointment, reflect the soon-to-be judges as lawyers, as politicians, and as the chosen few. We have a better understanding of the nature of judicial and political power from these accounts than we have from any other source on the topic. Simply put, the judges tell us who they are and how they got their lifetime appointments.

A number of patterns or relationships dominate the appointment stories in the oral histories. The most basic pattern is that of senatorial privilege, which occurs when a senator from the president's own party makes a recommendation for an appointment in the home state, which the White House honors.

There are, of course, several variants of this best-known and most typical process. Complications arise when the president is of one party and a state's senators are from the other party. There are further complications when the White House does not want to honor the senatorial privilege for a host of politically motivated reasons. Most strikingly, during the Carter administration, the senatorial privilege dynamic gave way to commissions for various parts of the country to interview candidates and make recommendations to the president.

The stories that follow touch on many of the variants in the nomination process and present in revealing details how the process works, not from the point of the view of the White House—where the attention is usually placed—but from the point of view of the nominee and just how he or she aligned the stars to get that nomination to a lifetime position.

In telling their stories, the judges reveal not just the mechanics of the nomination process—the mechanics of government, if you will—they also reveal a good deal about themselves. Their appointments, in most cases, were by far the biggest event in their lives. It was something they worked toward either explicitly or implicitly. As one judge put it, "Show me a trial lawyer and I'll show you someone who wants to be a federal judge."[113]

The patterns help account for the many forces that may come into play in an appointment. There are the political forces from a candidate's home state and the political forces in Washington. Sometimes the state political forces and the administration's political forces collide. Other forces apply. The dynamics are sometimes different in small jurisdictions, which we see described in the appointment stories. Sometimes quotas are the motivating reason for an appointment. Also on display are forces within the candidate himself or herself. We see varying levels of ambition and aggressiveness in securing nominations in the same way that we see a wide variety of personalities on display in the appointment stories.

These are their appointment stories. I often quote from the oral histories because the quotations best capture the candidate's personality. But whether I quote or summarize, these are the stories they have told and which we can trust are faithful, if for no other reason than because they are so often revealing in a not so flattering way about the candidate. Having arrived near the end of a career and telling the story of that career, the judges often seem to think of themselves as bulletproof, which is a boon to the reader. Nowhere else is this kind of information available. We learn from these histories the nature of a political judicial appointment.

Even those judges who only briefly describe their appointments (only a handful of judges make no reference to their appointments) say enough to indicate that their appointment story falls within one of the patterns I have described. For connections to political leaders or to power brokers, for example, we see that Robert Warren (E.D. Wis. 1974–98) had been the attorney general of Wisconsin (1969–74) and that John Reynolds (E.D. Wis. 1965–2002) had been attorney general (1959–63) and then governor (1963–65) of Wisconsin immediately prior to taking the bench.

William Schwarzer (N.D. Cal. 1976–present) knew Congressman Pete McCloskey at a time when California had no Republican senators and the

---

[113] Prentice Henry Marshall, "The Oral History of Retired Judge Prentice H. Marshall," Circuit Library, U.S. Court of Appeals for the Seventh Circuit (1999), p. 76.

congressional delegation was key to the selection process. Oliver Gasch (D.D.C. 1965–99), though a Republican, was a friend of legendary Democratic power broker Tom Corcoran. Corcoran, simply called Gasch and asked if he wanted to be a federal judge, because he knew that President Johnson wanted to appoint some Republicans.

Mary Lou Robinson (N.D. Tex. 1979–present) lobbied for her job and had U.S. Senator Lloyd Benson's support. Hubert Will (N.D. Ill. 1961–95) roomed with future U.S. Senator Paul Douglas while at the University of Chicago Law School. William Beatty (S.D. Ill.1979–2001) had a close friend who was friends with someone on Governor Stevenson's staff. Abraham Moravitz (N.D. Ill. 1963–2001) was close to the Chicago political machine and simply had to wait until the right opening appeared in the Kennedy administration. Dorothy Nelson (C.A.9 1979–present) was friendly with U.S. Attorney General Griffin Bell, who assessed the commission's recommendations for the White House.

These are only hints of what the histories reveal.

Presidential Connection

Perhaps the most powerful and political connection that a judicial office seeker can have is the personal support of the president. The president by definition has a free hand with the District of Columbia—with no meddlesome senators to deal with—but elsewhere there are political considerations on the president nominating to the federal bench those whom he knows personally and supports. Every personal appointment comes at the expense of the working relationship between a state's legislative delegation and the White House, but, then again, senatorial privilege on judicial nominees is simply tradition, not a constitutional directive. Clearly there are times when the White House directs a nomination.

The most striking example of a president personally directing a judicial appointment comes with Richard Nixon and the appointment of George MacKinnon (C.A.D.C. 1969–95) to the Court of Appeals for the District of Columbia. MacKinnon's presidential connection was so powerful, in fact, that his nomination became the first order of business for the president's new administration. MacKinnon had served in Congress with Richard Nixon. He sat next to him on the Labor Committee and greatly helped Nixon in the Alger Hiss affair by leading Nixon to some documents that exposed Hiss.

The issue involved the so-called Pumpkin Papers. The FBI knew or strongly suspected that the documents had been typed on Hiss's typewriter, but they had no way of proving that the typewriter was in Hiss's possession at the time the Pumpkin Papers were written. When MacKinnon heard of the problem, he remembered that alumni associations and insurance companies often kept correspondence. MacKinnon suggested to Nixon that the FBI check the files of Hiss's alumni association at Gaucher College and also his files at the New York Life Insurance Company. The search revealed letters written and signed by Hiss during the same period as the Pumpkin Papers. This helped lead to Hiss's conviction.

Nixon, who had been serving on the House Un-American Activities Committee, never forgot MacKinnon's help in this matter that was so close to him. When Nixon became president, MacKinnon got a call from the White House telling him that his friend the president wanted to know if he wanted to be appointed to the Court of Appeals for the District of Columbia. Later, MacKinnon explains, he learned from Richard Kleindienst that Nixon had called him over the minute the cabinet had been sworn in and said, "Dick, I want you to see if you can get MacKinnon to serve on the D.C. circuit."[114]

Appointed to the U.S. District Court for the District of Columbia, Gerhard Gessell (D.D.C. 1967–93) tells a revealing story—two stories, actually—about his connections to Lyndon Johnson and what he describes as a "truly personal presidential appointment."[115]

In the first story, Gessell explains that he had met Johnson in the 1940s, having dinner with him and their spouses. Everything seemed to go very well. The years passed, and, during the Kennedy administration, Gessell became chairman of the President's Committee on Equal Opportunity in the Armed Forces. After the Kennedy assassination, Gessell waited a bit and then went over to the White House to see Johnson's aide Bill Moyers to see if Johnson wanted Gessell to continue on the commission. Johnson himself wanted to see Gessell. The president, of course, remembered Gessell (though Gessell did not know if Johnson knew that he had worked on one of Johnson's campaigns) and said that he wanted Gessell to continue on the commission.

---

[114] George Edward MacKinnon, "Honorable George E. MacKinnon Oral History," Historical Society of the District of Columbia (1994), p. 13.
[115] Gerhardt Alden Gessell, "Honorable Gerhardt A. Gessell," Historical Society of the District of Columbia (1999, 2001), p. 72.

Then, in what Gessell calls an extraordinary meeting, Gessell was called over to the White House to a meeting Johnson was having with black leaders on the issue of appointing more blacks to the federal judiciary. Johnson was insisting to the black leaders that they were not sending him names of sufficiently distinguished candidates. Once he had those, he said, there would be more appointments. He explained to the leaders why various past suggestions had been inadequate and then, to make his point, he turned to Gessell and asked how many blacks worked at his distinguished Washington law firm. Gessell said that they had none because they had not gotten applications from any well-qualified blacks. Famous Washington lawyer Whitney North Seymour was the firm's lead partner, and it was the firm's policy not to make token hires. They wanted blacks in the firm, Seymour said, and they were always on the lookout for qualified candidates, but they simply had not had any such qualified candidates to date.

Sometime later, Gessell got a telephone call from Johnson himself asking Gessell if he wanted to be a judge on the District of Columbia federal bench. Gessell had not applied for a judgeship and had never even expressed an interest in the judgeship, so the offer was surprising. He was, as he put it, utterly dumbfounded, but he recovered enough to say that he thought it would be all right. Johnson then told Gessell that he should not be surprised if all sorts of FBI agents started asking questions about him.[116]

The second story comes from what Gessell later learned from other sources about what had actually happened. To fill the opening for solicitor general, Attorney General Ramsey Clark had recommended Gessell to the president, despite never having discussed the subject with Gessell. Johnson's advisor, Clark Clifford, suggested instead that Johnson appoint the dean of a law school to the post. The dean at Yale was ruled out because of his views on the war, so the job was offered to Harvard's dean, Erwin Griswold. Having had Gessell presented to him as such a distinguished candidate, and drawing on their personal connection, Johnson decided on his own to appoint Gessell. He did not talk to Clark about it, or anyone else. He just reached out to Gessell, making it, as Gessell notes, a truly personal presidential appointment.[117]

The path of Robert Grant (N.D. Ind. 1957–98) to the district court bench led directly to Dwight Eisenhower's White House, and while the

---

[116] *Ibid.* at 69–72.
[117] *Ibid.* at 73–74.

story of Eisenhower's loyalty to Grant is by itself worth recounting, the back story of his nomination is equally interesting.

Grant had been a successful, impressive lawyer in Indiana and followed his years of practice with a highly successful political career. He was sent to Congress five times by his district. It was only because of the surprising Democratic success in 1948 that Grant was not, as a Republican, returned to Congress. Grant had been a successful legislator, impressing the leadership and assuming significant responsibility in Congress. Out of office, he returned to practice and in 1952 made his bet on Eisenhower. The state's Republican leadership was for Taft, but Grant was for Eisenhower and ran his campaign in Indiana. Eisenhower did not forget this and wanted the man who supported him when he was in the wilderness to be rewarded.

Grant explains what happened in the Oval Office. He begins by describing his good fortune in life and the support of good friends:

> That is the one great advantage that I can really say that I have enjoyed. Maybe it was not even hard work, maybe it was the confidence of many friends. I recall one time, I was at a Republican state convention in Indianapolis. Bill Jenner told me that he and Senator Capehart had just had a meeting at the White House before they came out to the Indianapolis convention. That was about the time when they put Parkinson's name up for the court of appeals. They told me about the meeting they had just had with the president, when Ike said to them, "What I want to know is, do you have a place in this program for this fellow Grant?" They said, "Yes." He said that was what he wanted to know when they come up with a program. So, it is just support like that from fine people.[118]

But there was more to the story than the president reaching out and rewarding a deserving loyalist. The first suggestion that Grant might be appointed to the bench came in 1954. At that time, Lynn Parkinson, a Republican, on was on the district bench. The rumor was that Luther Swygert, a Democrat on the district bench, would be promoted to the Seventh Circuit and that Grant would replace Swygert.

Parkinson was desperate to get to the Seventh Circuit and tried to use Grant to get there. After hearing the rumor of what was being planned

---

[118] Robert A. Grant, "The Oral History of Judge Robert A. Grant," Circuit Library, U.S. Court of Appeals for the Seventh Circuit (1988), p. 89.

and hearing that Grant had met with Senator William Jenner and Attorney General Herb Brownell, which to Parkinson surely suggested that the levers were being pulled to get Grant on the bench, Parkinson called Grant over to his chambers and tried to shame him into not taking the position if it were offered to him. He argued that to take the position was to be part of a move that favored the Democrat Swygert over him, the Republican, and that any good Republican would refuse on principle to be part of the plan.

As Grants tells the story, Parkinson in effect threatened Grant with bad relations if the plan as described took effect and he and Grant were left on the district bench together. Grant explains,

> He said to me very definitely that if the thing was reversed, and he were the one who could be appointed to a district judgeship created by the promotion of a Democrat named Luther Swygert, he would tell them that he would have nothing to do with it. But, I told him that I would not do that. I would like to add this because it is a little better idea of the man, I said, "Lynn, I am sorry you feel that way because if Judge Swygert should be appointed to the circuit and I should be appointed here, I would be working with you and under you, and I would not like to think of your feeling for me in that light." He said, "Well, that's the way it is and that's the way it will continue to be." And, as I left him, he said, "You better think it over."[119]

As it turned out, though, Parkinson got the Seventh Circuit appointment in 1957, not Swygert, who waited until 1961 for his. Grant got his in 1957 and did not have to deal with the apparently unstable Parkinson, who served but two years before he walked into Lake Michigan and drowned himself.

A last example is that of William Campbell (N.D. Ill. 1940–88), who was a friend of Franklin Roosevelt and got his appointment as a result of a favor, but not a favor Campbell received. It was Campbell's favor to give to Roosevelt. Actually, it was the second favor he had given to Roosevelt. He did Roosevelt a favor earlier by taking the post of U.S. attorney for the Northern District of Illinois. Campbell had been doing quite well in private practice in Chicago, in no small part, he lets out, because of his connection to Roosevelt. Campbell took the job because corruption in Chicago had reached critical mass and Roosevelt turned to him as the

---

[119] *Ibid.* at 102–103.

only man capable of cleaning things up. Campbell was then so successful as the government's lawyer in Chicago prosecuting corruption, at least as Campbell explains it, that he had to be kicked upstairs to the district court to keep Chicagoans happy. Taking this position was his second favor to Roosevelt.[120]

Shirley Hufstedler (C.A.9 1968–79) speculated that her appointment had a presidential spousal connection rather than a presidential connection. She was not sure, but she suspected that Lady Bird Johnson was behind her appointment to the Ninth Circuit as only the second female appointment ever on the circuit bench—and the first in more than thirty years. Hufstedler had been close to Lady Bird, and she knew that the president wanted to appoint a woman to the circuit bench. She had been a highly respected judge in California, serving as an associate justice on the California Court of Appeals prior to her federal appointment. She later resigned the bench in 1979 to become United States Secretary of Education.[121]

Inner Administration Circle

If not the support of the president himself, it is extremely useful to have the support of high-ranking administration officials, preferably the attorney general. These are the folks who can make things happen.

Working for the attorney general, for example, led to the appointment of Harlington Wood (S.D. Ill. 1973–76 and C.A.7 1976–present) to the district bench. He had been an independent U.S. attorney in southern Illinois, so much so that he angered Senator Everitt Dirksen by refusing to back some of the prosecutions of prominent Republicans, which led Dirksen to proclaim that, if he had his way, Wood would never again get a government position requiring a presidential appointment.

Wood's performance as U.S. attorney led to him being chosen by Attorney General Richard Kleindienst to be the executive U.S. attorney, the person who rode herd over all ninety-four U.S. attorneys around the country. This led in turn to a promotion to the head of the civil division in the attorney general's office.

---

[120] William Joseph Campbell, "Oral History of the Honorable William J. Campbell," Federal Judiciary History Office, Federal Judicial Center (1982), pp. 1–2.

[121] Shirley Ann Mount Hufstedler, "Diversifying the Federal Judiciary: Interview with Judge Shirley A. Hufstedler," Federal Judicial Center, (1995), p. 21.

Undergirding both positions, aside from Wood's talent, was his dedication to Kleindienst. He, in fact, was in Africa on vacation when Kleindienst was forced out of office as part of the Watergate troubles. Wood cut his trip short and, losing several thousand dollars in the process, flew back to Washington. As he put it, he was not going to let Kleindienst walk out of the building alone. Not surprisingly, that kind of relationship led Kleindienst to want to help Wood. In explaining his appointment to the district bench, Wood says, "That's just because I was next door to Kleindienst and he had a lot to do with picking judges. He just asked me one day if I wanted that job back home, and I did."[122] His promotion to the Seventh Circuit three years later turned on a different friendship, this one with the nominating senator, Charles Percy.

Thomas Flannery (D.D.C. 1971–85) also had a friend in Kleindienst. He was the best kind of friend—one who owed a favor. Flannery had been United States attorney in the District of Columbia and had made it known that after a bit he wanted to move to the bench. He had been on the job about eighteen months when an opening on the district bench developed. He told Kliendienst that he was interested. Kliendienst told him that the opening was already spoken for, but he said that if another opening occurred, Flannery would be a leading candidate for it.

About a year later, Flannery learned, before anyone else knew—including the administration—that one of the judges was going to take senior status, which would create an opening for a new active judge. Flannery got this information by way of a telephone call from the judge himself, Lawrence Walsh. Armed with this information, Flannery arranged to meet Kliendienst. He reminded Kliendienst of his offer of a year earlier. Kliendienst indeed remembered and essentially repeated it, leaving the opening on the district bench as the only issue. Flannery then told Kliendienst that he had learned from Judge Walsh that he was going to take senior status and that the White House would get his letter in a couple of days. Kleindienst then said that he would handle it, and he did.[123]

Joseph Sneed (C.A.9 1973–2008) was the choice of the attorney general himself. Here, though, the nomination resulted not from friendship

---

[122] Harlington Wood Jr., "The Oral History of Judge Harlington Wood, Jr.," Circuit Library, U.S. Court of Appeals for the Seventh Circuit (1997), p. 54.
[123] Thomas Aquinas Flannery, "Honorable Thomas A. Flannery Oral History," Historical Society of the District of Columbia (1992), pp. 47–49.

but from high-level political maneuvering. His path to the bench is especially colorful and revealing of the way Washington works.

Sneed had been a career law professor. He had taught at a number of fine schools and was at Stanford in the late 1960s during that campus's period of student unrest. He was unhappy with radicalism and made his positions sufficiently known within the academic world so that when Duke was looking for a law-and-order dean of its law school, it turned to Sneed in 1971. But no sooner had Sneed begun to make changes at Duke than he was summoned to Washington to serve as the deputy to Attorney General Richard Kleindienst. In this case, the Nixon administration was trying to assume greater control of its various departments and selected Sneed as Kleindienst's deputy.

But soon enough, Kleindienst himself was out, as part of the fallout of the Watergate fiasco, and in came a new attorney general, Elliott Richardson. Richardson made it plain to Sneed that he wanted to have his own man as his deputy. Sneed agreed with Richardson about what he wanted, but that still left the problem of what to do with Sneed. As Sneed recounts it, Richardson first suggested that Sneed go back to Duke. Sneed rejected this and insisted on a lateral move. He would propose various positions and Richardson would look into them. And, though it was becoming obvious that a lateral move would be difficult, Sneed would not go away. He would have meetings with Richardson in which, as he recounts it, he simply would not leave, putting the pressure on Richardson.

Sneed then noticed that there was an opening on the Ninth Circuit that the administration was having difficulty filling. Sneed said he wanted the position. He had come to Washington to get a judgeship, he said, and he was not leaving without it. The failing candidate for the Ninth Circuit position was ruled out and, in a matter of days, Sneed had the nomination.

Sneed's description takes us into the heart of power politics.

One meeting was at his [Richardson's] house one Saturday afternoon. I never could quite put my finger on what it was he was after, except that he was appraising me. I never would give him the easy way out, which would have been to say, "Well, don't worry about it. I'll make my deal over at the White House; forget about me." But I never said that. I just sat there and talked and talked, thought up different jobs in the department that would make lateral movement feasible, like inspector general or this, that, and the other. Well, he didn't want any part of that. So one day I went up there—I think this was the latter part of June—and I said, "Look, there's a vacancy in the Ninth Circuit. A district judge has been suggested for it, William Smith has been lobbying for it, I have no objection to it, but nothing happens in the White House. It's been hanging there for quite a while. Obviously, somebody there doesn't like him. Why don't you take a look?" He said, "Well, that's a good idea." So, a couple of days later, he called me back and said, "You know, that thing is going like a house afire and you're a possibility for taking it on." I said, "Great, go."[124]

An appointment not starting with the attorney general is worth recounting. Stanley Weigel (N.D. Cal. 1962–97) of San Francisco had a friend and admirer in Kennedy's press secretary, Pierre Salinger, and because Salinger had so much influence within the administration, Weigel's nomination was the result of a phone call, though a football was also involved.

As Weigel tells it, he had represented some Berkeley faculty members in the 1950s and, as a result, had impressed Salinger, then a newspaper man in San Francisco. As he tells the story,

I came to know Pierre Salinger quite well. Pierre Salinger had been a reporter on the *San Francisco Chronicle*. He was the press secretary to President Kennedy. One Saturday when I happened to have been in Washington, probably during the prior week for some case or some work or other, I dropped in to see Pierre in the White House. We were chatting and I mentioned I would like to be a federal judge. Pierre said, "Stan, I'd like to see you be a federal judge." He picked up the phone—it was a Saturday morning—and called [Robert] Bobby Kennedy, who was then the attorney general. He said to Attorney General Kennedy, "A friend of mine, Stanley Weigel's here. I think he ought to be a federal judge and I'd like to have you see him this afternoon if you could." Apparently Kennedy said, "Well, let him come over." I wasted no time in going over, and he had a huge office. As I entered, he was wearing a crew neck sweater, and he had a football in his hand and I no sooner opened the door than he threw it at me and I caught it. And I think that that undoubtedly accounts for my having become a federal judge.

[124] Joseph T. Sneed III, "Oral History Interview with Hon. Joseph T. Sneed III," Ninth Judicial Circuit Historical Society (1994), pp. 196–197.

There was one complication, though:

> I believe that the California senator who would call the tune had some commitment looking toward the appointment to the federal bench in Los Angeles of a man named Carr. And Carr was apparently the son or brother to the United States attorney, or possibly district attorney in Los Angeles. He was not well thought of as I recall by the Department of Justice. It could have been that, to use the vernacular, that the senator in question said, "Well, I'll give you Weigel if you'll give me Carr."[125]

Recruited

June Green (D.D.C. 1968–2001) had no political connections, and certainly none to the White House, but out of nowhere she was asked if she wanted to be a district court judge on the District of Columbia bench. Her only qualification was that she was one of the leading lawyers in the area generally and certainly one of the leading women lawyers, if not the preeminent one. Her story has an element of mystery to it.

The star of her story is not President Johnson but Deputy Attorney General Warren Christopher, the man who wielded the power at the White House on judicial appointments. He had called Green and said that he wanted to see her. Time went by and nothing came of it. Then there was another call and, finally, months later, Christopher met with her. All the while Christopher had revealed nothing of his interest in seeing Green. Even when they were finally together, Christopher said nothing. Green recalls,

> So he said, finally, "Are you curious?" I said, "Oh, yes, I certainly am." He said, "Well, would you like to be a judge?" I said, "I'm not eligible [because I do not live in the District of Columbia]." He said, "I know that, too. I'm not talking about a local court. Would you like to be a federal judge?" I said, "I've never given it any contemplation, because I never thought that I would be asked." He said, "Well, think about it." I said, "I don't have any political connections."

[125] Stanley Alexander Weigel, "Stanley Weigel, Litigator and Federal Judge," Northern California U.S. District Court Oral History Series, Regional Oral History Office, The Bancroft Library, University of California, Berkeley (1988), pp. 80–81.

He said, "You don't need them." He said, "I don't know what's going to be done at the other end of Pennsylvania Avenue, but I certainly know what the recommendation is." [126]

It didn't take much for James Buckley (C.A.D.C. 1985–present) to sign on. He had served in the Senate, and though he had not practiced law for more than thirty years, he got a call from an assistant attorney general in Attorney General Ed Meese's office asking if Buckley were interested in going on the Court of Appeals for the District of Columbia. The assistant attorney general had once done some work for the magazine *National Review*, run by Buckley's brother Bill. At first, Buckley thought the idea was outrageous, but he soon warmed to it. He concluded that even if he did not take to the court, he could, because of having served as a court of appeals judge, make an easy entrance into a law firm later.[127]

It took more to secure Robert Bork (C.A.D.C. 1981–88). Bork was recruited directly by the White House for the Court of Appeals for the District of Columbia. Oddly enough, he was recruited not from the academic world but from private practice.

Bork had been a distinguished law professor at Yale for many years, but following the deaths of his wife and his best friend, fellow law professor Alexander Bickel, he decided to leave Yale and took up at the Washington branch of Kirkland & Ellis. Although Bork does not say so, the salary must have been tremendous.

Bork had been at the firm for only two months when the firm held a luncheon and invited Fred Fielding, then White House counsel to President Reagan, to speak. Bork sat next to Fielding at the luncheon, and Fielding whispered to Bork that he wanted Bork to join the court of appeals. Bork said that he could not do it because he had just joined the law firm. A couple of days later, Bork got a call from Jonathan Rose, the assistant attorney general for the Justice Department's Office of Legal Policy, urging him to take the appointment. Then, knowing that Bork had said no to Fielding and Rose, Deputy Attorney General Ed Schmults called and made the same pitch. The two argued for nearly an hour, with Schmults obviously not quitting. Bork finally said that he would think about it. Bork then talked it over with his children. The next morning, the attorney general

---

[126] June L. Green, "Honorable June L. Green Oral History," Historical Society of the District of Columbia (1998, 1999), p. 148.

[127] James Lane Buckley, "Honorable James L. Buckley Oral History," Historical Society of the District of Columbia (1995, 1996), pp. 129–131.

himself, William French Smith, called. Though he felt a little hesitant, because he had just joined the law firm, Bork capitulated and took the position.[128]

Senator

The essential dynamic in Article III appointments involves the senior senator of the president's own party making recommendations to the president, which he then honors with a nomination. There are variations of this practice, but, generally speaking, appointments come through a state's senator.

The oral history appointment stories shed light on the dynamic as it involves the candidate and the senator by describing the nature of the relationships that led to recommendations and appointments.

Albert Wollenberg (N.D. Cal. 1958–81), for example, was friends with both California senators, William Knowland and Thomas Kuchel, but when he decided after ten years on the state court bench that he wanted one of the two new openings on the federal bench, he had to lean on senior senator Knowland a bit.

Though he does not describe it, Wollenberg had been one of Earl Warren's closest advisors in his three terms as governor, and both Knowland and Kuchel had been elected to the Senate because of Warren. Knowland's father had been Warren's first patron, and when the opportunity arose to appoint a senator because the sitting senator had passed away, Warren showed his appreciation to the family by naming the son to the post. Knowland later won election in his own right, but Wollenberg must have thought the obligation still applied.

Wollenberg had heard of the opening on the federal bench and told Knowland of his interest. Knowland instructed Wollenberg to write him a letter declaring his interest and describing his qualifications, taking pains to tell Wollenberg that he was entering the competition late. Wollenberg remembers a subsequent telephone conversation during which he told Knowland that he was very interested in the job. Wollenberg describes the call.

---

[128] Robert Heron Bork, "Honorable Robert L. Bork," Historical Society of the District of Columbia (1992), p. 1.

I knew he was about to act in the matter, and I wanted his approval for the position. He told me I was awfully late in getting started, a lot of other people had applied for the job and so forth. I remember a remark he made, something about, "Why, there's a line clear from here to Baltimore," or "from my desk to Baltimore," some statement of that kind, "all of whom want consideration." I said, "That's great. The more the merrier. You'll get a good man. I'm at the head of the line, though. I'm standing right now [pounds desk for emphasis] in front of your desk. It's up to you to give me the answer. I'm not late. I'm in the front of the line, not in the back of the line." He said, "Okay, Al, we'll think about it." The next day he phoned me and told me he's sent my name to the president.[129]

Otto Skopil (D. Or. 1972–79 and C.A.9. 1979–present) was nominated twice, first for the district bench and then seven years later for the Ninth Circuit, and each time friends in high places helped.

Skopil had gone to high school with Mark Hatfield and had later done some legal work for Hatfield and his wife. He had only limited participation in Hatfield's political career, but clearly Hatfield always wanted to promote Skopil. As governor of Oregon, Hatfield several times tried to get Skopil to take a state court judicial position. And, as a U.S. senator, Hatfield encouraged Skopil to think of the federal bench. Skopil, an immensely successful practitioner, always put the idea off, but after a while he realized that the offers to join the federal bench would soon run out.

Then I began to think a little bit—well, if these opportunities are presenting themselves maybe I'm getting some direction. Maybe I should be, and maybe I do. Then I acknowledged that I did owe a debt to the profession. It was really for that reason that I decided to become a federal judge, because the compensation was not too good. I can remember I came on duty in the federal court in June and the fees that I made practicing law for that portion of the first six months of the year, the taxes that I had to pay on it exceeded what I got paid for the last six months as a federal judge. But I don't regret that, and I'm not saying that as a criticism. I think it is a

129 Albert Charles Wollenberg, "To Do the Job Well: A Life in Legislative, Judicial, and Community Service: Interviews," Northern California U.S. District Court Oral History Series, Regional Oral History Office, The Bancroft Library, University of California, Berkeley (1997), p. 258.

responsibility, and it's something that we have to perform. Our society is entitled to it, you know. Our system may not be perfect, but I would be hard pressed to find a better one.

For Skopil, his success lay with Hatfield's support. Describing the appointment, he notes that "Mark was instrumental and there isn't any question about that. He was very, very, very helpful in that situation."[130]

Hatfield's support was not enough to get Skopil from the district bench to the Ninth Circuit. The support was still there, but, in the Carter administration, appointments to the court of appeals began with a committee review process. Skopil did not even think there was any point in trying for the opening on the Ninth Circuit. He was a Republican, and a Democrat was in the White House.

As a testament to his qualifications, some sitting judges on the Ninth Circuit sought Skopil out and encouraged him to apply. As Skopil recounts it,

> So I thought, well, here I am a Republican. We got a Democrat in office. I don't know why I'm going to be applying. But I was encouraged by members of the Ninth Circuit—by Blaine Anderson, who has since died, and by Jim Browning, who later of course was the chief of the court, and of course Ted Goodwin—and also by [U.S. District Judge] Gus [Solomon] (D. Or. 1949–87). So I thought, you know, if these people think I'm capable of doing this, well, ... So I did.

It was here that another friend stepped in to help Skopil. Skopil had gotten close to Griffin Bell, former Fifth Circuit judge and later attorney general in the Carter administration, when they worked together on judicial administration matters. It was Griffin to whom the commission gave its short list of recommendations. The head of the commission for Skopil's northwest part of the country, he recalls, was a very close friend of Bell's. Bell had encouraged Skopil at the committee level, and, of course, once Skopil was recommended by the committee chaired by Bell's friend, Bell himself made the selection.[131]

Eugene Wright (C.A.9 1969–2002) had gone to law school with Henry Jackson, who later became one of Washington's leading politicians and was a United States senator. Wright was lucky to learn of three new positions

[130] Otto Richard Skopil, "Oral History Interview with Judge Otto Skopil," U.S. District Court Collection, Oregon Historical Society (2006), pp. 4–5.
[131] *Ibid.* at 21.

for the Ninth Circuit. He did not know about the openings and just happened to talk with someone who did. Once he learned of them, he contacted John Ehrlichman in the White House. Ehrlichman had tried two cases before Wright when Wright was a state court trial judge. Later, Wright moved to the Washington Supreme Court. He had praised Ehrlichman for his work in the two trials, and apparently the compliment stuck with Ehrlichman because he had followed Wright's career and while in the White House he wanted to help him. It was through Henry Jackson, though, that Wright got the position. Jackson was running interference for Wright. As Wright put it, he had Henry Jackson to thank for his appointment.[132]

Being close to your state's senators, to be sure, helps in getting a nomination. This was true for Thomas Fairchild (C.A.7 1966–present) and his nomination to the Seventh Circuit in 1966. Fairchild had been elected to the Wisconsin Supreme Court and was poised to become the next chief justice of that court when the opening on the appellate bench opened. Fairchild had long been involved in Wisconsin politics and was a member of a small group that could be described as revitalizing the party. As he puts it,

> Well, you might say I had it the easy way. The two Democratic senators in Wisconsin, in 1966, were William Proxmire, the senior senator, and Gaylord Nelson, the junior senator. I had been very close to both in Democratic politics as the revitalization of the state Democratic Party was under way. And both, in a sense, may have felt a little politically indebted to me. Of course, Lyndon Johnson was president, and he was a Democrat. This job opened up, and I don't know of any real chance that anybody else had at this appointment. In fact, my big problem was deciding whether I wanted to take it.

How he went about deciding whether to take the job is worth hearing.

> I made quite a canvass of people asking their opinion on the subject, should I, or shouldn't I? I talked to Justice Walter Schaefer of the Illinois Supreme Court, and Chief Justice Roger Traynor of the California Supreme Court, and people that I knew in Wisconsin. One had been briefly a colleague on our court, but had been

---

[132] Eugene Allen Wright, "Oral History Interview with Judge Eugene A. Wright," Ninth Judicial Circuit Historical Society (1987), pp. 24–25.

defeated. I talked to Williard Hurst, who was on the law school faculty at Madison. I talked to Leon Feingold, who had contributed greatly to any political success I had had. I didn't want to leave the Wisconsin court without at least talking to Leon, who had a lot to do with my getting there. And certainly Jim Doyle, who was a district judge in Madison then and had been very instrumental in the whole reorganization of the Democratic Party, and had helped me in all my campaigns.[133]

Herbert Choy (C.A.9 1971–2004) owed his seat on the Ninth Circuit to Hawaii senator Hiram Fong, who put his name forward to the Nixon administration. How that came about is perhaps symptomatic of the nomination dynamics of small jurisdictions. As Choy, who had gone off to Harvard Law School, recounts it, he met Hiram Fong on Merchant Street in Honolulu, where he had gone to buy an article of clothing at McInerney's Men's Shop, after returning to the city in 1946: "Hiram asked me what I was planning to do, now that I had returned from military service. I said that I was looking around for a position, but had not yet decided on anything particular. He invited me to confer with him and his partner, Katsuro Miho, who were a two-man law firm, about joining them." He joined them but Fong left in 1959 to become one of the state's first two senators.

In 1968, legislation increased the number of judges on the Ninth Circuit from nine to thirteen, and Fong was determined to have one of the new seats go to an Hawaiian. When it did not, and the spot that Fong thought should go to Hawaii went to Arizona instead, he blocked the nomination on the judiciary but relented when Barry Goldwater promised that he would support Fong's candidate when the time came. Fong then went to Nixon and argued that Hawaii had wrongly lost out to Arizona for the group of new openings, which prompted Nixon to promise that the next opening would go to an Hawaiian. That opening came up in 1971 when Stanley Barnes took senior status. Fong had the sitting district judge on the island, C. Nils Tavares, in mind for the spot, but he was deemed to be, at sixty-six, too old. This, in turn, led Fong to turn to his former law partner and offer him the position.[134]

[133] Thomas E. Fairchild, "The Oral History of Judge Thomas E. Fairchild," Circuit Library, U.S. Court of Appeals for the Seventh Circuit (1999), p. 73.
[134] Herbert Young Cho Choy, "Oral History Interview with Hon. Herbert Y.C. Choy," Ninth Judicial Circuit Historical Society (1990), pp. 52–53.

Fong also put Samuel King (D. Haw. 1972–present) on the district bench. King's father had been governor of Hawaii and King himself had been active in politics. He had been chairman of the Republican Party in the 1950s, which led to his taking a position on the Hawaii state court bench. In 1972, when the district court opening developed, King was a Republican National Committeeman.

Nixon was traveling through Hawaii when King got a phone call from Fong asking to meet. King thought it was because he was to help out with Nixon's visit, but instead Fong asked King if he wanted to be a district judge. He would be meeting with Nixon and wanted to present King as his candidate of choice. How King describes the events lend flavor to their level of familiarity.

> I was having breakfast in the breakfast room up at our home in Nuuanu, and Hiram Fong called me: he was a Senator. He said, "Sam, how soon can I see you?" And I said, "Oh, in fifteen minutes, I'll just come down the hill," and he said, "Fine, come down as soon as you can." So I said, "I'll be there in twenty minutes." So I went down to see him, and he said, "Do you want to be a federal judge?" I said, "Well, let me put it this way. Yes! But, that's not what I thought you called me for; I thought you wanted to get together because Nixon is coming to Hawaii, since I am the National Committeeman." "Oh, no, no," he said, "he's got it all arranged, he's going to go down and stay with the Marines at the military base and all that sort of thing. No, no," he said, "but I've got an appointment with them and I want to tell them you're my choice."[135]

James Moran (N.D. Ill. 1979–present) had the right kind of friend to get to the district court. He had been friends with Adlai Stevenson in law school and they remained good friends when they served in the Illinois General Assembly together. After leaving the assembly, Moran helped Stevenson out when Stevenson moved on to the post of state treasurer, running for him a division that efficiently turned state deposits into money for agricultural and low-income housing loans. Stevenson, when he got to the Senate, asked Moran if he wanted to go on the bench, but for some time Moran said no because the money was not adequate. To this, Stevenson replied that the political winds were changing and that the offer

---

[135] Samuel Pailthorpe King, "Oral History Interview with Judge Samuel P. King," Ninth Judicial Circuit Historical Society (1991), p. 60.

would not be good with a Republican administration. Knowing that his chance would not come around again, Moran accepted the offer from his good friend Stevenson and took the bench.

Two fights had to be won for Richard Mills (C.D. Ill. 1985–present) to get his nomination. The first fight was a function of the fact that, although there was a Republican in the White House in 1984, both of Illinois' senators were Democrats. The question—the fight—was over whether the Republican congressional delegation from Illinois or the Republican governor of Illinois would make the choice for the district bench and then pass that name to the White House. The delegation won out.

The second fight was within that delegation over a candidate. Here, Mills had an advantage. Bob Michel, his supporter and promoter, was not only the leader of the congressional delegation, he was also the minority leader, which made it even clearer that his choice would prevail. Thus, it was with his connection to Michel that Richard Mills got his seat on the district court bench.[136]

There could have been a third fight, between the winning party and the White House, but in this case the White House yielded. It gave way to the Congressional delegation, which had in back rooms fought with the governor and won.

For Gene Brooks (S.D. Ind. 1979–96), getting a favor from a friend in the Senate can also mean returning that favor by promising to make patronage appointments. His senate friend was Birch Bayh. They had gone to law school together and in fact forged a special relationship of sorts. They played on the school's softball team (Brooks was so good he played semi-professionally), with Brooks pitching and Bayh catching. Years later, after remaining friends throughout, the now-senator Bayh had first put Brooks forward as a bankruptcy referee, the predecessor position to U.S. bankruptcy judge, and, when an opening developed on the district, he turned again to his friend Brooks. This is where the patronage issue comes in. In the phone call in which Bayh asked Brooks if he wanted the job, Brooks said that he did, but he was then confronted with Bayh's desire that Brooks, if appointed, make particular appointments on behalf of Bayh. To this Brooks said, "Whatever you want, Senator."

Later, Bayh's son Evan, who had succeeded his father as a U.S. senator, phoned Brooks and called in a favor. Bayh was not forcing Brooks out,

---

[136] Richard Henry Mills, "The Oral History of Judge Richard H. Mills," Circuit Library, U.S. Court of Appeals for the Seventh Circuit (2000), pp. 59–60.

but if he left his seat, then Bayh could, with a friendly administration in Washington, appoint Brooks' successor. The risk otherwise would be that Brooks would retire or take senior status under a Republican administration, leaving Bayh with the appointment. Brooks complied, leaving the bench.

At about the time of his decision to retire, he got a call from a local law firm wondering if he would be interested in joining it and, in the process, make much more money. Brooks left the bench and joined the firm.[137]

Illinois senator Charles Percy, others have reported, did seek out those best qualified for judgeships. He was, in fact, quite proud of his record in choosing judges and, according to one political insider, often boasted of his accomplishment. Percy also considered personal relationships. For James Foreman (N.D. Ill. 1972–present) it was a combination of both factors.

Foreman explains that once he learned of the opening, he decided to "throw [his] name in for the position and let it be known to Chuck Percy that I was interested." Percy, he recounts, had formed a committee to investigate the applicants, and both the committee and Percy thought he was qualified, which led to his recommendation to Nixon. And then he candidly added, "Chuck thought I was qualified and our personal relationship was very helpful to me in getting the position. I don't think that's terribly unusual, or wasn't at that time."[138]

Alfred Goodwin (D. Or. 1969–71 and C.A.9 1971–present) owes his judicial appointment success to the support of Mark Hatfield. They had known each other their entire careers and were good friends. Hatfield first appointed Goodwin to the Oregon Supreme Court, where he served for nearly a decade. It was, in fact, Hatfield's only appointment to the state's supreme court. He thought so highly of Goodwin that he began to push Goodwin for the United States Supreme Court.

Goodwin's and Hatfield's party was out of office, so the argument for Goodwin was that he would make a good moderate Republican candidate if the opportunity ever arose. Nixon was elected, and the talk became more serious about Goodwin. Hatfield had a close connection to Attorney General John Mitchell, and Mitchell let Goodwin know that the White House was interested in him. "John Mitchell made that rather clear

---

[137] Gene E. Brooks, "The Oral History of Retired Judge Gene E. Brooks," Circuit Library, U.S. Court of Appeals for the Seventh Circuit (1994), pp. 33–35.

[138] James L. Foreman, "The Oral History of Judge James L. Foreman," Circuit Library, U.S. Court of Appeals for the Seventh Circuit (1985), pp. 13–14.

to me in a private conversation," Goodwin explains, "but his language was ambiguous enough so that he could have denied it later if he ever wanted to. But he said, 'Well this isn't the end of the line for you, Ted; the president has high hopes for you.'"[139]

But then a position on the district court opened up and Hatfield put Goodwin forward for that. There were actually two openings, one on the district court and one on the Ninth Circuit. Hatfield wanted Goodwin for the circuit court judgeship, but a deal was struck that put one of the older district judges, John Kilkenny, on the circuit bench with the understanding that he would take senior status in two years to once again open up the seat, this time for Goodwin. Kilkenny, then sixty-eight years old, was appointed and served his two years, taking senior status at seventy. Goodwin was appointed to replace him. The Supreme Court appointment never materialized, but because of Hatfield Goodwin was appointed not once but twice.

Rosemary Barkett (C.A.11 1994–present), appointed to the Eleventh Circuit in 1994, was the favorite judge, it seems, of Bob Graham, who was first Florida's governor and then one of its senators. Graham had appointed Barkett to three different judicial posts in the Florida state system, first as a trial judge, then as a court of appeals judge, and then as a justice on the Florida Supreme Court. Graham thought so well of Barkett that he suggested her as a replacement for Byron White of the United States Supreme Court when White retired in 1992. There is no indication, as there is for Goodwin, though, that her consideration for the Supreme Court got to the inner offices of the White House. Barkett was flattered but shrugged off the heady suggestion of a Supreme Court appointment and mentioned to some supporters instead that she would not mind the United States Court of Appeals for the Eleventh Circuit. That hint turned out to be enough, so that when an opening developed shortly thereafter, Senator Graham used his influence to have her appointed.

The wonderfully named William Justice (E.D. Tex. 1968–present) of Texas had a friend in Senator Ralph Yarborough. It was Yarborough who had to fight it out with former Texas senator Lyndon Johnson, who was in the White House at that time. Justice recalls,

I had been a United States attorney at that time for about six and a half years. I decided that I would like to have the job of U.S. district

[139] Alfred T. Goodwin "Oral History Interview with Alfred T. Goodwin," U.S. District Court Collection, Oregon Historical Society (1986), p. 456.

judge. I decided that I might be qualified for it in view of the feelings that I formed about the judges I had been appearing before. I notified Senator Yarborough of my desire and he told me he'd take it under consideration. He then proceeded to tell me about the method of appointment that was then going on. Back in 1961 when Kennedy came in, Lyndon Johnson became vice president and he had also run for his job as senator the same time he was running for vice president. He won both of them. So on that basis he decided that he was entitled to half of the patronage from Texas, which was unusual because that was ordinarily given to the senior senator from the party that was in power. Yarborough regarded that as a transgression on his territory but there wasn't anything he could do about it, certainly if Kennedy wasn't going to go against his own vice president. They in effect reached that agreement that Johnson would get half and Yarborough would get half. They would consult with each other on occasion about who they wanted to get nominated and they had vast disagreements. One of them would put up one candidate and the other, for example, for the Western District of Texas U.S. attorney, Yarborough would put up a nominee and Johnson would put up one. They didn't know how to resolve this difficulty and they finally settled it on this basis. If a particular person being under consideration had not called either Johnson or Yarborough a SOB in public then that person was eligible [laughter]. It might have been a little more formal than that, but that's the impression I was given by Senator Yarborough.

When Johnson came aboard as president, he continued the same system. He demanded and got half of the patronage from Texas. Yarborough told me about some of their meetings. He said the world would be in turmoil—India was about to invade Pakistan or something of that nature. He said they'd get up there on Saturday afternoon and discuss and re-discuss whether or not Joe Blow would get the customs collector job in Port Arthur, Texas.

In my particular case, Yarborough advanced my name and the president suggested a lawyer practicing in Bonham, Texas, who enjoyed the favor of Sam Rayburn, Speaker of the House. They went back and forth for several months about all that. Finally, a vacancy came out in the Western District of Texas for U.S. district judge. The president suggested a guy by the name of Woodward, Hal Woodward. I forget who it was that Yarborough settled on.

Finally, it got to I'll give you the Eastern District or I'll give you the Western District or whatever it was. They finally agreed on which one would get which district and the president got the Western District of Texas and he nominated Hal Woodward. Yarborough got the Eastern District of Texas and he nominated me.

Before that all came about, there was a very crucial experience. I learned that the president was also suggesting a lawyer from Marshall, Texas, by the name of Baldwin. What disturbed me particularly was that Lady Bird Johnson grew up just outside of Marshall in a little country place which I can't recall its name right now [Karnack, Texas]. Her best friend in Marshall was the wife of Mr. Baldwin. When I learned that, I just thought that this was it and I've lost. I was certain the president's wife would have a great influence over this. I got the nomination. I wondered what happened to Baldwin. They had solved that, too. The president nominated him for a position on the Court of Customs and Patent Appeals in Washington, D.C., the equivalent of a circuit judgeship. That recital is too long but that's what happened.[140]

Governor or High Ranking State Official

Myron Gordon (E.D. Wis. 1967–present) had been successful in judicial electoral politics, having been elected to the Wisconsin Supreme Court. This success ironically posed a threat to his federal court nomination. On one hand, there was a movement for him to be put on the district bench once an opening occurred. The mayor of Milwaukee, Henry Maier, and a leader in the Milwaukee business world named Jim Wyndham both supported him, and his base of support broadened. "For a short time", he recalls,

> it looked as if my selection might be a breeze. Well, it surely wasn't, because other people developed their own interests. Some labor

---

[140] William Wayne Justice, "Oral History Interview with Judge William Wayne Justice," Fifth Circuit Court of Appeals Library, New Orleans, LA (2002), pp. 41–43.

leaders objected to my departure from the Wisconsin Supreme Court because the then-governor was a Republican who would be appointing my successor on that court. When the senators declined to make me their only nominee, it opened the field to others such as the two Milwaukee congressmen. Each had a favorite son.[141]

Gordon's broadly based support, though, carried him through.

The appointment of Samuel Dillin (S.D. Ind. 1961–2006) gives insight into both the way a governor's inner circle operates and the nature of the relationship between the White House and a state's senators in choosing nominees.

Dillin, a Democrat, had been a legislative wizard beginning from the time he was in law school and serving in the Indiana state legislature. He rose to be in the governor's inner circle because of his legislative skills. He had brilliantly managed the state senate in 1961 and was told he could either have the nomination to the U.S. Senate for the following year or the nomination to the governorship when the current governor stepped down. While he was trying to choose between doors one and two, the opening to the district court developed and he knew in an instant that it was the court that he wanted. He then called Senator Vance Hartke, to whom the promised favor also applied, and the nomination followed.

An interesting wrinkle then developed. There had been two openings on the district bench. Dillin was nominated for one and David Kiley was nominated for the other. But then the White House under Kennedy cut into what had been senatorial privilege and explained that the Republicans were insisting on one of the nominations in partial payment for going along with a bill authorizing 143 judgeships nationwide. Attorney General Bobby Kennedy told the Indiana Democrats that the White House felt it owed nothing to Indiana, because the state had gone for Nixon, and that it was going to take away one of the two nominations from the Democrats. After extensive negotiations, a compromise allowed Hartke the chance to name the Republican to be nominated for the second judgeship. This deal could have scuttled Dillin's chances, but because he was so close to the governor

---

[141] Myron L. Gordon, "The Oral History of Judge Myron L. Gordon," Circuit Library, U.S. Court of Appeals for the Seventh Circuit (1999), p. 42.

and to Hartke, he was the Democratic pick that the White House did not object to. Kiley, on the other hand, lost out.[142]

Luther Swygert (N.D. Ind. 1943–61 and C.A.7 1961–88) had the support of Democratic National Committeeman Frank McHale and Democratic U.S. senator Frederick Van Nuys for his 1943 appointment to the district bench. He also had a friend in the Justice Department who was especially close to Tom Clark who was, to hear Swygert explain it, in on the nomination.

There were others interested in the district court job, but Swygert had two additional factors helping him. One was that then sitting Judge Tom Slick wanted to see Swygert succeed him. Second, Slick told Swygert and his supporters that he was going to take senior status and put the judgeship in play. This was not public knowledge. The day after the announcement, Van Nuys submitted Swygert's name to head off the challenges of the others.

The stars were not so aligned the next time Swygert was up for a nomination. In 1957, Swygert's cause for an appointment to the Seventh Circuit was led by former U.S. senator William Jenner, who was then serving in the Justice Department. Jenner was a Republican. As Swygert explains, "The reason that he did that was not just because of our friendship but he felt that there was more patronage on the district court than the court of appeals."

Jenner promoted Swygert to Attorney General Brownell, who asked Swygert to meet with him. At about the same time, though, Lynn Parkinson pushed for the job by having his wife, as Swygert put it, start to throw sharp knives into him. She gossiped that Swygert was unfit for the job in part because of his chronic bouts with depression and in part because it was Parkinson, she said, who was doing Swygert's work on the district bench. Swygert opted for discretion as the better part of valor and waited until 1961 for his appointment to the Seventh Circuit. This time it was James Fleming, former U.S. attorney and political heavyweight, who advanced his cause. Fleming had been there at the beginning, when he pushed for Swygert to replace Slick, and he continued thereafter to promote Swygert's interest.[143]

---

[142] S. Hugh Dillin, "The Oral History of Judge S. Hugh Dillin," Circuit Library, U.S. Court of Appeals for the Seventh Circuit (1994), pp. 42, 60.

[143] Luther Merritt Swygert, "The Oral History of Judge Luther M. Swygert," Circuit Library, U.S. Court of Appeals for the Seventh Circuit (1985), pp. 23–24.

William Steckler (S.D. Ind. 1950–95), only thirty-six at the time of his appointment, had highly placed supporters for his nomination, and, oddly enough they were more enthusiastic about the position than he was. Steckler was close to Frank McHale, a Democratic National Committeeman, and he was even closer to Frank McKinney, who was close to President Truman. Indiana's two senators were Republicans, which gave McKinney additional leverage with Truman. His best connection was with Truman himself. He had met with him several times and was questioned by one of Truman's aides—but only about his young age and his lone competitor for the job, the U.S. attorney for the district. Satisfied by his answers, Steckler's appointment followed.

To hear Steckler tell the story, he had been doing very well in private practice and was balking at giving that up. Finally, he decided he wanted the position, as much to make his supporters happy as anything else. He summed it up, saying, "I felt it would have been unfair for me to back out after all of the efforts that had been expended in my behalf. And of course it was a great honor to have your name submitted to the president."[144]

Andrew Hauk (C.D. Cal. 1966–2004) secured his nomination to the Central District of California through political connections, and therein lies an intriguing story. Hauk had been a Johnson man in the 1960 presidential campaign. Once Kennedy had secured the path to the presidential nomination, being a Johnson supporter was not a useful political credential. But, as Hauk tells the story, Johnson's selection as vice president brought him back into the fold. As he describes it, he began to become known. He was invited, for example, to $1,000 a plate dinners. The oil money paid for the dinners, he says, but then he adds that "how invitations were passed to me is going to stay secret, nobody's going to see it until I'm gone."[145]

Kennedy's assassination brought opportunity for Hauk. Following the event, his close political supporter, Carmen Warshaw, a Democratic National Committeewoman and leading Jewish fund-raiser, called Hauk and told him that he now had a chance. Warshaw not only secured Hauk's nomination, but in a contest between Hauk and William Gray, another Central District judge nominated at the same time, Warshaw's connection in the Johnson White House arranged to have Hauk's commission

---

[144] William Elwood Steckler, "The Oral History of Judge William E. Steckler," Circuit Library, U.S. Court of Appeals for the Seventh Circuit (1988), pp. 56, 107.

[145] A. Andrew Hauk, "Oral History Interview with Hon. A. Andrew Hauk," Ninth Judicial Circuit Historical Society (1990), p. 60.

signed before Gray's, thereby giving him seniority, which ultimately resulted in Hauk serving as chief judge while Gray never did.[146]

The question of how Hauk got himself invited to the dinners he describes comes elsewhere in the interview. Hauk in his interviews was, to say the least, freewheeling. The interviewer would essentially flip a switch by asking a question and Hauk would be off, sometimes going on for what amounted to several single-spaced pages at a time. Moreover, Hauk would frequently digress and repeat himself, sometimes with slight variations. This matters because elsewhere in the oral history, Hauk explains how he settled a matter with the federal government for his client, the Union Oil Company.

Hauk served as assistant counsel for the oil company from 1952 until he went onto the Superior Court bench in 1964. The problem was that the client needed its oil quota raised and only the Secretary of the Interior could make the adjustment. Access to the administration was tightly controlled, however. Hauk describes having a meeting with Big Daddy Jesse Unruh in his Cadillac in which Unruh told him that $100,000 needed to be contributed to the party for Hauk to meet with the right person in the administration. The money was paid, Hauk got his meeting, and the client's quota was raised.[147] The suspicion Hauk's oral history creates is that this contribution led to the insider status and dinner invitations he describes.

Stephen Reinhardt (C.A.9 1979–present) had friends who had very influential friends. Reinhardt got his appointment during the Carter administration and through its commission process. Reinhardt had been a member of the Los Angeles Police Commission, the chair of which was Sam Williams. Williams was important for two reasons. He and Reinhardt were close and were, perhaps, Mayor Tom Bradley's two closest advisors. Sam Williams was also head of the selection commission in Southern California. Tom Bradley, in turn, was personally close to President Carter. Reinhardt got the recommendation of the commission and then the nomination of the president.[148]

Robert Kelleher (C.D. Cal. 1970–present) had highly places friends in the governor's office in California. The one he was closest to was William French Smith, who would later be the attorney general in the Reagan administration, but at the time of Kelleher's appointment in 1970, Smith

[146] *Ibid.* at 58–67.
[147] *Ibid.* at 59.
[148] Stephen Roy Reinhardt, "Oral History Interview with Judge Stephen Reinhardt," Ninth Judicial Circuit Historical Society (1993), p. 23.

was a leading member of Reagan's inner circle. Smith had gotten to know Kelleher because of tennis. Smith was a big fan; Kelleher had been a great player and was captain of the U.S. Davis Cup team in the early 1960s. Kelleher was also a well-respected litigator and had, in fact, tried several cases against Smith's firm, though Smith himself was not personally involved. Kelleher was thus not just a dashing tennis player, he was an impressive lawyer as well.

His story unfolds simply. He had let it known during the Eisenhower administration that he wanted to go onto the federal bench. He mentioned to Smith during the Nixon administration that he wanted to be appointed. Smith was close to the White House and also to Republican Senator George Murphy. The nomination followed. It was the support that he got from the state's Democratic senator John Tunney that got him the job. Tunney had beaten Murphy, leaving Kelleher's nomination in limbo. Tunney was familiar with Kelleher and was sufficiently impressed that he backed the nomination.[149]

Fight

Prentice Marshall (N.D. Ill. 1973–96) was an immensely successful and well-respected trial lawyer who, to his good fortune, decided to leave private practice to teach at the University of Illinois Law School. This was good fortune because Senator Charles Percy had decided, after his earlier candidate did not review well, that he wanted to nominate an academic to the bench. But Marshall was more than an academic; he continued to try cases as part of the school's clinical program.

Percy had long stressed qualifications over patronage in his choices for the federal bench and had stringers troll for the best-qualified candidates. He had his office call Marshall to see if he was interested in going onto the federal bench. Marshall spoke for many others when he answered, "Show me a lawyer who has devoted his life to litigation and I will show you somebody who would like to be a federal judge."[150]

It did not trouble Percy that Marshall, a Democrat, was from the wrong party. The state's top Republicans were not so generous, however.

149 Robert Joseph Kelleher, "Oral History Interview with Judge Robert J. Kelleher," Ninth Judicial Circuit Historical Society (1990), pp. 30–31.
150 See fn. 113.

They did not want to give the prized post to the opposing party and resisted Percy. They brought their beef to the attorney general, Richard Kleindienst, which proved to be another stroke of good fortune for Marshall. In resolving the dispute in Percy's and Marshall's favor, Kleindienst was to have said that the constitution calls for the advice and consent of the Senate, not the advice and consent of the Republican Caucus and Illinois General Assembly.[151]

Tension Between White House and State Political Forces

Tugs of war between the party in the White House and that party's state delegation can involve the spoils of patronage, but they can also have an ideological aspect to them.

Robert Jones (D. Or. 1990–present) found that, even though he was a Republican sponsored by his state's two senators, the state's entire delegation, and the state's current and past Republican governors, he was not passing the conservative litmus test applied by the White House. There were several villains of the piece. Both the president's chief of staff, John Sununu, and Attorney General Richard Thornberg had to be convinced that Jones was conservative enough. They had heard that Jones had written supposedly liberal opinions while on the Oregon Supreme Court. One had involved a Native American tribe and its ceremonial use of peyote. Sununu gave the opinions first to Robert Bork for analysis. Bork couldn't determine whether there was a liberal bias. Knowing he was in a firefight, Jones had the dean of the University of Oregon Law School report on all of his opinions. This led to a joint letter from them and the sponsoring senators Hatfield and Packwood reporting that Jones was the most qualified person in the state, that he was the man they wanted, and that they did not want the White House to consider anyone else.

Still the White House was not satisfied. There was for Jones a certain nastiness in the White House's whole approach. Michael Luttig, who later took a seat on the Fourth Circuit and was often on the very short list for the Supreme Court, was one of Jones's White House interrogators. He was, Jones reports, a mean person.

---

[151] Prentice H. Marshall, "The Oral History of Retired Judge Prentice H. Marshall," Circuit Library, U.S. Court of Appeals for the Seventh Circuit (1999), pp. 76–79.

He treated me, a Supreme Court justice, like dirt, and in my mind is unfit to serve on any court. He promoted himself onto the Fourth Circuit, where he's been sitting since. But after getting appointed to the Fourth Circuit, he withheld and stood his time to fight the Anita Hill and the Clarence Thomas battle, which I thought was totally inappropriate. If he's a judge, he's a judge. He wasn't a politician, especially one at that level. So, they say nice things about him. I don't say nice things about him.

The impasse was eventually broken by a remarkable demonstration of home state support. Senator Packwood went to see Sununu and brought with him a medal Jones had received for a speech he had given to the Sons of the American Revolution. "It was a beautiful ribbon—like a Congressional Medal of Honor—and underneath the medal said, 'Patriotism Award.' Packwood said to Sununu, 'Here, look at this. The Sons of the American Revolution think Judge Jones is a patriot.' Sununu said, 'That's good enough for me' [both laugh]. That's how I got in. Isn't that funny?"[152]

There was a fight over the nomination of Alfonso Zirpoli (N.D. Cal. 1961–95) to the Northern District of California. Zirpoli had been an extremely successful practitioner and U.S. attorney. During the Kennedy administration, he was asked by Attorney General Robert Kennedy if he wanted to go onto the district bench. The problem came not from within the administration but from the governor's office in California. Pat Brown as governor was strongly pushing the candidacy of his brother Harold Brown for the district court judgeship. Brown in fact took Zirpoli aside and asked him to stand down so that his brother could get the nomination. Zirpoli said he would not do this. Foiled, Brown then approached the mayor of San Francisco to ask him to ask Zirpoli to stand down. The mayor also said no. In Washington there was not much doubt as to Zirpoli's nomination. Zirpoli went to see Deputy Attorney General Byron White in his office in Washington. White asked him to sit down for a minute while he called for someone. As Zirpoli tells the story, "He sent for a fellow named Andretta who handles all of the business of the attorney general's office and the financing. When Andretta stepped into the room,

---

[152] Robert Edward Jones, "Oral History Interview with Robert E. Jones," U.S. District Court Collection, Oregon Historical Society (2005), pp. 92–93.

he turned to Andretta and he said, 'I want you to meet the next Italian judge.'" [153]

Small States

The dynamics for judicial nominations in small jurisdiction are such that the most impressive lawyers in the jurisdiction become a force in their own right. Political connections are necessary, but the lawyer whom others consider the most impressive has a built-in advantage.

This was true for Harold Ryan (D. Id. 1981–95). He rose to the top of the profession in Idaho and was asked by his friend, Senator Jim McClure, if he wanted to join the bench. He turned McClure down in 1976 because he had a son in school and didn't want to relocate his family. In 1981, McClure called and offered the job again. Ryan explained to McClure that he had been telling everyone that he was still not interested. Ryan recalls that conversation:

> McClure then said, "Well, you would be doing me a great favor if you would consider taking it." I says, "Well, you have never put it that way before." And so I says, "Well, give me a chance to think about it. How long would you need before I give you an answer?" I think this was a Wednesday morning, and he says, "Well, I'd like to know by Friday." So I hung up the phone and my wife and I started talking about it. For several days before that, lawyers had been calling me around the state seeking my support to come on the bench, and I had told all of them that I had no intention of doing it, but now I was about to go backwards on what I had said there. My wife pointed out to me that in many respects she had noticed that I was getting kind of bored with some of the aspects of the practice of law, which I didn't realize, and I got to thinking that some of that was absolutely true. Parts of it I enjoyed, parts of it I didn't anymore.
>
> So then I called up my old friend, Ray McNichols. He and I had gone to law school together, and said I'd like to talk with him.

---

[153] Alfonso Joseph Zirpoli, "Faith in Justice: Alfonso J. Zirpoli and the United States District Court for the Northern District of California," Northern California U.S. District Court Oral History Series, Regional Oral History Office, The Bancroft Library, University of California, Berkeley (1982–1983), pp. 115–116.

And so my wife, Ann, and I came to Boise, and right here in these chambers, which was Judge McNichols' chambers at that time, sat down and had a long visit with him as to what this job was all about and what it entailed, and I kidded with Ray at the time, I said, "You know, Ray, since we got out of law school, I've never really had a job." And he caught the gist of it all right and he says, "Well, one thing about this job; you are your own boss." I said, "Well, it does make a big difference." We visited awhile, and my wife and I talked about it all the way home. By Friday I made the call back to Senator McClure and said that if he wished to nominate me, I'd be happy to take it. So that came out in the paper about a day later, and by December I was being sworn in. I think I—if my dates are right, I got a call from President Reagan the 4th or 5th of December and my nomination was put in place by him.[154]

The appointment of Bruce Thompson (D. Nev. 1963–92) in the small jurisdiction of Nevada turned on his support from his state's two senators. The story begins with Thompson at the county courthouse one day when somebody asked a group of lawyers if anyone was interested in the job. Thompson said he was and later got a phone call from one of the lawyers in the group, who told Thompson that if he was interested he ought to head over to the local hotel and see Senator Alan Bible because he was in town and staying there.

At the hotel, Bible told him that he wanted to make the appointment as soon as possible. The longer he waited the more enemies he would necessarily make. Was he interested in the job, Bible asked? One senator down, one to go. Thompson knew the other senator, Howard Cannon, well. They had once gone on a whistle stop campaign together, but Thompson needed to know for sure. As Thompson recounts,

> So then I found out that Senator Cannon was down in Las Vegas so I flew to Las Vegas and made an appointment to see him and told him that Senator Bible had indicated he was willing to recommend me, and I just wanted to find out that Senator Cannon wouldn't take the position that I was personally obnoxious to him, and he said he

[154] Harold L. Ryan, "District Judge Harold Ryan," Ninth Circuit Library, Boise, Idaho (1990), pp. 57–58.

would approve the appointment, so they made the recommendation to the Department of Justice.[155]

The best get pushed to the front more often, it seems, in small jurisdictions. This was the story of the appointment of Procter Hug (C.A.9 1977–present) to the Ninth Circuit in 1977. He first had to decide whether he wanted to try for the nomination. There was an opportunity, since the commission set up under President Carter to make recommendations for the circuit bench, to its credit, actively sought out qualified candidates. But even with the oppportunity there, Hug was reluctant. District judge Bruce Thompson sent Hug a brief letter and encouraged him to apply, but even this was not enough. First, he was under the impression that any new appointee would have to move to the circuit's headquarters in San Francisco, something he did not want to do because of family concerns. Second, he had assumed that the current chief justice of the Nevada Supreme Court, Al Gundersen, would be recommended. Gundersen had made appointment to the circuit court the crowning achievement in his career and had been working with Nevada senator Cannon for the appointment. He had let everyone know that he wanted the position.

Not everyone wanted Gundersen, though. One of the members of the commission, rather than seeking out letters in support of Gundersen as part of the committee's process, took the occasion of the Nevada state bar convention to hand out questionnaires to the lawyers asking them what they thought about the judicial temperament and legal ability of those who had applied to the commission. Responses to Gundersen were not flattering and he dropped out of contention.

About that time, Hug got a call from Eugene Wright on the Ninth Circuit. Wright and Hug had never met, but Wright knew of Hug through people he knew at the Judicial College in Hug's hometown of Reno. Wright encouraged Hug to apply to the commission and settled, to Hug's relief, the question of moving to San Francisco. Apparently that was not required. Hug then thought through the matter and realized that if he were ever to leave practice and go onto the bench, this was the time. Energized, Hug applied to the commission and made the final cut through interviews. He then had to endure a vigorous campaign, likely run by the disappointed Gundersen, against the candidates who made the final cut.

---

[155] Bruce Rutherford Thompson, "Oral History Interview with Hon. Bruce R. Thompson," Ninth Judicial Circuit Historical Society (1988), pp. 58–59.

The fault with Hug, the campaign against him argued, was that he had no judicial experience, in contrast to Gundersen, of course. The campaign failed and Hug got the recommendation of the committee and then the nomination.[156]

Quotas

James Parsons (N.D. Ill. 1961–93), the first black to be appointed to the district bench, describes his appointment, at least in part, as a quota appointment of President Kennedy. There was also, to be sure, a personal relationship with Kennedy that also explains the appointment. On two occasions during the 1960 presidential campaign, Parsons toured Chicago with Kennedy. After the election, Kennedy seemed surprised that there had never been a black appointed to the district bench. He assembled a group to solve the problem and, according to a Chicago ally of Parsons at this meeting, Kennedy began the meeting by turning to him and asking, "Well, what about your man out there in Chicago."[157] The appointment promptly followed.

Leon Higginbotham (E.D. Pa. 1964–77 and C.A.3 1977–93) had no doubt that his nomination to the district bench in Pennsylvania was a quota appointment. There had been appointments to blacks in Chicago and Detroit, and the political forces of Philadelphia essentially demanded one of their own. Higginbotham had become known to the White House—something that in effect settled a tie. One Philadelphia congressman wanted a particular candidate while the other wanted someone else. Neither promoted Higginbotham. The administration, by way of Robert Kennedy, sternly told the two that if they could not agree on a candidate then the White House would nominate Higginbotham. They could not agree and Higginbotham got the nomination. Amusingly, both congressmen called Higginbotham once they knew their candidates failed and tried to convince Higginbotham that he had been their candidate all along. Each congressman even tried to gild the lily by saying that he

[156] Procter Ralph Hug Jr., "Oral History Interview with Hon. Procter Hug, Jr.," Ninth Judicial Circuit Historical Society (1995), pp. 135–141.
[157] James Benton Parsons, "The Unfinished Oral History of Judge James B. Parsons," Circuit Library, U.S. Court of Appeals for the Seventh Circuit (1996), p. 74.

had to overcome the resistance of the other congressman to get his choice—Higginbotham—through.[158]

Lobbying

Except in rare cases in which candidates are recruited, those interested in federal judgeships actively pursue the position they want, though the degree of aggressiveness in this pursuit varies. We see examples of how the more aggressively inclined sought their judgeships in the stories of Raul Ramirez (E.D. Cal. 1979–89) and Thomas Tang (C.A.9 1977–95).

Raul Ramirez's approach was that, if he was in, he was all the way in. He was not sure he wanted to apply for one of the new positions in the Eastern District of California, but a friend helped persuade him that he should apply. Then, as Ramirez explained, he did all that he could to get the job.

> If I was going to throw it in, I was going to throw it in like a bull in a china shop. I started talking to legislators, senators, lawyers, DAs, politicians, police officers, business people, etc., etc. Because I had some very, very stiff competition and, of course, I was the youngest and least experienced out of all the other candidates. So, I figured if you're gonna go for it and after what they put me through on the application form, I figured, it's horrendous. Put as much power behind it as you can, which I did.[159]

Tang of the Ninth Circuit tried to get to the source when he made the short list of candidates chosen by the Carter commission. He had been encouraged to apply by senator Dennis DeConcini, not a bad connection to have, but, to improve his chances, Tang decided not so much to crash an American Bar Association convention to make his case but to go out of his way to attend. He had been to only one ABA convention before, but, at about the time his candidacy was being considered, there was an ABA convention that Attorney General Griffin Bell would be attending. Tang says, "I know that I made particular efforts to make my presence known to the then-Attorney General Griffin Bell. I traveled to and

---

[158] Aloyisus Leon Higginbotham Jr., "Interview With The Honorable A. Leon Higginbotham," Historical Society of the United States Court of Appeals for the Third Circuit (n.d.), pp. 53–57.

[159] Raul Ramirez, "Oral History Interview with Hon. Raul Ramirez," Ninth Judicial Circuit Historical Society (1990), pp. 17–18.

attended an ABA convention precisely to be there to meet with the attorney general." As it turned out, Bell told Tang that he did not need to see him. Nonetheless, Tang's selection followed.[160]

Easy

For some judges, the appointment seems to have been easily done. That, at least, is what their descriptions suggest.

Carolyn Dimmick (W.D. Wa. 1985–present) explains that she was busy and happy running for another term on the Washington Supreme Court when an opening on the district court developed. She had not submitted an application, but, at a social function, one of the members on the committee searching for the new appointment told her that the senator was not happy with the list of candidates and asked her to consider putting her name into contention. "And I said, 'You know, I wouldn't put in my application but if someone handed me the job, I certainly wouldn't refuse it.' And fortunately somebody handed me the job. And that was how simple it was. I know people who are clamoring for the job, but, as I say, it was just very easy."[161]

For Charles Merrill (C.A.9 1959–96), the appointment was so quick and so painless that he can't quite remember how it happened.

I'm not sure [how it happened]. I was told that on one occasion, giving one of my speeches, historical-type speeches, at a convention in Las Vegas, a bar convention of some sort, and a couple of prominent attorneys and judges at one of the tables remarked that I would be a good candidate for the court of appeals when a vacancy occurred there in which the state of Nevada might have an interest. I know that some of my legal friends asked me at the time whether I'd be interested and I said, "No, I'm perfectly happy being on the Supreme Court."[162] And then later I did decide that I would be

---

160 Thomas Tang, "Oral History Interview with Hon. Thomas Tang," Ninth Judicial Circuit Historical Society (1998), pp. 21–22, 25.
161 Carolyn R. Dimmick, "Oral History Interview with Judge Carolyn R. Dimmick," Ninth Judicial Circuit Historical Society (1991), p. 13.
162 Charles Merton Merrill, "Oral History Interview with Judge Charles A. Merrill," Ninth Judicial Circuit Historical Society (1989), p. 10.

interested and I would accept if it was offered. But other than that I have no knowledge of exactly how it was my name came up.

Arthur Alarcon (C.A.9 1979–present) describes his appointment to the Ninth Circuit and suggests that for him it was just a matter of his interest. Once he decided he wanted the job, it naturally followed that he should get it. Alarcon had seen the newspaper advertisement run by the Carter commission to fill the vacancy, but he did not respond to it, and it was not until a friend persuaded him to apply, arguing that he might not get another chance, that Alarcon sent in his application.

My self confidence is so healthy, thanks to my father, that it did not occur to me that my application might be rejected. I had always believed that whatever I strived for I would achieve. For that reason I was taken aback by my friend's advice. I sent in the application on the last day of filing. I promptly forgot about it for a while.

He was interviewed by the merit committee in the federal courthouse and admits that it was only the second time he had been in the building. The first time was when he was sworn in as a member of the California bar. His only obstacle in getting the job, Alarcon explains, was his political affiliation. The White House apparently did not know that he was of the wrong party when he was chosen, but even when it came to light it was not enough to stop the ordained Alarcon.[163]

Paul Rosenblatt (D. Ariz. 1984–present) used a personal connection to Barry Goldwater, the nominating senator, and in short order he got the job. As he explains it, he saw an announcement that a vacancy had been created by one of the judges taking senior status. "I expressed an interest to Senator Goldwater. Lo and behold, he recommended me to President Reagan and I got appointed in 1984." The back story, he explains, is that one of his sisters had dated Barry Goldwater when they were in college. They remained close thereafter. This in turn led Rosenblatt to note that he owed a lot of his career success to his sister.[164]

Cynthia Hall (C.D. Cal. 1981–84 and C.A.9 1984–97) certainly makes it seem as though she had no difficulty getting onto the bench, not once but twice. She had served for nine years on the United States Tax

[163] Arthur Lawrence Alarcon, "Oral History Interview with Judge Arthur L. Alarcon," Ninth Judicial Circuit Historical Society (1991), pp. 92–100.
[164] Paul G. Rosenblatt, "Oral History Interview with Judge Paul G. Rosenblatt," Ninth Judicial Circuit Historical Society (1998), pp. 89–90.

Court—not an Article III court—and decided she wanted to leave. She would either go back to private practice, she said, or she would seek out a position on the district court. She wrote to Senator Hayakawa, was interviewed by his office, "and eventually I was his first choice." After three years on the bench in the Central District of California, she simply got a call from the Justice Department saying that the president wanted to consider her for a position on the Ninth Circuit. Nothing more is said, or need be said.[165]

Presidential Deal Making

White House political calculations sometimes take precedence over senatorial privilege, and a president feels the need to appoint judges from the other party. Deals that are struck requiring the president to appoint from the other party yield benefits to the White House and create openings for candidates from the other party who would otherwise never have a chance at an appointment.

One such deal involved Leland Nielsen (S.D. Cal. 1971–99). His story has the added wrinkle of being the only one in the oral histories in which an appointment turned on the candidate favorably impressing an influential party member. To his credit, Nielsen refused to jump through the hoops and lost out on the nomination; a few years later it came around again, but on better terms. In its first form, Mr. and Mrs. C. Arnholt Smith, because of their close ties to Nixon and their financial standing in the party, had acquired a veto over federal court nominations in San Diego. In early 1970, Nielsen was offered a district judgeship by Republican senator George Murphy. While in Washington, Nielsen spoke to Murphy's administrative assistant, who told Nielsen that everything had been cleared for the nomination and that all he needed to do was clear with the Smiths.

"I said, 'There is no way in the world that I would ask either one of them for the time of day, much less their clearance for me to become a federal judge.' So, when the nominations came, I wasn't nominated."

In just a few months, though, Murphy had been beaten by Democrat John Tunney. California now had two Democrats in the Senate, complicating matters for the Republican White House. A deal was then struck

---

[165] Cynthia Holcomb Hall, "Diversifying the Federal Judiciary: Interview with Cynthia H. Hall," United States Court of Appeals for the Ninth Circuit (1995), pp. 45, 61.

for the two openings: one Republican district judge for one Democratic judge. Nielsen was the Republican. As he explains it, in the spring of 1971,

> I was on my [state court] bench one day when a call came from the attorney general. I went into my chambers and took it, and he said, "Are you still interested in the federal bench?" And I said, "Not under the circumstances that it was laid down to me before." He says, "No strings attached." I said, "Yes, I am." I was nominated practically the next day, along with Matt Byrne in Los Angeles, who, of course, is a very active Democrat and a very, very close friend of Senator Tunney. I learned later that there had been a deal made with the administration for California. One Democrat for one Republican. I was the Republican, and he was the Democrat.[166]

In the late 1970s, Arnholt Smith was convicted in San Diego's federal district court of embezzlement and tax evasion and served eight months in prison.

Collins Seitz (C.A.3 1966–98) was the recipient, literally, of sleight of hand in getting his appointment to the Third Circuit. Seitz, a Democrat, had struggled to get the two senators of his state, both Republicans, to recommend him. That the Democratic governor of the state wanted him certainly helped. But the struggle was not over. Seitz tells the story:

> When my name was surfaced, Lyndon Johnson, who was a famous wheeler dealer, was trying to placate the Republicans. Even though he first said he would appoint me, we found out through the grapevine that he was going to trade me for another appointment in California and name a Republican from Delaware to placate the Republicans. I well remember the night I heard the news and my old partner, William S. Potter, who was Democratic state chairman, was attending a dinner and I went into the dinner and I told him what was happening. He went outside and made a telephone call to Jenkins, who was Lyndon Johnson's right-hand man. And he and Potter were good friends and he talked to him on the phone like a Dutch uncle and finally Potter says, well, Jenkins is going to switch the papers on the president's desk. Believe this or not. And I

---

[166] Leland Chris Nielsen, "Oral History Memoir of Leland C. Nielsen," Ninth Judicial Circuit Historical Society (1998), pp. 17–19.

haven't checked it yet but I think either the *Wall Street Journal* or *The New York Times* has an account of this deal and maybe it can be found out about that period, what actually happened, what they tried to do.[167]

Lyndon Johnson, a Democrat, appointed William Gray (C.D. Cal. 1966–92), a Republican, to the bench of the Central District of California because the man he wanted fell badly out of favor and Johnson thought he had to appoint a Republican to save face. Deputy Attorney General Ramsay Clark, with whom Gray had worked in the 1950s, urged Johnson to appoint Gray, which meant that only California's Democratic leadership had to be persuaded. Both California senators at that time were Republicans, and Gray had connections to each. They were for him. Moreover, Gray had two connections to the head of the Democratic party and to the Democratic governor, Pat Brown, so, in the end, the Democrats had no opposition to him and the trade went through.[168]

Commissions

The commissions that President Carter, through Attorney General Griffin Bell, set up around the country were designed to take away senatorial privilege in the nomination process and strive instead to find the best-qualified candidates. Bell takes us inside the decision-making process in his oral history and throughout it describes his role in the selection commissions that President Carter established as part of his judicial appointment process.[169]

Bell, a former judge on the Fifth Circuit, was serving as both attorney general and as a Carter confidant. He had known Carter since their childhood and enjoyed a relationship of great trust with him. Carter directed him, he recounts in his oral history, to make the federal judiciary more reflective of the population. The goal was to seek out more qualified women and minorities for appointment to the federal bench. A few

---

[167] Collins Jacques Seitz, "Interview with the Honorable Collins Jacques Seitz," Historical Society of the United States Court of Appeals for the Third Circuit (1993), pp. 54–55.

[168] William Percival Gray, "Oral History Interview William P. Gray," Ninth Judicial Circuit Historical Society (1998), pp. 25–27.

[169] Griffin Boyette Bell, "Diversifying the Federal Judiciary: Interview with Judge Griffin Bell," Federal Judicial Center (1995).

commissions were set up for various parts of the country. Some commission members were named by the White House and some by senators, if they were Democrats. If the senators were Republicans, they suggested names but did not control appointment to the commission. Bell reserved the right to name the chairmen of the various commissions. Sometimes individual senators, like Kennedy in Massachusetts, set up their own committees.

The real task was to find qualified candidates, which happened in a variety of ways. Bell and his staff would sometimes just beat the bushes; in other instances the senators had their own suggestions. One approach was to raid the state court benches for qualified women candidates. High-stakes politics were played on occasion when senators insisted that particular candidates make the commission's short list of suggested candidates. There was relatively little horse trading when a senator held out for a particular candidate to be appointed, but there was some. After all, the White House was impinging on the near-sacred right of senators to select judicial candidates for acceptance by the White House. There had always been struggles between the White House and the senators, with horse trading always going on, but it had never been suggested until then that the role of the senators should be diminished. The commissions Carter set up had the effect, to the dismay of the senators, of doing exactly that: diminishing their role in the judicial appointment process.

There were political fights within the individual commissions and between the commissions and the White House. When Bell was dissatisfied with the candidates that a commission recommended, the White House exerted pressure to get the commission to more directly follow the diversity mandate. The White House by way of Bell would not accept the excuse tendered occasionally that there simply were not any women or minorities that could be found.

Bell also reserved for himself the ranking of the candidates for each appointment. For each appointment, the various commissions were to present five candidates. Bell then took the five and ranked them. In all but a couple of instances, Bell recounts, President Carter appointed the candidate he had ranked first. The president in making his selection did not factor in the goal of diversity. Bell had already done that in ranking the candidates. Bell, then, was the force driving the selection process.

We get some insights into the Carter initiative from a series of interviews with women judges appointed by Carter conducted by the Federal Judicial Center under the title *Diversifying the Federal Judiciary*.

Barbara Rothstein (W.D. Wa. 1979–present) was one of two women on the state court bench, a position she had secured in part at the urging of the Washington Women Lawyers group, a separate bar association for women. When the Omnibus Judgeship Act created a new position in the Western District of Washington, the group approached Rothstein and urged her to apply. Rothstein explained to the group that she was not even sure she wanted the position, but the group insisted, saying it wanted to be able to put forth some good names. She agreed and her name was submitted. The merit selection commission then called and the interviews began.[170]

Rya Zobel (D. Mass. 1979–present) had become the first woman partner at one of Boston's biggest and best-respected firms. She had also served for ten years as the law clerk to the chief judge of the federal district and in that position had been entrusted with great responsibility, including all of the judge's opinion writing. She was sent a questionnaire by someone on Senator Kennedy's nominating commission after a new position had been created by the Omnibus Judgeship Act. She filled it in and was interviewed by Senator Kennedy and then by the merit commission committee.[171]

Ellen Burns (D. Conn. 1978–present) was serving on the Connecticut Superior Court bench prior to her appointment by President Carter to the district court bench. This Carter appointment, however, did not come by way of a merit selection commission. Instead, it was the direct result of Connecticut's most influential politician, Abraham Ribicoff. Ribicoff was Connecticut's senior senator, having been elected in 1963, and he had likewise been a very popular governor of the state. He had also served in the Kennedy administration as cabinet secretary for Health, Education, and Welfare.

As Burns recounts it, she received a call from a spokesman for Senator Ribicoff. The candidate Ribicoff had been pushing had run into difficulty and dropped out of the running. The spokesman on a Monday asked if Burns would be interested in the job, and she said that she would like to be considered for the position. The spokesman then made it clear that he was not asking if Burns wanted to be considered for the position. He was asking if she wanted it. She said that she did and was instructed to fly to Washington on Thursday to meet with Ribicoff. She met with Ribicoff, who then brought

---

170 Barbara Jacobs Rothstein, "Diversifying the Federal Judiciary: Interview with Judge Barbara J. Rothstein," Federal Judicial Center (1995), pp. 28–29.
171 Rya Weickert Zobel, "Diversifying the Federal Judiciary: Interview with Judge Rya Zobel," Federal Judicial Center (1995), pp. 33–34.

her to see Connecticut's other senator, Lowell Weicker. By the time Burns flew home that afternoon, Ribicoff had announced that she was the candidate for the job. Getting the hearing and being confirmed took a bit longer, but the choice was made, by Ribicoff, within just a few days.[172]

Barbara Crabb (W.D. Wis. 1979–present) had been appointed in 1971 as one of the first United States magistrates. The position in the beginning was only half-time. When a new judgeship for the Eastern District of Wisconsin was created as part of the Omnibus Judgeship Act, the merit commission announced the new position and asked for applications. With her experience as a United States magistrate, Crabb was a particularly well-qualified applicant. The interesting part of her appointment story is that the commission almost did not come about. One of the Wisconsin senators wanted a commission, but the other did not. That senator had a particular legislator in mind for the new judgeship and did not want a commission to interfere with his plans. But because one of the senators wanted it, the other had to agree publicly that a commission was a good idea. With the commission in place, Crabb secured her nomination.[173]

Although there was a directive from President Carter to Attorney General Bell to find women and minorities, the vast majority of appointments made under the commission system went to white males. We see the commission process at work, adapted, as it sometimes was, to achieve certain goals.

Take the example of Abner Mikva (C.A.D.C. 1979–94) of the U.S. Court of Appeals for the District of Columbia. Mikva had followed a clerkship on the United States Supreme Court with years of highly successful private practice before turning to politics. He had served five terms in Congress when he got the idea that he should seek out the federal bench. His jogging buddy David Bazelon, then chief judge of the court, pushed Mikva to think about the court. Once Mikva decided that his political appetite was sated forever, he asked Bazelon what to do.

Bazelon told him to call the chairman of the commission, Senator Joseph Tydings of Maryland. Tydings then sent Mikva forms to fill out, and a spot before the nominating committee was found. The committee had lawyers, judges, and laypersons. The lawyers—all from the District of Columbia—opposed Mikva because they wanted a local candidate,

---

[172] Ellen Bree Burns, "Diversifying the Federal Judiciary: Interview with Judge Ellen Burns," Federal Judicial Center (1995), pp. 31–32.

[173] Barbara Brandriff Crabb, "Diversifying the Federal Judiciary: Interview with Judge Barbara Crabb," Federal Judicial Center (1995), pp. 21–23.

believing that the district was in essence a state and that, as a state, the president should select a candidate from it.

At least one layperson opposed Mikva, but not because of his qualifications. Mikva had been so effective in Congress, he was told, that he should stay there, where he could do the most good. Tydings, not surprisingly, then made Mikva's one of the ten names he sent to the president.

There were two openings to be filled. Tydings called Mikva to say that he was in, and Mikva responded, "Joe, I'm not a modest person, but that's an awfully overwhelming list." On it were state supreme court justices, law school deans, and very prominent members of the bar. Tydings said, "No, you're in because the president is going to look at that list and he is going to see ten names and only one face." Mikva continues, "And it is true. Of the ten names, I was the only one that the president knew. We'd had contact in Congress, we'd campaigned together in '78 and in '76; and sure enough it came to pass. Judge Wald and I were the two people that the president nominated."

Tydings had also advised Mikva that he should call the president personally, arguing that the president might well like to know that one of his strong supporters on the Ways and Means Committee was up for a judgeship. So Mikva called.

> I said to the president, "I just want you to know that I'm seeking to become a judge on the U.S. Court of Appeals here in Washington; and my name is going to appear on the list that is coming to you with some of the recommended people." He had not really focused on this at all, hadn't even thought about it. He said, "Oh, well I hope you have talked to Senator Stevenson about it because we take a lot of weight from home-state senators." I said, "Mr. President, Senator Stevenson doesn't have anything to say about this. This is one of these appointments that is yours exclusively. I hope he'll vote for me and support me, but it's your call." He said, "Oh really, I guess I didn't know that." Anyway, he said, "Thank you," and shortly thereafter I ended up being one of his nominees.[174]

Milton Schwartz (E.D. Cal. 1979–2005) had a different experience with a merit commission. Schwartz had heard that there were going to be two new seats for his district from then-Ninth Circuit judge Anthony

---

[174] Abner Mikva, "Honorable Abner J. Mikva Oral History," Historical Society of the District of Columbia (1996, 1999), pp. 169–173.

Kennedy. He explained that the funding for the two seats had not yet been approved but that it was, in his words, a done deal. This sent Schwartz to his desk to put his name in, as Kennedy had suggested, for one of the new spots. Senator Alan Cranston had organized the commission and used district judge Thomas MacBride for initial interviews. Schwartz had known MacBride all his life, though not well, and the interview was very businesslike. According to Schwartz, MacBride said, "Well, I don't see any reason why you wouldn't be qualified. You've got a few things against you. You're the wrong sex, the wrong color, you're way too old."

It was then on to the full committee, made up of lawyers, civic leaders, and ordinary citizens. Schwartz was anxious about this interview, worrying that his lack of federal practice might trip him up. He reviewed evidence and procedure materials the night before the interview but found that the questions he struggled with had nothing to do with law. One commission member asked him, for example, how many pro bono cases he had taken on in which the client was Mexican–American. He had no way of preparing for such a question, he recalled.

There was a friendly face on the commission, a lawyer Schwartz had known from state bar activities, and eventually the interview concluded. There was one question that Schwartz could shine on, as he put it. He was asked about his age—sixty—and whether he had missed many days from work due to illness.

Schwartz recalls, "I was so happy to field a question that I could run with. And I said, 'I have never missed a single day from the office for illness or injury since the day I was admitted to practice in 1949.'"

Schwartz' biggest support came from a leading Democratic political insider. Schwartz was a Republican, but his friend supported him anyway, "kicking and screaming" as he describes it. His qualifications and support led to the call from Senator Cranston that he was going to recommend Schwartz to the president.[175]

[175] Milton L. Schwartz, "Hon. Milton L. Schwartz Oral History," Historical Society for the United States District Court for Eastern District of California (n.d.), pp. 74–75.

CHAPTER FOUR

ONCE APPOINTED, TRANSITION
TO THE JOB

No matter what federal judges did before getting their appointments, there is a transition to the new job that takes place. Sometimes the transition involves the substantive aspects of the new job—all that federal law, both civil and criminal. As Gene Brooks (S.D. Ind. 1979–96) puts it,

> This is a big transition for anybody. I don't care where you have been. I don't think anyone is qualified to be a federal district judge. I don't know any lawyer I ever knew that was qualified to be a federal judge. I don't know any lawyer that has had to deal with that many areas of the law. It is what you get the first day you are there, whether it would be discrimination, bankruptcy, or labor law, or patent law, or contract law, whatever it may be, you are going to get them all. Maybe several of them in the same day. You simply cannot believe for starting what you don't know.[176]

For some, such as Harold Ryan (D. Id. 1981–95), it was going back to subjects that they had not touched in a while.

> I had laid off criminal law for so long that I was very rusty at it, so that was probably the hardest thing for me to get onto right at the first, was criminal cases, and two of the first early ones that I had were really tough ones from the day one. So I had to learn and learn fast and get onto it. From a judge's standpoint, some of these criminal cases

---

[176] Gene E. Brooks, "The Oral History of Retired Judge Gene E. Brooks," Circuit Library, U.S. Court of Appeals for the Seventh Circuit (1994), p. 32.

are like watching a soap opera—they're kind of interesting, some of the witnesses that cross through the witness stand that you see.[177]

There's a lot of work waiting for a new judge. James Moran (N.D. Ill. 1979–present) explains, "I ended up with about 125 fully briefed motions, some of which were three years old, so it took me quite a while to dig out from under. I don't think of anything as being terribly difficult. It was fun right from the start."[178]

For Paul Rosenblatt (D. Ariz. 1984–present), who had been a state court judge, the new challenge was invigorating. "Going back to federal court jurisdiction," he said, " was a real reawakening for me, because after twelve years on the state court, I was really kind of burning out, so when I was given this new responsibility, it recharged the batteries."[179]

As with any job, there is an initial learning curve. Given the vast areas over which the federal courts have jurisdiction, the learning curve for new federal judges can take a while to move through. Aubrey Robinson (D.D.C. 1966–2000) thought that it took him about two years to feel comfortable on the bench.[180] Leon Higginbotham (E.D. Pa. 1964–77 and C.A.3 1977–93), on the other hand, thought it took five years.

> I think that everyone who talks to federal judges—new federal judges—suggests that it takes about five years for you to become completely comfortable. And I think that it's between five to seven years because you deal with a whole plethora of legal issues which you have never had to deal with in depth. If you've done personal injury, you very well may not have done securities. You aren't familiar with the nuances of 10(b)(5). You are not familiar with some of the nuances of product liability law. So that in the beginning, in the first year, maybe eighty percent of the number of cases you'd deal with are on issues to which you've had only a marginal exposure. Now, I guess there are two ways in which you can handle that.

[177] Harold L. Ryan, "District Judge Harold Ryan," Ninth Circuit Library, Boise, Idaho (1990), p. 65.
[178] James B. Moran, "The Oral History of James B. Moran, Senior District Court Judge of the United States District Court for the Northern District of Illinois," Circuit Library, U.S. Court of Appeals for the Seventh Circuit (1994), p. 51.
[179] Paul G. Rosenblatt, "Oral History Interview with Judge Paul G. Rosenblatt," Ninth Judicial Circuit Historical Society (1998), p. 103.
[180] Aubrey E. Robinson, "Honorable Aubrey E. Robinson, Jr. Oral History," Historical Society of the District of Columbia (1992), p. 67.

One, you can sort of just say I'm going to learn on the job and take my time, or you can go at it with great intensity.

And I guess for the first five years, I just gave ninety-nine percent of my spare time on the adjudication process, learning how to put the pieces together, reading all the advance sheets. I mean it—now, when I think about it, I wonder about the wisdom of reading all of the Fed Seconds. Not the Third Circuit, but all of the Fed Seconds. I would speed read through them. I sped read through the Supreme Court opinions. But that was a great on-the-job training process. And within a short period of time, I found, after two or three years, someone would come in and would be taking a position, I could say to them, "You know, I read about something in the Seventh Circuit, and isn't there some law on this issue?" And I think you then start to have a very different relationship with lawyers. [181]

Appellate judges have their own adjustments to make. For James Buckley (C.A.D.C. 1985–present), who had not even practiced law for thirty years, the change was dramatic.

I was obviously dropped into a great big cold bath and assumed responsibilities for which I had little traditional preparation. Nevertheless, after talking to one Supreme Court justice and several circuit court judges, I was satisfied that I was competent to do the job. I had been warned that I would have to spend a great deal of extra time at the outset getting up to speed on various aspects of the job, but that was doable.

The amount of reading required for the job, however, posed a problem for Buckley.

What I hadn't counted on was the problem I would be facing as a result of my being a very slow reader with a very poor memory for details. I was overwhelmed by the volume of reading I had to do in preparing for my first hearings—the job of having to absorb and sort out quantities of factual information and questions of law that were completely new to me. So, it was a little bit like going to law school and plunging into your first assignments in which you were

---

[181] Aloyisus Leon Higginbotham Jr., "Interview with the Honorable A. Leon Higginbotham," Historical Society of the United States Court of Appeals for the Third Circuit (n.d.), pp. 70–72.

required to read a dozen difficult opinions and start making some sense out of the law.

Luckily, he could grapple with what he read.

I found, however, that I hadn't forgotten how to think like a lawyer and was soon satisfied that I had nothing to be scared of in terms of my ability to do the job. But there were myriad details to be absorbed and learned—the ABC's of the FCC, FERC, ICC, and things of that sort. And initially I had to get on top of all this without the benefit of a clerk, because my first clerk didn't report for duty until after I heard my first cases. I guess what this all adds up to is a huge amount of concentration on a type of work that I hadn't been exposed to in years, in the hope that I would get to the root of the key questions with sufficient confidence not to make a fool of myself when I asked my first question in open court.[182]

For Procter Hug (C.A.9 1977–present), it wasn't the law that daunted him. It was, instead, getting the office up and running.

It was a big shock because I was here alone and really nobody to actually, you know, show me anything. All of a sudden these boxes of paper started arriving. I had my secretary, who had been with me for a long time in the law firm, but she didn't know anything about the court, nor did I, and I didn't have any law clerks yet but I got them fairly soon. None of us were much in tune with how the court was operating so for the first few months it was quite interesting.

The other thing is that when I'd moved over to this office building, one of the things they didn't have is any bookshelves for quite a long time, it seemed like several months. No bookshelves around and we were serpentining the books on the floor [laughter]. Actually, the members of the court were very helpful and it was just the fact that they were away, but when I went around to talk to them, you know, and got some good ideas and I went down to Judge Kennedy's chambers and talked to him as to how he had his office set up and then I went down and spent a few days in San Francisco and went

[182] James Lane Buckley, "Honorable James L. Buckley," Historical Society of the District of Columbia (1995, 1996), pp. 145–146.

around to the various judges to get ideas of how to do it and that all was very helpful. But in the end, after I'd gone through all this, they suggested that maybe it would be a good thing to have a manual for new judges, so they thought that I'd be the one to whip up the new manual, which I did.[183]

In talking about their transitions to the bench, some judges describe what they lost. For some, it was money. Bruce Thompson (D. Nev. 1963–92) recalls,

All I ever missed, I guess, was the income. At the time I was appointed I was exceptionally busy. I had a pretty good practice and it was kind of wearing on me. The ringing of the telephone and all that stuff—it just drives you up the wall after a while. I don't think there's any convenient way to postpone telephone calls when a client calls you about something. I know lawyers do do that, but in any event at the time in 1963 when I was appointed I was fifty-two years old and I was really ready for a change and I enjoyed it ever since I did it.[184]

For some, especially those who had been state court judges, there was a loss of autonomy. According to Robert Jones (D. Or. 1990–present),

It seemed to me there was an awful lot of loss of autonomy. I was used to controlling my court reporter; if I wanted a transcript immediately, I'd say give me a transcript. Well, I told this court reporter on a motion to suppress down there, give me a transcript. "Oh, well, that'd have to be ordered by someone. One of the parties has to pay for it and I'm backed up, so I couldn't get one out for two months." I said, "Well that's all very interesting, but I'm going to have my transcript here within two days or you'll hear further from me." We had to get a little bit rough with them. They were just used to just letting things drift. I found a tremendous disorganization of matters where the judge had clerks handling your calendar, and court reporters who are not your own, and the law clerks were fine. But anyway, we worked it all out. I finally got a real-time

---

[183] Procter Ralph Hug Jr., "Oral History Interview with Hon. Procter Hug, Jr.," Ninth Judicial Circuit Historical Society (1995), pp. 146–147.
[184] Bruce Rutherford Thompson, "Oral History Interview with Hon. Bruce R. Thompson," Ninth Judicial Circuit Historical Society (1988), p. 74.

reporter that I hired who's still with us, Amanda Gore. She's our chief reporter here now. I screen the reporters for their talent and we got rid of the old ones that wanted to still not have real time, and take their sweet time as to when and where they did their work. We worked it out with the courtroom deputies so that the courtroom deputies would respond to us, to me, and not to some clerk in a different area.[185]

William Beatty (S.D. Ill. 1979–2001) lost his state court minimalist ways. As a state trial judge, Beatty had a much bigger docket. But he also had no staff. "You just had a court reporter to get it done. Other than that you had no staff. So I get this job and I get two law clerks, a full time secretary, plus the support from the clerk's office, so man that was like dying and going to heaven."

In state court, one sentence orders were the standard and briefing of motion was discouraged, making for an almost paperless operation.

> In the state court when we ruled on something we just wrote out an order, you know, motion denied or motion allowed. If it was a post-trial motion you might use three or four sentences instead of one. Motion denied because that's the way you think it should be. That was it. Or we would rule orally from the bench. Well, I felt that had worked pretty well in the state court and didn't see any reason why it shouldn't work as well in the federal court, so that was the way I proceeded until the first time I got an opinion back from the Seventh Circuit stating that "the learned trial judge did not see fit to give us the reasons for his rulings." It suddenly dawned on me that "Aha, I am supposed to write all this stuff out."[186]

Some judges, once they took to the bench, got tutoring from more experienced judges. Two judges in Indiana report this.

Robert Grant (N.D. Ind. 1957–98) remembers that Luther Swygert (N.D. Ind. 1943–61 and C.A.7 1961–88) "invited me up, and I remember going to Fort Wayne where I sat on the bench with him one day as an

[185] Robert Edward Jones, "Oral History Interview with Robert E.. Jones," U.S. District Court Collection, Oregon Historical Society (2005), p. 97.
[186] William Louis Beatty, "The Oral History of William L. Beatty Senior District Court Judge of the United States District Court for the Southern District of Illinois," Circuit Library, U.S. Court of Appeals for the Seventh Circuit (1999), pp. 28–29.

onlooker, watching him and taking advice from him. He helped indoctrinate me in the job. Oh, we got along very, very well."[187]

Swygert made a habit of helping new judges. He says,

> I remember that Bill Steckler came to Hammond. I put him up at the Hammond hotel and he stayed for a few days. I invited him to sit with me on the bench for a few days to get used to it. That for me, myself, was a traumatic event. I could tell, his whole demeanor was different, and when he left I took him over and put him on a train and he had a different attitude.[188]

For Spencer Williams (N.D. Cal. 1971–87), it was being thrown into the pit. He remembers,

> I saw Bob Schnacke and went to chambers with him. He loaned me a robe and said, "Come on, we're going to select a jury." So I sat with him while he selected a jury. That was my first sitting on the bench. I learned a lot about that at the time. I think maybe two other times I went into court and sat with him to watch what happened. Then he said, "Okay, you're on your own. Do it."[189]

His only other help came from fellow judge Al Zirpoli, who called Williams after he was appointed but before he was sworn in. "'You know, you are your own boss,'" Williams recalls Zirpoli telling him. "'Don't ever forget that. You can do whatever you want to do'" [laughter]. "And then he said, 'Let your law clerks do your research for you. That's what they're there for. And then make the decisions.'"[190]

Alfred Goodwin (D. Or. 1969–71 and C.A.9 1971–present) had some trouble with some of the well-worn exchanges between the bench and counsel and needed to use cue cards to keep him on script. His courtroom deputy provided the help.

---

187 Robert A. Grant, "The Oral History of Judge Robert A. Grant," Circuit Library, U.S. Court of Appeals for the Seventh Circuit (1988), p. 108.

188 Luther Merritt Swygert, "The Oral History of Judge Luther M. Swygert," Circuit Library, U.S. Court of Appeals for the Seventh Circuit (1985), p. 28.

189 Spencer Mortimer Williams, "Law, Politics, and the Judiciary: The Honorable Spencer M. Williams," Northern California U.S. District Court Oral History Series, Regional Oral History Office, The Bancroft Library, University of California, Berkeley (1992, 1998, 2000, 2001), pp. 42, 45.

190 *Ibid.* at 45.

Claire was just the perfect helper for me because I was a little unfamiliar with federal court. I was rather unfamiliar with federal court practice and procedure. I hadn't used the Federal Rules of Civil Procedure for fifteen years and didn't remember much about when I did use it, it had been a long time ago. Claire said, "Well now I'll hand you up a little cue card to tell you what comes next so you just wait until I hand up a little card." And she'd reach around and hand up a little card that said now you do this and now you do that. And it was wonderful. I just followed her cues and she just led me through each step of the procedure. She just put down one word usually. For example, the cue would be "allocution."[191]

Some made missteps once on the bench, but only literally. Stanley Weigel (N.D. Cal. 1962–97) remembers that when he mounted the bench at the induction ceremony, he tripped over his robe. "I didn't fall," he explains,

but I stumbled over my robe. I had a wonderful bailiff named Hugh Lemo and a very knowledgeable, streetwise courtroom deputy named Walter Moniz, and afterwards, when I expressed some embarrassment at having tripped, I remember a juror said, "Well, Judge, don't worry about that. You're not used to wearing skirts." That was a nice remark. It was absolutely exhilarating. I thought it was really sort of Valhalla. I think I was in my fifties then. I had looked forward to being on the federal bench, and I thought then and still think now, what more could someone trained in law ask for than to be in a position to try to do justice unto the law? That seemed to me to be a wonderful thing, and I found it very exhilarating, and to some extent I still do, despite the fact that the novelty has worn off.

Dorothy Nelson (C.A.9 1979–present) had her own slipup.

I got sort of a bad start that first day because I went into the courtroom—it's a lovely courtroom in the Old Pioneer Courthouse in Portland, has a fireplace, has an old John Adams desk, has a lovely antique clock ticking away. It was raining outside, there was a fire in the fireplace, and I came in—the last of the three judges to walk in. The presiding judge had come in and sat in his chair and leaned way

---

[191] Alfred T. Goodwin, "Oral History Interview with Alfred T. Goodwin," U.S. District Court Collection, Oregon Historical Society (1986), pp. 398–399.

back, and the next judge had come in and sat in the chair and leaned way back. I came in and sat in my chair and leaned way back and went right to the floor. My head banged on the floor, and I was a little disoriented because it was these old, old chairs that are wonderful for men but simply don't fit short women.

So I came into the first conference sort of a little embarrassed about what had happened; and I began talking about the case, it was an Indian rights case, and I really guess I got very excited about the case, and the presiding judge said, "Well, Judge Nelson, I'm going to let you write that opinion." In the first place I said, "Well, there are many issues here. I'd like to know how you all feel." And he said to me, "Well, are you for the Indians or against the Indians?" And I said, "Well I'm coming down, if all these other issues work out, I'm probably going to hold for the Indians in this case." He said, "Fine, write it that way." And I said, "But . . . but . . . but I'd like to know how you feel on these other issues." He said, "Well, write it, and we'll see how it comes out."[192]

For district judges promoted to the court of appeals, there was a transition period of a different sort. The work is altogether different on the appellate bench, and for district judges accustomed to seeing people every day and being in the mix of things, the document-intensive work of the appellate court can leave the former district judges looking for more contact with the familiar.

Otto Skopil (D. Or. 1972–79 and C.A.9 1979–present), for example, recounts, "I missed the trial work principally because I was doing nothing but reading. I never saw any people, and I'm a sort of a people person. I didn't like that because I enjoyed the trial work that I did as an attorney, and I enjoyed the trial work that I did as a judge, principally because I knew most of the attorneys who were trying cases in front of me."[193]

Milton Schwartz (E.D. Cal. 1979–2005) provides in his oral history the most extended and thoughtful examination of the changes brought by the judicial appointment. His life, he says,

changed dramatically and drastically. I had not had any judicial experience at all, either the volunteer kind where you would sit

---

[192] Dorothy Wright Nelson, "Oral History Interview with Hon. Dorothy W. Nelson," Ninth Judicial Circuit Historical Society (1988), pp. 10–11.

[193] Otto Richard Skopil, "Oral History Interview with Judge Otto Skopil," U.S. District Court Collection, Oregon Historical Society (2006), pp. 24–25.

in some of the departments to help them out and that sort of thing, so I didn't have anything that constituted background in judicial work. And I knew that I was almost sixty years old when I was appointed and that I was therefore expected to be an expert. When you're that old, you're older than anyone that ever comes into your courtroom as a lawyer, and they assume that you are much better trained and experienced than they are, and they look to you for these things, and most of the things that I was presented with while on the court I had no experience whatsoever with, or even come close to it. And I thought very seriously about packing up and going back to where I came from.[194]

Schwartz's relationship to the bar, to his own firm, and to his own practice influenced his decision to go onto the bench and his reaction to the move. It was not a simple matter. He went to the bench, in effect, to get away from lawyers—certain types of lawyers—but, once on the bench, being away from lawyers and being restrained in his ability to respond to what he saw before him in court made him wonder if he had made the right choice.

Lawyers, to be sure, had worn him out and prompted him to go onto the bench. Lawyering had become too much of a struggle. Cordiality and collegiality had faded away and all he had were fights on all fronts.

I was really tired at age sixty of getting pushed around and getting dumb-clucked by rude, unpleasant lawyers, and it was the same thing getting worse and worse as we went along and as you get more and more impatient. I was tired of fighting with unpleasant, rude lawyers who would never automatically accord any courtesy at all. Their belief was that if you just say no and are hard-nosed and make them struggle you will get what you want, because they'll fold pretty soon. They won't like this kind of treatment. And so they'll probably settle on my terms, or whatever crazy theory they have. All of which was a terrible mistake because I've never, ever, in all these years found a lawyer that I could intimidate and beat up on. All it does it make him madder at you and then it becomes a personal thing. He's going to vindicate himself because you have insulted him by insulting his client. And so it never worked, and the few dirty tricks

---

[194] Milton L. Schwartz, "Hon. Milton L. Schwartz Oral History," Historical Society for the United States District Court for Eastern District of California (n.d.), p. 108.

that—I guess the statute of limitations has run on whatever ones there are that I indulged in—I got paid back in spades by my opponent. I was never able to get away with anything that was worthwhile. Quite the opposite. They were able to get even with me, and there came a time when I needed a courtesy from an opposing attorney and, in effect, he or she would say no. And it made the work a lot harder.[195]

He had some moments in the beginning when he questioned the wisdom of his decision to become a judge. He felt panic in his first days.

I had my first law and motion calendar, and I took every case under submission to think about it some more, and reread things, and I came back to chambers and put all of those files on the back bar, and I never got to them for about three or four weeks. I mean there was so much immediately and I'd forgotten everything. I'd forgotten what was in the briefs. I'd forgotten what the major issues were. It just went right out. And I said, "I'm never, ever going to do that again."[196]

The best part about being on the bench was that he no longer had to worry about running his law firm.

And for me it was a wonderful thing because it was kind of a rebirth. It was quite a different thing than just moving from one legal job to another. The focus was different, and the great thing about it is that almost all of the time that you spend in this job is what theoretically you were trained to do. And all of the years that I practiced law it seemed to me that I was most of the time doing—worrying about personnel, worrying about money, worrying about what the firm was going to do, and whether we were going to move, and whether we should add people—all things that I didn't even pretend to be trained in. And that was the most wonderful benefit of everything.[197]

But at the same time that he was glad to be free of lawyering and the law firm, he felt isolated on the bench. All those lawyers he had known for

---

[195] *Ibid.* at 109–110.
[196] *Ibid.* at 93.
[197] *Ibid.* at 122.

so long did not come to see him as they would have if he were in practice. Meeting with other judges is not enough.

> There's nobody to come and visit and you've just got your two law clerks and your secretary and the court reporter and the courtroom clerk. That's all you can have to talk to. And it does get very lonesome. Lonely. And you don't have this great collegiality of being able to trade thoughts and ideas back and forth. We struggle to have one meeting—one meeting a quarter, really, with the whole court. And we don't get very much accomplished because it's at noon, and everybody is in a hurry, and you do the best you can with it. And that's what was tough for me, and I don't think I ever have gotten used to it.[198]

The ironic twist in his relationship with the bar deepened his sense of isolation. The familiarity with longtime colleagues in practice, which had enriched his professional life, was not only yanked from him, its replacement did nothing but irritate him. All of a sudden, he explains, being on the bench had a reverse effect on his friendships with lawyers.

> Your friends did not want to ask normal courtesies or favors from you, even if a stranger lawyer would not even hesitate to come in and say, you know, I simply can't get to court on that third day of trial because I've got something terrible that's happening. Is there any possibility that we could skip that day, or whatever. Your friends would never do that, and they would always assume you would figure they were taking advantage of a personal relationship to get a favor. And that would be kind of sad, because I'd get all these hamburgers that would come in and they'd say, "How about taking a day or two off here, because—ahhhhh," and it worked in reverse. And that bothered me.
>
> It also bothered me that when I saw really good lawyering and well-done work that I couldn't automatically award the decision to the good lawyer who did a good job and saved me lots of time and effort. The only way you can pay him is have him win his case, and a good part of the time I'd have to rule the other way, but you'd have to dig it all out yourself. And that seemed to be a

---

[198] *Ibid.* at 108–109.

rotten system. That you rewarded the bad lawyer by doing his work for him, and then almost hearing him rush out and say to the client—"I was able to straighten him out. I mean, he was off the track there, but I got him straightened out so that we're going to get a decision in our favor." That sort of thing. So there were a lot of unpleasant things that were hard for me to handle. A number of my friends and colleagues did not like it either and I kept thinking, I'm giving up a lot of money and a lot of possibilities, and maybe I made a mistake. I never felt I made a mistake, because I was tired by the time I was sixty.[199]

Schwartz went to the bench at sixty, a full decade later than the average age for other judges. Being older had its advantages and disadvantages, both of which were part of his transition from private practice to the bench. Age had given Schwartz maturity and distance.

I don't think that I've had a lawyer in my courtroom that was as old as I was when he was in my courtroom. And that is a big, big help. I would gladly trade much greater mental, academic acumen in place of seasoning. When you are older than the lawyer and have been around quite a bit longer than the lawyer, for some reason or other the macho aspects of his character and the taking you on kind of thing are greatly diminished. I'm shocked when I hear—when we have young judges where the lawyer is older and been around longer, they just can't contain themselves if they disagree with the judge's ruling. They simply can't. And I've thought back to see if I was subject to that same sort of thing and I really find that I was. If I felt that a relatively new judge I didn't particularly like, and he was not sympathetic to my position, I would get a lot angrier and get a lot more combative than I ever would with an older judge. And I think that's nice.[200]

On the down side, though, there are the problems brought on by being older. "The older you get and all the problems, you know, memory— you can't remember anybody's name and all of those things. You worry, worry, worry all the time. Because you know that nobody is going to tell you that."

---

[199] *Ibid.* at 109.
[200] *Ibid.* at 100–101.

He recalls having to call the wife of one of his colleagues on the bench and tell her that her husband was irrevocably slipping. He found out from his own wife, when he told her what he had done, that it would be irresponsible not to take action when a colleague is slipping. The question for Schwartz turned on embarrassing the slipping judge. His wife's response was stern.

> "You mean you've been arguing whether you should or shouldn't tell her?" I said, "Yeah." And she said, "Well, that's a wonderful, macho kind of thing to do." She said, "I want everybody in your courthouse to be told that the first time they notice anything different, even if they think it's no worse than what you've always done, anytime they notice anything different they tell me first and give me a shot at finding out." But you can't hide these things, and it's certainly no kindness to save somebody.

Then there is the problem of staying awake, which Schwartz addresses with great candor. He no longer had the law firm to protect him.

> When I have a bad time at certain hours in the afternoon when it's just deadly. And I've tried everything. I've tried eating no lunch at all. I've tried having just juice. I've tried eating a big lunch. Everything. It's the same—you've got a circadian cycle and there are certain times of the day when you are going be sleepy. And when I was at the law firm, they used to schedule all of my appointments with clients for the afternoon because I wouldn't fall asleep in the afternoon while interchanging. And then anything that had to do with reading, or reading briefs or anything, that was in the morning because, boy, in the afternoon you're gone. And sometimes during a trial, particularly if it's putting in tedious exhibits, long descriptions of them and then just all this stuff, particularly in long criminal cases where they have to put in all these things, I would go through these things as if I were having low back trouble and I would get up and stand behind the chair as if to rest my back, which translated meant the judge is falling asleep.[201]

---

[201] *Ibid.* at 125–126.

CHAPTER FIVE

NATURE OF THE JOB

The United States Code sets out all of the law that a federal judge needs to apply, but it says nothing about the nature of the federal judgeship. It can be defined and perhaps even described by reference to statutory authority, but its nature can be described only by those who have held the position. They understand what the job does to the judge.

A few of the district judges describe how they see their jobs. William Campbell (N.D. Ill. 1940–88), for one, tried not to lose sight of the power of his office.

> I would tell them at the new judges' seminar that they have the most awesome power in the whole federal government. No other job, no member in the Supreme Court, including the chief justice, has the power that you do. No members of Congress, not the president, no one has the power you have, but you are entrusted with that power by your fellow citizens, in their own good, and use it in their good. That's why you were given that.[202]

John Reynolds (E.D. Wis. 1965–2002) reinterprets the idea of power and says that "being a judge is a passive job. And I think being a good judge—it's necessary to be passive. You have to assume the lawyers know something about their cases before you decide it. And so I listen to the lawyers, and they usually know something. They know more than I do, that's for sure."[203]

---

[202] William Joseph Campbell, "Oral History of the Honorable William J. Campbell," Federal Judiciary History Office, Federal Judicial Center (1982).

[203] John W. Reynolds, "The Oral History of Judge John W. Reynolds," Circuit Library, U.S. Court of Appeals for the Seventh Circuit (1997), p. 50.

But if judging has an element of passivity as Reynolds describes it, there's also the element of action. After all, the judge is there is make decisions. Reynolds says, "I keep preaching, but haven't convinced anybody, that probably the most important thing that a judge can do is decide things."[204]

For Oliver Gasch (D.D.C. 1965–99), the decisions need to come quickly. "You've got to be fast. It's like being at the seashore and the breakers are coming in, and if you seek to walk through the waves they're going to knock you down. But if you dive in and start swimming, you're going to have a hell of a good time. I try to think that way when tough decisions come up."[205]

Aubrey Robinson (D.D.C. 1966–2000) agreed. "I think the job of a United States District Court judge is to dispose of the litigation for which he or she is responsible as fairly and expeditiously as is reasonable, consistent with all the things that he or she is involved in." [206]

For Andrew Hauk (C.D. Cal. 1966–2004), the job is to "move the case along, keep it moving. Don't tolerate delays in the course of the trial or before trial. That's the most important in my view, moving the case along. And how do you do that? Ruling from the bench, number one. Don't take things under submission, number two. Number three, courteous but firm, courtesy but firmness with all the lawyers."[207]

Richard Mills (C.D. Ill. 1985–present) gets to the heart of the challenge.

> There are so many things about the trial court action. You have got it always going through your mind, and it is like bridge, it is a game of decisions. You make them right, you make them wrong, but you make them now. You don't have time to reflect. You have got to hustle, you've got to move them out. We have become case managers, that is exactly what we are, case managers in most situations. So you've got to hustle. It seems to me that the challenge of the trial bench, any bench for that matter, but particularly the trial bench, is to try and find new ways, new innovations, in how to move these

[204] *Ibid.* at 22.
[205] Oliver Gasch, "Honorable Oliver Gasch," Historical Society of the District of Columbia (1991, 1992), p. 18.
[206] Aubrey E. Robinson Jr., "Honorable Aubrey E. Robinson, Jr. Oral History," Historical Society of the District of Columbia (1992), p. 70.
[207] A. Andrew Hauk, "Oral History Interview with Hon. A. Andrew Hauk," Ninth Judicial Circuit Historical Society (1990), p. 89.

cases through because people don't give a damn whether they win or lose or the reasons for that, they want to know the bottom line so they can get on with their life. Half of them are going to win, half of them are going to lose. And everybody wants to move forward. So we shouldn't spend an eon contemplating our legal navels. We just can't do it. We've got to hustle those cases through. Sure, we're going to make some mistakes in the process, but then man isn't perfect.[208]

Only a few judges have misgivings about the nature of the job and having taken the appointment. Most are ebullient about the job and the decision to take it. For Alfred Goodwin (D. Or. 1969–71 and C.A.9 1971–present),

The great thing about the independence of a lifetime appointment is that you can be pretty candid in dealing with questions about what can be done better. You don't have to worry about offending anybody. They can't cut your pay, and chances are they can't even reduce your workload, and they probably won't impeach you. I don't claim to be audacious or a carping critic of the establishment, but I do enjoy the independence that I have because I know if I have something to say I don't have to worry about it. Fortunately I don't think I use it much. I don't have a lot to say publicly about the way things are being run. If somebody asks me and I have an opinion I'll tell them.[209]

For some there is constant learning. For Paul Rosenblatt (D. Ariz. 1984–present), "the wonderful thing about being a federal court judge is that it opens the legal horizons dramatically because of the broad range of subjects and issues and conflicts that come before the court."[210] For David Williams (C.D. Cal. 1969–2000) says,

You never learn enough about the law, and you're always encountering something new. On federal court we have seminars where the judges gather in a certain city, and sometimes once a year. In fact, we're obliged to do it once a year. And we have college professors and some lawyers and some of the judges, they come and lecture to

[208] Richard Henry Mills, "The Oral History of Judge Richard H. Mills," Circuit Library, U.S. Court of Appeals for the Seventh Circuit (2000), p. 61.

[209] Alfred T. Goodwin, "Oral History Interview with Alfred T. Goodwin," U.S. District Court Collection, Oregon Historical Society (1986), p. 468.

[210] Paul G. Rosenblatt, "Oral History Interview with Judge Paul G. Rosenblatt," Ninth Judicial Circuit Historical Society (1998), p. 98.

us on the changes in the law, and we are privileged to learn what the changes are. We learn other techniques, such as the technique of writing opinions, and so it's a constant, ongoing thing. And I am very proud of the way the government has arranged these meetings that keep judges on their toes and let us stay abreast of the law and try to do a good job.[211]

There are dissenters, some on particular issues, some on the whole. For Bruce Thompson (D. Nev. 1963–92),

the worst part of being a judge is being in a situation where you are way behind in your work and it doesn't look like you're going to be able to catch up. That would apply now as well as from the time I was appointed. Initially, the District of Nevada didn't have an overwhelming case load. Then, the judges from Nevada served frequently in other districts. By 1978, when I retired, well at least at that time, the caseload was way too heavy for one judge and it had been accumulating for five or six years prior to that time. It is hard to know what to do.[212]

Fred Taylor (D. Id. 1954–88) has greater misgivings and questions whether lawyering does not have more appeal. For him, there was the thought of leaving the bench and going back to private practice.

Most people won't believe it, but if I had had this job for, say ten years, I'd like to have gone back into private practice. I always felt that I could do something for somebody in private practice. But in this business, all I do is something to somebody. I'll put it this way. I enjoyed the private practice in many respects. I don't discount this job. I've enjoyed it in many ways very much.[213]

On this very point, contrasting the roles of judges and lawyers, we have the opposite view from James Moran (N.D. Ill. 1979–present): "I will say one nice thing about being a judge is that things more often than not come out the way you think they should, more often than if you're a

---

[211] David W. Williams, "Oral History Interview with Hon. David W. Williams," Ninth Judicial Circuit Historical Society (1998), p. 97.
[212] Bruce Rutherford Thompson, "Oral History Interview with Hon. Bruce R. Thompson," Ninth Judicial Circuit Historical Society (1988), p. 105.
[213] Frederick Monroe Taylor, "Oral History Interview with Hon. Frederick Monroe Taylor," Ninth Circuit Library, Boise, Idaho (1987), p. 31.

lawyer, and you can have an influence on why that happens. So that's satisfying. I certainly think the job of a judge is to resolve disputes."[214]

It is the contrast to their lives as practitioners that judges often refer to when they consider their role as judges, which necessarily has them removed from the legal community.

Paul Rosenblatt (D. Ariz. 1984–present) identifies the isolation inherent in the job. The job is "terribly isolating. The worst part about being a judge is the isolation. Your friends don't call you."[215]

Mary Lou Robinson (N.D. Tex. 1979–present), notes that "federal court is a little more isolated. Lawyers don't come in and just sit down and tell you about the case they're trying down the hall. And it's—so it is more isolated and there are many lawyers that I don't know well now, lawyers who don't come to federal court at all. But the lawyers, they may be your good friend but they know in the courtroom that's a whole different ball game."[216]

Another district judge, William Justice (E.D. Tex. 1968–present), gives an example to explain how the isolation works.

> You can't get too close to an attorney because if other attorneys see you out eating with him or whatever they form the conclusion that maybe you favor that particular person. You have to keep yourself pretty aloof from the lawyer unless it's a big gathering. That was very hard for me to do because I had some very close friends that would appear before me from time to time. Of course I tried to be impartial. I had a former law partner appear before me. I gave his client a pretty hefty sentence and he didn't like that. We didn't talk about it.[217]

Two district judges did not feel as constrained on the social front. In the opinion of Fred Taylor (D. Id. 1954–88), "I think a judge has to be more or less circumspect in what he does. I think he's somewhat in a position like that of a school teacher. But I don't see any reason why a

---

[214] James B. Moran, "The Oral History of James B. Moran, Senior District Court Judge of the United States District Court for the Northern District of Illinois," Circuit Library, U.S. Court of Appeals for the Seventh Circuit (1994), p. 70.

[215] Paul G. Rosenblatt, "Oral History Interview with Judge Paul G. Rosenblatt," Ninth Judicial Circuit Historical Society (1998), p. 83.

[216] Mary Lou Robinson, "The Oral History of Judge Mary Lou Robinson," Circuit Library, U.S. Court of Appeals for the Fifth Circuit (2006), p. 33.

[217] William Wayne Justice, "Oral History Interview with Judge William Wayne Justice," Fifth Circuit Court of Appeals Library, New Orleans, LA (2002), p. 55.

judge should be a recluse. He does have to be kind of tactful. We've had situations in the state where its judges have been accused of being preferential."[218]

William Gray (C.D. Cal. 1966–92) responds this way to the notion of isolation and notes an amusing role reversal.

> No, I don't think it's a lonely life. I belong to the Chancery Club, and I go to the meetings, and I know that there are going to be several of my friends there whose company I enjoy, and I make the most of it. I do find that when I went on the bench, two things happened. My friends did not call to suggest lunch like they used to do, so I have to make my own advances, like when I go to the Chancery Club. An attorney from Paul Hastings still will not call me "Bill." He calls me Judge, and heavens, I've known him forever. And so my friends tend to take two steps backward, people that I really care about. The other thing is that, when I became a judge I became "Bill" to people I couldn't identify. It's amazing. People I really didn't know too well, and the ones in which I wasn't interested so much, took about two steps forward.[219]

The isolation of the job is more pronounced at the appellate level. Abner Mikva (C.A.D.C. 1979–94), a former congressman, describes the isolation of appellate judges. Both district and circuit judges do their work alone, he notes, but at least the district judges can get together for lunch. But he found that awkwardness follows the appellate judge who wants to join in. He says,

> The judge's work is so uniquely alone. A district judge does most of his work alone. A court of appeals judge, aside from the oral argument and the conference, does most of his work alone. And, even on the opinions, even after the conference, almost everything is done by mail, by written word or, at the best, telephone conversation. But it's very seldom that the judge will go back and talk to a colleague about a case after there has been a conference on it. The district judges had lunch together—that was the one break—and I would sometimes go to the lunch room. I found that while I

---

[218] Frederick Monroe Taylor, "Oral History Interview with Hon. Frederick Monroe Taylor," Ninth Circuit Library, Boise, Idaho (1987), p. 40.

[219] William Percival Gray, "Oral History Interview with Hon. William P. Gray," Ninth Judicial Circuit Historical Society (1994), pp. 37–38.

would do it every once in awhile just to show the flag, especially when I was chief judge, it either did or should have chilled their conversation because frequently they would be talking about cases that were happening, and many of those ended up coming up on appeal.[220]

Robert Bork (C.A.D.C. 1981–88) puts a special twist on the isolation. He notes,

I was then a widower, and I guess I still am, but at the time I hadn't remarried. You sit all day in chambers by yourself working on these things, and then you go home and talk to the dog at night. It's a very isolated lifestyle. Everybody's busy and you don't drop in on a judge to kick around a legal question because the judging has become much too much of an assembly line process—get the stuff out. And it was regarded as an imposition on somebody to drop in to talk over a case, particularly if they weren't involved in it. Even if they were involved in it, they communicate by sending drafts back and forth—memoranda and dissents and so forth. Rarely do you get together. We'd get together right after the argument.[221]

James Buckley (C.A.D.C. 1985– present), who served with Bork, says.

One of the strange things about this job is that we almost never see one another. I can literally go three weeks without laying my eyes on another judge. It's a very weird situation. In my first years on the job people asked me what it was like, and I said it's like entering a monastery. And then after a while I realized this was wrong because monks get together about five times a day at inconvenient times to pray together. By contrast, this court consists of a series of hermitages. We each live our own quite separate existences.[222]

Luther Swygert (N.D. Ind. 1943–61 and C.A.7 1961–88) takes the monastery idea and looks to the nature of the monastic life, not the number of times monks confer.

---

[220] Abner Mikva, "Honorable Abner J. Mikva Oral History," Historical Society of the District of Columbia (1996, 1999), p. 296.

[221] Robert Heron Bork, "Honorable Robert H. Bork," Historical Society of the District of Columbia (1992), p. 14.

[222] James Lane Buckley, "Honorable James L. Buckley," Historical Society of the District of Columbia (1995, 1996), pp. 182–83.

I have often said that I think there is some relationship between monastic life, it ought to be, and judges. While judges can't be of course cooped up in a monastery behind cloisters, I think that there ought to be sort of a kind of devotion and a commitment to their job. It seems to me that there should be some relationship between monastic kind of existence and attitude and judging.[223]

Thomas Tang (C.A.9 1977–95) more fully sums up the nature of the isolation problem.

There is a kind of isolation. But sometimes you wonder whether it's just the result of the job itself or whether or not that is just a function of the complexity in society itself. For instance, whereas I used to know more lawyers, I know very few lawyers personally now. Although I come into contact with them, I don't finally come into contact with them on the same basis as I did when I was a trial judge. So in that respect it's lonelier. You don't have the contact. But on the other hand, even as a judge your contact with individual lawyers is different than when it was lawyer to lawyer. When a former associate of yours refers to you as judge, you say, well, you know, why that kind of difference? And so you know with that kind of difference the relationship is not the same as it used to be.[224]

Stress

If it's not the isolation, it's the stress, or at least it can be the stress. The judges report that it is sentencing in criminal matters that produces the stress. They do it, but no one seems to like doing it. And the higher the stakes, the greater the stress. Alfred Goodwin (D. Or. 1969–71 and C.A.9 1971–present) says,

Well, I don't know of any judge who is of sound mental health who enjoys sentencing. There are some sick people out there that enjoy sentencing. You can read about it in the tabloids that pick them up nationwide. Bizarre sentences are meted out by judges who are

---

[223] Luther Merritt Swygert, "The Oral History of Judge Luther M. Swygert," Circuit Library, U.S. Court of Appeals for the Seventh Circuit (1985), p. 208.
[224] Thomas Tang, "Oral History Interview with Hon. Thomas Tang," Ninth Judicial Circuit Historical Society (1998), p. 38.

obviously laboring under some sort of system of delusions or something about their role in society. But mentally healthy judges don't
enjoy sentencing.[225]

William Steckler (S.D. Ind. 1950–95) tells a stunning story about his
predecessor, Robert Baltzell (S.D. Ind. 1925–50), and how having to sentence a man to death stayed with him the rest of his life. But as part of his
story he makes plain that he has been similarly affected by the job. He
explains that Judge Baltzell had been persuaded to stay on the bench as
long as he could, but that

> his health broke rather suddenly during the last three years he was
> on the bench. I think what Judge Baltzell suffered most from was
> some of the same things I have suffered here in the last four to five
> years—that's the criminal case load. The criminal case load that a
> federal judge has to handle on the district level is so taxing. It takes
> so much out of the judge that it affects his health. Judge Baltzell had
> the unpleasant task—I would say the horrible task—of sentencing
> a man to die. The man was in a wheelchair when the judge pro-
> nounced the sentence. Judge Baltzell was required to conduct the
> trial and sentence the man to die. The fellow was hanged over here
> on the old Marion County jailhouse lawn. That preyed upon Judge
> Baltzell's mind.
>
> I came over to talk to Judge Baltzell, and we were talking about
> the unpleasant things that a district judge is required to do. Tears
> came to his eyes, and he made the remark that he hoped I would
> never, ever have to do what he had to do—sentence a man to die.
> He looked at me with the tears in his eyes, and said, "I often wonder
> whether I will reach heaven as a result of having to pronounce a
> death sentence." I said, "Well, Judge, you were doing your duty; you
> were doing what you had taken an oath to perform." Then I said, "I
> agree, I hope I never ever have to do that." But, I said, "I'm sure the
> Good Lord will forgive you and accept you for what you really are,
> the good man that you have been." I was hard pressed to know what
> to say.[226]

---

[225] Alfred T. Goodwin, "Oral History Interview with Alfred T. Goodwin," U.S. District
Court Collection, Oregon Historical Society (1986), pp. 434–435.
[226] William Elwood Steckler, "The Oral History of Judge William E. Steckler," Circuit
Library, U.S. Court of Appeals for the Seventh Circuit (1987), pp. 11–12.

Joyce Hens Green (D.D.C. 1979–present) knew that she could be required to sentence a defendant to death and wondered if she could steel herself to do it. Her analysis is revealing.

> Since the federal district court has jurisdiction over the death pen-alty statute, I've asked myself repeatedly whether I would be able to handle such a case, since I have always been opposed to capital pun-ishment. Inhumanity to victims does not require the ultimate inhu-manity to the perpetrator (except, I believe, in a handful of instances, like the intentional Oklahoma bombing of the Federal Building causing 168 deaths). Statistically, we are told, the death penalty does not deter others from the commission of heinous crimes. How did I feel? It was a very difficult decision. When I received the case [*Cooper*] and knew that it was death penalty eligible, my prosecutor son asked if I could do this. I acknowledged that I had searched within and I could. In the first instance, it is the jury that makes the decision whether or not the defendant receives the death penalty, and then, and only then, the judge could, under the law, set aside that decision, lowering the penalty to life. I decided that I would be able to see the *Cooper* case all the way through, as my duty as a fed-eral judge required. As it turned out, I never had to face the ultimate question, for which I am grateful. I do believe in the *Cooper* case that the decision reached by the prosecution and the defense was the most appropriate one also for the victims' families, each of whom had agreed to the life sentences.[227]

United States Sentencing Guidelines

In addition to the stress that seems endemic to the nature of sentencing defendants in criminal cases, the United States Sentencing Guidelines (USSG) passed into law in the 1980s have frustrated just about everyone. The USSG were the congressional response to the perception that judges around the country were meting out widely varied sentences for commis-sion of the same crime.

Uniformity in sentencing was sought by creating a complex system that considered at its core an offense level designated for each crime in

---

[227] Joyce Hens Green, "Honorable Joyce Hens Green Oral History," Historical Society of the District of Columbia (1999, 2001), p. 229.

the United States Code and a criminal history category for each defendant that was a function of prior misdemeanor and felony convictions in the past ten and fifteen years, respectively. Added to what became these two axes—vertical for offense level and horizontal for criminal history category—were all sorts of possible adjustments relating to the offense and to the individual being sentenced. In the main, though, the essential calculation flowing from the matrix of crime and criminal history was meant to control disparities between sentencing judges. It became known as the heartland approach, as in an approach that reflected core sentencing values. There would have to be something quite unusual or compelling to deviate from the heartland calculation.

What this meant in practice was that district judges were essentially stripped of their discretion in imposing sentences. The whole point of the USSG was to cabin that discretion. Some discretion remained with the adjustments, but that discretion, narrow as it was, was not ordinarily to be applied. We now have a whole generation of district judges who have known only the USSG. Although their responses are, of course, important, the responses from those judges who had been handing out pre-USSG, purely discretionary sentences—bound only by the statutory maximum and, in a few cases, by a statutory minimum—tell us more about the nature of judging and their particular responses to carrying out their obligations.

Samuel Dillin (S.D. Ind. 1961–2006), for example, says,

> I find the sentencing guidelines much more difficult because I don't think they are accurate at all. There are many cases where I would give a much harsher sentence than provided by the guidelines and in others I would put the defendant on probation and they won't let me. So I don't like the guidelines at all, although in a way it makes it easier. You don't have to really think. I don't know why somebody doesn't come out with something like a candy machine where you punch in the ingredients and a card comes out at the bottom and tells you what the sentence is because that is about what it amounts to.[228]

According to Andrew Hauk (C.D. Cal. 1966–2004),

> the guidelines are for the birds. They are terrible. They take away all the discretion a judge has to do justice in a case, either in lowering

---

[228] S. Hugh Dillin, "The Oral History of Judge S. Hugh Dillin," Circuit Library, U.S. Court of Appeals for the Seventh Circuit (1994), p. 68.

it or raising it, and they make it absolutely stiff and solid by rules that are set there, and you can find the rules just by using a computer, an adding machine, or keeping notes and then going back to your notes. It's crazy, without concern for the individual.[229]

The ironic consequence of the USSG, Hauk notes, is "that nobody pleads anymore. Why? Because no matter what he does, if he pleads guilty the sentencing guidelines stick it to him, and if he fights it and lose it, the sentencing guidelines stick it to him in the same amount. Weird, but that's what the situation is."[230]

John Reynolds (E.D. Wis. 1965–2002) from the start thought that the USSG were a bad idea.

I was the minority of one on these sentencing guidelines in the judicial conference. I had no support from the other judges because there's a mind-set against judicial review of sentencing. I thought we should have judicial review of sentencing because I think any judge can be a little goofy at times. In case he's irrational, for whatever reason, and reaches an irrational result, let somebody review his decision to see whether it's reasonable and rational.[231]

He then gives a short, angled view of the history of the USSG.

Judge Gerald Tjoflat, who was chairman of the committee, had a powerful personality. He was convinced that Congress was going to pass something, and therefore we should have, as he put it, some input into it. And so, of course, you had this unholy alliance between liberals and conservatives to make these guidelines. The liberals were concerned about the issue of fairness. They thought the disparity was unfair in the sentencing, which is true. And the conservatives wanted to get rid of these soft-headed judges who were giving all these light sentences. And there's a little truth to that, too. So they had this unholy alliance, and Steve Breyer went and engineered it for Ted Kennedy. They put it through and put Breyer on the commission.[232]

---

[229] A. Andrew Hauk, "Oral History Interview with Hon. A. Andrew Hauk," Ninth Judicial Circuit Historical Society (1990), p. 74.

[230] *Ibid.*

[231] John Reynolds, "The Oral History of Judge John W. Reynolds," Historical Society of the District of Columbia 1992), pp. 26–27.

[232] *Ibid.* at 27.

Samuel King (D. Haw. 1972–present) continues with the criticism.

And somehow, some way, they thought this was a great idea for the entire nation. They can have guidelines and have explanations as to why you don't, why you go below or above them, or something like that. But these are almost mandatory. We used to have a piece of paper that we sent around among ourselves. When it was Judge Pence and I, just the two of us, and with Judge Tavares there were three of us. We sent out what we thought we were going to sentence and they took a look at it and said what they thought the sentence was, to try to get a little feel on sentencing. And then you say, oh well, I was going to give him ten years, but the national is only five, then you should rethink that. If I'm going to give him ten, I had better make a good record as to why I'm doing it. Well, if that is all the guidelines did, then there would be no objection. But they say this kind of crime, this kind of a person, throughout the country is getting this kind of sentence.[233]

Harold Ryan (D. Id. 1981–95) gives the broader view of the USSG and explains why the judge's role is diminished under the USSG.

Even though it would seem to judges many times that they should go above or below the sentencing guidelines, unless you can come up with these new and different reasons of which may or may not have been considered by the guidelines commission, and that's rather foggy sometimes and hard to see just what they did cover and what they didn't cover in their thinking, so you generally stay within the guidelines and there isn't really much to it as far as a judge is concerned. I think our probation department could sentence these people just as easily as we do.[234]

Joyce Hens Green (D.D.C. 1979–present) gives the most recent oral history view of the USSG from the bench.

While many judges continue to rebel inwardly at the injustice we believe the guidelines promoted, we have no choice but to follow them. Let me give some background on this. Literally, we use a grid

---

[233] Samuel Pailthorpe King, "Oral History Interview with Judge Samuel P. King," Ninth Judicial Circuit Historical Society (1991), p. 82.

[234] Harold L. Ryan, "District Judge Harold Ryan," Ninth Circuit Library, Boise, Idaho (1990), p. 82.

to determine the fate of a defendant for the particular offense of which he or she was convicted. Most judges believe that judgment and discretion and common sense and individual application are essential when sentencing another human being, but now judges are required to say, "Mr. Jones, the guidelines show you are in criminal category IV, the offense level is 32; therefore, my discretion is 168 to 210 months. I sentence you to the lower end, 168 months." Departures from the guidelines are uncommon.

And just how bad are the guidelines, we can ask? Green continues with a startling story about another judge.

One of my colleagues, known as a law and order judge, a former U.S. attorney, told the judges he was brought to tears by the uneven justice he had to administer. He described a scenario much like the one I've just outlined. He related how he had to turn away from the audience in the courtroom and face the wall so that no one would see the tears trickling down his face as he had to impose a very heavy sentence on the lowest member of the conspiracy, while he gave more lenient sentences to others at, or near, the top of this conspiracy. We do this every day; we know it is unjust. It is so difficult for a judge to ladle out sentences you are absolutely certain are unfair, but you have no choice, you must follow the law. Very sad, very disturbing.[235]

The reader should know, however, that there has been a potentially major shift in the way sentencing is handed out in the federal system. Under a Supreme Court case of 2005, *United States v. Booker*,[236] the federal judges are no longer mandatorily required to apply the USSG. Now the sentencing judge must consult the USSG, but he or she has the discretion to apply, instead of the USSG, the sentencing factors in 18 U.S.C. 3553(a)—the very factors that controlled sentencing before the USSG. Most judges, perhaps because they have always worked in a USSG regime, invoke their discretion to apply the 18 U.S.C. 3553(a) factors sparingly, leaving the USSG system largely intact, replete with what many consider to be overly harsh sentences for various crimes, including drug crimes.

---

[235] Joyce Hens Green, "Honorable Joyce Hens Green Oral History," Historical Society of the District of Columbia (1999, 2001), pp. 236–241.
[236] 543 U.S. 220, 125 S.Ct. 738 (2005).

CHAPTER SIX

IN CHAMBERS, IN COURT, AND
GETTING ALONG WITH OTHERS

When it comes to what judges do in court and in chambers, we have, as an exception to the general dearth of federal judicial autobiographical materials, two fine resources—one from the district bench and one from the circuit bench—that provide extensive and illuminating detail as to how the particular judges worked.[237] But the oral histories not only present more judges describing their work habits and procedures, we get the added bonus of them going beyond the published sources and describing the relationships between bench and bar in the courtroom and the relationships among the judges behind the scenes. Some of what they describe is startling.

For district judges, we can look at two topics within the subject of how judges do their jobs. One is to look at the way judges manage their work in chambers, while another is to look at how the judges manage what they do in court, which includes how they handle the lawyers practicing before them. For appellate judges, the essential issue is how they manage their work as they prepare for oral arguments.

The goal in judging, of course, is to get the job done. Harold Ryan (D. Id. 1981–95) gives some perspective on the objective and the interest he and all other judges have in getting help from everyone involved in the process. As he puts it,

> You learn to use your law clerks, you use your secretary, everyone's around that can be helpful on this, you learn to put them to the

---

[237] Prentice H. Marshall, "Some Reflections on the Quality of Life of a United States District Judge," 27 Arizona Law Review 593 (1985) and Frank M. Coffin, The Ways of a Judge: Reflections from the Federal Appellate Bench (Houghton Mifflin 1980).

highest and best use. Then on top of that you learn to use your attorneys in asking for the briefs and for all the help you can get out of the attorneys, and they're more than willing as advocates to do everything they can to serve their side of the case. So there isn't anything you ask attorneys to do along those lines but that they don't give it their best shot.

On his general approach, he says,

I guess a certain amount of it is administrative. You sort of run it so the thing works, and so you can get a product out and get the cases closed and decided. The court only serves one function—we're here to serve the people in the district and the litigants, and so we try in such organizing to give them the best, the fastest possible service in getting their lawsuits completed.[238]

Pretrial Conferences

As often as they can, judges try to get cases settled short of trial through pretrial conferences. Such conferences have the benefit of being less formal.

James Moran (N.D. Ill. 1979–present) explains, "I always have status conferences in chambers because lawyers are much more candid sitting around a table without a court reporter than standing up in open court with a court reporter and with an audience of other lawyers."[239]

William Campbell (N.D. Ill. 1940–88) wanted the lawyers as comfortable as possible. "They could smoke," he says, "and if they wanted to cuss me out that's all right. There's no rules. There's no contempt. If they think I'm dumb, tell me."[240]

Campbell became a crusader for pretrial conferences when he became chief judge in his district. He had long gotten the parties together at such a conference and in effect read them the riot act about the dangers of

---

[238] Harold L. Ryan, "District Judge Harold Ryan," Ninth Circuit Library, Boise, Idaho (1990), p. 69.

[239] James B. Moran, "The Oral History of James B. Moran, Senior District Court Judge of the United States District Court for the Northern District of Illinois," Circuit Library, U.S. Court of Appeals for the Seventh Circuit (1994), p. 54.

[240] William Joseph Campbell, "Oral History of the Honorable William J. Campbell," Federal Judiciary History Office, Federal Judicial Center (1982), p. 16.

going to trial. He had his ways in persuading lawyers to do the right thing. He emphasized that he was in control.

> Now you get the occasional recalcitrant lawyer who won't give in a thing. "All right," you say to them, "now look, you're stuck with me. I'm going to try this case, not some other judge down the hall. I'm going to try it. You can act like a son-of-a-bitch. You want me to be a son-of-a-bitch at the trial? I can be. If you don't believe it, I'll give you names of lawyers who can tell you. Also, I can be a reasonably nice guy at the trial. Now get one thing through your head. I'm running this lawsuit. You're not. You may have brought it, but I'm running it, and you are going to run it by my rules or you are going to be the sorriest practicing lawyer in Chicago." And usually they will come along.[241]

In trying to overcome the resistance of other judges, his core belief was that these judges did not want to hold pretrial conferences because of their elitism and refusal to jump into the mix. In the judicial education seminars he would hold around the country, he would give to those outside his district what he gave to the judges within his district.

> They regard themselves as something above the legal profession. Well, they are still part of our legal profession. I keep hammering that into them at these seminars. "Never forget you were appointed, not anointed. Nobody anointed you. You are not God. You are not His representative. You are another member of the legal profession. Act like one. Give the poor devil in front of you the same break that you would want if you were there. A lot of people are unable to do it, and it isn't their fault. They are psychologically, or by background or birth or training, unable to adopt that attitude toward their fellow human beings. And if they are thus psychologically disadvantaged I say—they think it's an advantage—you are never going to become a good pretrial judge."[242]

How tough Campbell was and how insistent he was on pretrials, when he was chief judge, is illustrated by his anecdote involving an older judge.

---

[241] *Ibid.* at 14.
[242] *Ibid.* at 29.

When he had gotten resistance from the older judge, Campbell said,

> "Now, don't talk back to me, Judge Barnes." I said, "I know you are
> old enough to be my father but I want to tell you something else.
> You are getting more disagreements from your juries than any other
> judge in this court. And the reason is your God damn haughty attitude
> on holding pretrial." I said, "Who in the hell do you think you are,
> God?" I said, "What's wrong with meeting lawyers? You used to prac-
> tice law. Bring them in and meet them." I said, "You will be surprised
> how nice they are. They really are when you get to know 'em."[243]

Not surprisingly, given this insistence, Campbell continued to have
settlement conferences in criminal cases even when the rules changed
and judges were prohibited from holding such conferences. He proudly
notes in his oral history, "Now I can't do it. Rule 11 says I can't. I can't sit
in on any plea bargaining. So what I do now is send my probation officer.
It says he can go. And I send him. He says, 'Maybe I can talk the judge into
something if he pleads guilty, or something like this.'"[244]

Motions

District judges, of course, preside over trials. They also, though, hear
motions on matters short of trials relating to the cases. The experience of
William Beatty (S.D. Ill. 1979–2001) in Illinois, including his dissatisfac-
tion with the process, is fairly representative of what has gone on throughout the country over the last few decades.

It had been Beatty's practice to have a motion day, usually a Monday,
and have all of the lawyers appear that day when they had a pending
motion. Beatty would then call each of the motions and try to resolve the
issue then and there, with each side making its pitch orally and then
having Beatty rule on the spot. The problem with this approach is that it
tends to be paperless, with the judge's decision rather than the reasoning
being recorded. Beatty was able to maintain his paperless approach to
motion practice until new additions to the Southern District outvoted
him and put into place the briefing schedules that were applying elsewhere in the federal system. With a growing docket in the district, motion
day as Beatty envisioned it could not be maintained.

---

[243] *Ibid*. at 22.
[244] *Ibid*. at 28.

Judge Foreman and Judge Stiehl wanted to do it one way, I wanted to do it another. They won. We went to a system where everything was done on paper. We didn't have oral arguments, we didn't have hearings. You file a motion, you have to file a pleading, the other side files a brief, then a reply brief is filed. It is a defense lawyer's dream as far as running up billable hours. We never see the lawyers—all the discovery is handled by the magistrate judges. They just crank out the briefs and, of course, they have those little elves that stay back in the law library just cranking out all these briefs and charging so many hours for them. I think this is one reason it has gotten so expensive for insurance companies. I will say one thing, though, it has gotten a lot of cases settled. They figure it is cheaper to settle them than to stick around and try them.[245]

James Moran (N.D. Ill. 1979–present) took an interesting approach to criminal case motions and never gave his law clerks work to do on them. "Criminal motions are almost invariably very pedestrian and just to protect the record," he explains. "I can dictate or write three pages and do motions. Everybody knows what the answer is going to be. It's just to keep the record clear. I know what the answer is. Why inflict that on a law clerk?"[246]

Milton Schwartz (E.D. Cal. 1979–2005) describes how he handled preparing and deciding all those legal issues. He prepared carefully and did everything he could to read the briefs and to talk with the law clerks and think about the motion in making a tentative decision before going onto the bench.

> And I figured that at the end of the oral arguments I was in the best position to decide the case that I ever could be in. And I really believe that, that I'm—we're in a better position to resolve the case right after arguments and the briefs have been read. And I profited by it in a way that I didn't expect. A bonus. And that was that I'd tentatively make up my mind that the plaintiff should win, or whatever decision the tentative was, probably in ninety percent of the hearings I would stick with that tentative decision.

---

[245] William Louis Beatty, "The Oral History of William L. Beatty, Senior District Court Judge of the United States District Court for the Southern District of Illinois," Circuit Library, U.S. Court of Appeals for the Seventh Circuit (1999), p. 35.

[246] James B. Moran, "The Oral History of James B. Moran, Senior District Court Judge of the United States District Court for the Northern District of Illinois," Circuit Library, U.S. Court of Appeals for the Seventh Circuit (1994), pp. 66–67.

But it was more important than that because many of those decisions I was better, I was more certain that I was right than before the argument, because the more I flushed it out with questions and the more I argued with the lawyers, the easier it would be for me to say this has some surface appeal to me as an issue, but it doesn't hold up well under the light, and now I feel better about my tentative decision than I did before. And that was a bonus that I didn't expect.[247]

There was, Schwartz concludes, value in pulling the trigger on the decision rather than holding off and returning to it later. That way lay more work. "And the other thing about it," he says, "really was that you have to decide it then, and you can't take it under submission because you may never get back to it, but if you do it will be a brand new case and you just have to start all over again, and read all the briefs, and go through that whole process."[248]

Fred Taylor (D. Id. 1954–88) says,

I tried very hard to do my job. I was there when I was supposed to be every day and got everything done that I was supposed to do. I didn't take very many vacations. I take the file, go through all the pleadings and briefs, find out what the issues are, and, if necessary, do some research to determine what should be or shouldn't be done. Of course after oral argument, I might take something under advisement if I am not sure which way to go. But I always try to determine from the pleadings and briefs and pre-trial, which is quite important, what the real issues are and what I think should be done.[249]

In Court

Judges have to run their courtrooms so that the business of the court gets done. William Beatty (S.D. Ill. 1979–2001) might have been forced to give up his motion days, but what he did not give up was the relaxed yet tolerant way he managed matters in his courtroom. In an age in which more and more judges stressed formality and insisted that lawyers stay at the

[247] Milton L. Schwartz, "Hon. Milton L. Schwartz Oral History," Historical Society for the United States District Court for Eastern District of California (n.d.), p. 93.
[248] *Ibid.*
[249] Frederick Monroe Taylor, "Oral History Interview with Hon. Frederick Monroe Taylor," Ninth Circuit Library, Boise, Idaho (1987), p. 11.

lectern, Beatty gave free reign to the lawyers. In perhaps the most striking part of his oral history, he explains,

> The job of trying cases for a lawyer is hard enough without making it any harder. The first thing I tell any lawyer who comes up here before me is you do whatever you want to in the courtroom. I don't care whether you stand. They always ask, do you want us to stand up, judge? Do you want us to sit down? Do we get permission to approach the witness? I say, I don't care what you do, within certain bounds of decorum, you do whatever you want to in the court-room. You are out there to win your case. If you think you can win you case by spitting on the floor or making me look like a fool, or whatever you want to do, it's all right with me.[250]

Myron Gordon (E.D. Wis. 1967–present), on the other hand, stresses formality. When his oral history interviewer brought up the topic by saying that he ran a fairly formal courtroom, Gordon told him to strike the word *fairly*. Gordon was a stickler for punctuality, which was based on his own experiences, he says. And during trials, he would impose severe time limitations on the lawyers, so much so that the Seventh Circuit had to intervene and chasten him. "On the level of not tolerating a waste of time," he says,

> there, too, I found that lawyers could move a case along if the judge gave them reasonable time limitations. That effort has not flown, and I no longer have any trial time limitations. I limit the opening statement and at the end of the trial discuss with counsel how long they'll need for closing summations. Other than that, if the case takes two days or two weeks, I don't intrude. This is because the court of appeals has been critical of that procedure.[251]

William Justice (E.D. Tex. 1968–present) also prefers the formal.

> I had been disgusted when I was in the state court system with the infor-mality of things. There was not enough dignity in the proceedings. There in Athens and other state courts that I attended you could

---

[250] William Louis Beatty, "The Oral History of William L. Beatty Senior District Court Judge of the United States District Court for the Southern District of Illinois," Circuit Library, U.S. Court of Appeals for the Seventh Circuit (1999), pp. 35–36.

[251] Myron Gordon, "The Oral History of Judge Myron L. Gordon," Circuit Library, U.S. Court of Appeals for the Seventh Circuit (1999), p. 52.

smoke. You didn't rise when you talked to the judge. You just made your objection from your chair. Some of the lawyers would put their feet up on the desk while they were questioning witnesses and all of that, and I thought that was not good. Judge Sheehy kept decorum on his courts. Lawyers had to rise, and they had to ask permission to approach the bench and that kind of thing. That appealed to me. Things moved quickly and lawyers were kept under control, so I adopted much of the same procedures.

My courtroom was pretty close to an English-style courtroom. I did my best to make it that way. Later on it came in good because I had lawyers that were in a state of semi-rebellion in these cases that involved integration and anything that was racial. When they came into the federal court they were not accustomed to it. They were used to the state procedure. There was a formal opening of court with the "Hear ye, hear ye." The judge would be up there in that robe. That was uncommon in the state court in those days. It kind of served to intimidate them a little bit. It's easier to keep them under control, so I just kept that system.[252]

Ordinarily, lawyers present more control problems for judges, but spectators and even the litigants themselves can cause problems. Alfred Goodwin (D. Or. 1969–71 and C.A.9 1971–present) recounts the special problems posed by young protestors engaging in what was termed *guerilla theater*. He explains,

That was also the period when guerrilla theater became an important part of the jurisprudence of the federal courts. Judges would take classes in how to deal with bizarre exercises of the First Amendment in the courtroom. Of course, the old-time federal judge was typically a no-nonsense character, something of a martinet who maintained not only order in the court but a high level of decorum and conventional behavior, including dress and tone and just the ambience of the courtroom. A federal courtroom was always rather hushed and dignified and businesslike.

Well, guerrilla theater took great delight in upsetting that applecart that federal courts enjoyed, and the young people would come in the courtroom wearing the most bizarre costumes emblazoned

---

[252] William Wayne Justice, "Oral History Interview with Judge William Wayne Justice," Fifth Circuit Court of Appeals Library, New Orleans, LA (2002), pp. 47–48.

with slogans and sometimes with four-letter words which weren't ordinarily used by nice people, and so on. And they'd sit in the courtroom, and they wouldn't say anything because they knew that they'd be removed from the courtroom if they said anything. But they would sit there and silently do pantomimes or other things, displaying little placards or posters or do card stunts, reminiscent of the card stunts at a football game. And then they'd be removed from the courtroom. But there was always this kind of interesting gamesmanship going on between the producers of guerrilla theater and the federal judges and their bailiffs as to how to maintain order and still not violate First Amendment rights.[253]

It is with lawyers that judges have the most problems. Tensions flare with lawyers who are overly aggressive with regard to each other and with lawyers who show a lack of sufficient respect to the court itself.

Milton Schwartz (E.D. Cal. 1979–2005) recalls instances in which lawyers angered him enough that he lost his temper. There was one lawyer, he recalls, who would slouch in his chair to the extent that he slid down in his chair and splayed his legs out. Schwartz asked him if he was comfortable, to which the lawyer said, "Yeah." "And I said 'Get up,'" Schwartz recalls. "I just shrieked at him. I clashed with him something fierce. He was arrogant."[254]

While useful, Schwartz's anecdote is much less illuminating on the issue of the need for judges to control lawyers than the account he gives of the advice he gave fellow judge David Levi (E.D. Cal. 1990–2007) when Levi was new to the bench. He had heard that Levi was having trouble with the effrontery of some lawyers—one lawyer in particular—and asked him about it.

The lawyers were apparently treating Levi in a way that they would never treat Schwartz. Schwartz knew that these lawyers would not treat him badly because he had them in his courtroom frequently and had experienced no problems with them. So something must be going on, Schwartz assumed. He begins his account by saying that "people like David Levi are as gentle and as kind and they don't attack, they're not confrontational, and yet he'll take a lot of flack that I've heard about that

---

253 Alfred T. Goodwin, "Oral History Interview with Alfred T. Goodwin," U.S. District Court Collection, Oregon Historical Society (1986), pp. 428–29.
254 Milton L. Schwartz, "Hon. Milton L. Schwartz Oral History," Historical Society for the United States District Court for Eastern District of California (n.d.), p. 61.

I can't believe he would be subjected to, and particularly by people that I know who have been in my court a lot and have never evidenced those characteristics to me."

"When he first talked to me about it," Schwartz continues, "[Levi] said, 'It's upsetting to me because I know that this man is a very good lawyer, and has a good reputation, and his stuff is good. Obviously I don't agree with everything he says, and when he doesn't like the rulings I make he can get just really out of line.'"

Then, in the most revealing part of the exchange, Schwartz presses Levi on what he thought was conduct beyond the pale. Hearing that the conduct was indeed outrageous, he tells Levi that he should never take that kind of abuse, especially from a lawyer who plainly knows better. He concludes by telling Levi that he needs to take action.

> And I said like, "What is out of line for you?" And he told me and I said, "That's out of line. You shouldn't put up with that, you should not be subjected to it. You can put up with anything you want in your own courtroom but you should never be subjected to that kind of thing, and particularly from a lawyer who is as sophisticated and as good and knows what he's doing as much as this one does. I can't believe it." And he said, "Well, I couldn't either, and I don't know where to go from here, and I don't want to get too tough," and all that. And he said, "Do you have any idea why?" And I said, "Sure, he's threatened by you. His masculinity is threatened. You're much younger than he is, and he's been around a long time, and he's acquired a reputation in which he undoubtedly believes, believes his own press notices, and he knows he's good. And he just can't handle something like this, and it just offends all of these things that get started. And it's too bad because I would not have guessed that he was susceptible of this, but he's a fighter and he's a trial lawyer, and it's too bad. But I would sit him down real hard. You just don't have any business subjecting yourself to this."[255]

Schwartz takes the position that judges need to be aggressive in their own way. The danger of not being assertive is being a weak judge. In an

---

[255] *Ibid.* at 101.

important explanation, he says,

> The big mistake, I think, that's made about judges, is this foolishness about how he's supposed to be even tempered and even handed and quiet and thoughtful, and we call that good judicial temperament. That, I believe to be a terrible misnomer. Because I think that a person who is well liked by all of his colleagues, and is a fine, gentle person, polite, is also running the risk of being a very weak judge. And I think some of the roughest, toughest advocates whom you would never say have judicial temperament frequently turn out to be the best judges, because they know what their obligations are, and they know what it is to be mean and tough if they have to be, and they don't hesitate. That's their job anyway. But I think that a good part of the time those who are considered fine fellows, good companions, congenial, frequently are very weak people and become weak judges.[256]

One of the the fiercest courtroom managers was Andrew Hauk (C.D. Cal. 1966–2004). Beyond being extraordinarily aggressive in controlling lawyers, he plainly delights in telling stories of his courtroom management style in his oral history. As a general matter, he engages in a form of outrageous rudeness carried out in the name of efficiency in oral arguments. He expects—reasonably so—the lawyers to submit a memorandum of law that is thorough but with short points of law and authorities. And then, in court, Hauk says, "Well, I've read all your points and authorities. You got anything to add to them?" "No." "Ready to roll."[257]

This means that Hauk will not give lawyers a chance to say anything by way of argument. Hauk's delight in exercising power over the lawyers comes through when he explains, "and then they start screaming. They didn't have their chance to argue. Well I gave them their chance. They had nothing to add, so I rule right from the bench. So they have to be alert as well as prepared."[258]

A fair reading of this explanation is that Hauk is having a bit of fun with the lawyers, indifferent to the insult being delivered from the bench to the lawyer. He has, after all, set up a Hobson's choice. If the lawyers say that

---

[256] *Ibid.* at 104.
[257] A. Andrew Hauk, "Oral History Interview with Hon. A. Andrew Hauk," Ninth Judicial Circuit Historical Society (1990), p. 101.
[258] *Ibid.*

they have more to argue than what is in their briefs, then Hauk will attack because the briefs were not sufficiently comprehensive. And if they say that they have nothing to add, then they are simply cut off. That the lawyers before him are powerless is what seems to please him most. He boasts, for example, of sanctioning lawyers with fines and also sending them to jail for a fews hours so that when they return they will be chastened.[259]

In his oral history interview, Hauk is so outrageous, and so filled with anger at young lawyers—in contrast to the lawyers of days gone by—that he needs to be heard in a torrent to fully appreciate the level of his outrageousness. Asked how lawyers should present themselves in court, both in the way they dress and in the way they move in the courtroom, he says,

Come in clean shaven so they don't look like a bunch of yuppie hippies. At least wash their faces. You know, some come in with unwashed faces. You wouldn't believe it unless you saw it. Some of them don't know how to act in court. I mean they don't follow the protocol of the court. They wander around like gypsies or Sears Roebuck floor walkers. It's unbelievable. What do they call them, floor walkers, used to call them in department stores, didn't they? Salesmen or floor walkers trying to hunt down customers. Where are they going to find the customer? The customer is the judge.[260]

Stand on the podium and talk into the mike and talk distinctly and don't mumble. So many of them do, you know. But preparation, that's the key to it and intellectual honesty, that's another one. Don't misquote cases. Don't give half quotes. Don't try to pull any shenanigans because most of the judges will tell you the same thing I do, now don't try to kid an old kidder, I've been through the mill, I know what you're trying to do. Don't do it. Most of these punkos that are practicing law come in like they own the place, try to push the judge around, they're not going to get away with it, with a good judge.[261]

Harkening back, Hauk continues,

When I first came on it was a different situation. There weren't so many young squirts practicing law it seemed to me. And all of the old timers were excellent lawyers and very respectful of one another and of the court and all the proprieties that you expect from good

---

[259] *Ibid.* at 106.
[260] *Ibid.* at 101.
[261] *Ibid.* at 105.

lawyers, including the protocol that you would expect good lawyers to practice with one another and toward the court and the courtesies just went without saying in those days. And it's deteriorated. And I don't know what the reason is except that some of these yuppie lawyers I guess think that they've suddenly become big shots because they put on three piece suits and can grab up to $85,000 a year their first year out of law school, or first year away from a judge anyhow, and make more money than the judges.

And they all have been doing that, although lately, I must say, is a little different attitude. They're not doing so well and it shows in their fear of the court if not respect. Particularly the yuppies, the smart alecks, and you can do it in a nice way, just tell them if they don't stop it they might spend the night in the cooler. If they keep it up maybe they'll be sanctioned and they'll pay it, not their clients if it's monetary. If it's not it's probably a good lesson for some of them, and it's been a good lesson. They go down and a couple of hours in the cooler they come back and they're much chastened and they're much more apt to follow the orders of the judge, if you want to call them orders, I call them suggestions. And they'll say, "Don't get angry, Judge." "I never get angry. I get vigorous, but I don't get angry." Because I'm enjoying the exchange, and I do, I enjoy the exchange with lawyers, even the bad ones because they think they're getting away with something, but on the inside I'm giggling, you know, I'm laughing at how idiotic they are, some of them.[262]

Appellate Judging

At the appellate level, three judges detail their work habits. Otto Skopil (D. Or. 1972–79 and C.A.9 1979–present) says,

We go through cases pretty thoroughly. I'll sort of outline the procedure that has been followed since I've been on the court. Maybe it has changed a little bit more recently. But as soon as we get the calendar and the cases that are on that calendar, what happens is I go through the briefs. My clerk goes through the briefs and he or she writes up what we call a bench memo indicating what the issues are

---

[262] *Ibid.* at 106.

and what his research, or her research, reveals. At the same time, I'm going through it and I go ahead and indicate problems that are bothering me if they appear from the brief. Then when we sit down at the table, then we go ahead and compare. I find out whether they've answered all of my concerns. If they haven't, then we send them back.

I've been a great believer in communication. So I've always indicated to all the clerks that I've ever had that everybody has an equal voice in this situation. "I *want* your input on it. I was raised in a different era than you were. What may be important to you I don't even recognize or realize. So that input is very great to me. However, when we get down to the end there's only one vote." That has been a policy that I have followed. So from that standpoint I'm well prepared. I then send my bench memo to the other judges, which indicates what my feeling is on this case, before we ever hear arguments. So they have an opportunity to [review mine] and I get theirs. So I know ahead of time, basically, where we're going to disagree. Then of course, we hear the oral arguments if it's an argument case. We then sit down at conference afterwards and go through it pretty knowledgeably because we've already been through this thing with one thing in our mind. Now we go to the arguments and we know where each one of us stand, so we try to hash those things out. Generally we can hash them out. Sometimes you can't. Then of course after the writing assignment is given to one of the judges, well the final product is circulated, and again input—again input.[263]

Dorothy Nelson (C.A.9 1979–present) explains,

We have what we call a hot court. All of our judges read all of the briefs. We have our clerks—most judges have clerks do it—prepare neutral bench memoranda telling us what they think are the real hard issues and the kinds of questions that might be helpful to ask on appeal. I found as a new judge that sometimes I have all these questions and I wouldn't get them in. And I think it's helpful if we all agree on what is really bothering us. Sometimes we still might not have enough time. But then I feel it is very helpful to discuss

---

[263] Otto Richard Skopil, "Oral History Interview with Judge Otto Skopil," U.S. District Court Collection, Oregon Historical Society (2006), p. 34.

the cases when we are looking at each other. It saves a lot of memos that go over our computer. I think it's much easier to talk out issues, since we are all well prepared for oral argument, without exception, rather than coming back to chambers and then trying to send mail to the other two and try to work them out in the end.

So input is the way I work when I preside, and now I'm halfway up the totem pole in seniority. I preside a good deal these days. When I preside, I ask the judges to come an hour early—if it's in the morning, I'll bring a continental breakfast; if it's in the afternoon, I'll promise to bring sandwiches—to sort of, first of all, ask what bothers us about the briefs. Generally, in chambers, when we get summaries of what our cases are to be six weeks hence, I sit around with my clerks and we say, "What looks good? What would we like to work on?" And we negotiate with the other chambers. We will take some of the cases that we think are better than others. They'll take some. We'll take some that we really are not so excited about. They'll take some. And it balances out. And I try to let my clerks have input so that at least every other month they are all working on some case that they really care a lot about, which I think is very important. But we have a very collegial atmosphere. The clerks help to select the cases. In preparing bench memos my door is always open. They walk in and out. And they talk to each other all the time. They write draft opinions, and they check them out with each other. Nothing goes out of my chambers unless it has been reviewed by at least two of us very thoroughly.[264]

In contrast, James Buckley (C.A.D.C. 1985–present) relies more extensively on his clerks.

It has changed to a degree. From the beginning, I have required my clerks to prepare fairly detailed bench memoranda to compensate for the slowness of my reading and my poor memory for details, but I nevertheless used to read each of the briefs from beginning to end and to duplicate a lot of the other work my clerks were doing. I now begin by reading the bench memoranda and then check those portions of the briefs that address the legal questions at issue in the

---

[264] Dorothy Wright Nelson, "Oral History Interview with Hon. Dorothy W. Nelson," Ninth Judicial Circuit Historical Society (1988), pp. 10–11.

case. In this way, I have a firsthand knowledge of how each of the parties frames the argument but spare myself an awful lot of the background and excess verbiage. In other words, I've learned how to make more intelligent use of my clerks' bench memoranda. This in turn has freed up time for a closer scrutiny of cited sources, which can often prove misleading.

In describing the work his clerks do, Buckley says,

I am able to hire very able clerks, and many of them have an ability to grasp technical details and relationships that entirely escape me. Let's face it; I try to get clerks who are significantly brighter than I am. In preparing for a case, I take notes on a legal pad as I go along. Usually, these take the form of questions that I'll ask each party. These will be interspersed with "CQ's," which are questions I will need to follow up with my clerk. I find that by going through my ten to fifteen yellow sheets of notes before oral argument, I can quickly recall the details of a case before oral argument. Then I will have, "TC's," which stands for "tentative conclusion," with an emphasis on the tentative, because I will often conclude that my initial conclusion was wrong, based on what I learn at oral argument and in discussions with the other judges on my panel. In three quarters of the cases, however, the issues are not really in doubt.

I am a very untypical judge in that I am truly very slow. It takes me significantly more time to do my job than it takes the other judges here. When I mention this, people say that I must be more thorough than the others. But this is not so, I'm not better prepared. I am often less well prepared than many of the people on the panel. I am just painfully slow at reading and writing, which is ninety-nine percent of an appellate judge's work. I have always been a workaholic, but I have never put in more hours in any job in my life; I work most weekends and I get here at 8:15 in the morning, I leave here at 6:30 in the evening, and I usually put in an hour or two at home at night.[265]

---

[265] James Lane Buckley, "Honorable James L. Buckley," Historical Society of the District of Columbia (1995, 1996), p. 184.

Getting Along

Though Article III judges are by definition self-contained entities responsible only unto themselves—that is, with only impeachment as a curb to their autonomy—they must nonetheless work with each other at both the district court and circuit court levels. Judges within a district, for example, have a chief judge and an ongoing need to coordinate their efforts. At the circuit court level, there is also a chief judge—for the circuit court and all of the district courts within the jurisdiction of the circuit court—with administrative responsibilities. Moreover, at the circuit court level, the judges always work together in hearing and deciding cases, either as panels of three or *en banc*.

The oral histories of the Seventh Circuit, both from judges of the circuit court and of the various district courts, present an unprecedented look at how federal judges get along, or, in several instances, not get along. In fact, they do not get along so often that the circuit can be dubbed The Fighting Seventh.

Tensions between judges that amount to conflicts should not be confused with the tensions that routinely occur over run-of-the-mill problems. Thomas Fairchild (C.A.7 1966–present) for example, who served as the circuit chief judge, recounts problems that came up with the senior district judge system. It had been the case that the yearly designations to sit had no limitations. Problems arose with two elderly judges who presided, unsuccessfully, over long trials. It was clear that their age hindered their ability to preside and action needed to be taken. Fairchild hit on the idea of specific designations, which would go out to a senior judge but not make him eligible to sit on the longer, more controversial trials. Withdrawing a designation would have been too harsh a result, so the specific designation rule was used to solve the problem. The senior judges, however, did not think the solution was the right one, Fairchild recalls.

Most of the problems can be solved by the jawbone method, Fairchild explains. The chief judge would confront the judge whose work had raised concerns and persuade him that changes had to be made. With one elderly judge, for example, an agreement was reached that the judge would no longer participate in cases. The judge agreed to having a desk in a small room and a secretary to write letters for him, but no case participation. Then there was the older bankruptcy judge who was urinating on the courthouse. Fairchild recalls that he had to come in to "take care of that particular situation."

There were, in contrast, real tensions in the circuit, almost all of them the result of clashing personalities. There was an ongoing tension between Luther Swygert (N.D. Ind. 1943–61 and C.A.7 1961–88) and William Lynn Parkinson (N.D. Ind. 1954–57 and C.A.7 1957–59), when they served together on the district bench in the Northern District of Indiana. There, according to Swygert, they struggled over matters as minor as scheduling vacations. More generally, Swygert explains that Parkinson had a tactic "in trying to get his way" that particularly irritated Swygert.

> Most of the time he wouldn't even talk with people in negotiating situations. He would say things in a tentative way and he may concede a little bit and say I might do this or I may do that. Parkinson had this unhappy faculty where he would say, "You promised this, you just got through committing yourself." It is hard to deal with a person like that. He would have you tied-up. I probably should have been more assertive and said, "No, I am the chief. Let's do it this way." It was the same thing with vacations. He would say, "I want to take this vacation" and go away. He would never consult me. I don't know too much about his problem here [the Seventh Circuit] except that he didn't get along. He was a loner, an extreme loner. And I had a terrible, I had a lot of difficulties with him.[266]

Not only could Parkinson be difficult, but apparently Parkinson's wife exacerbated the tension between them. When both judges were on the Northern District bench, a contest of sorts developed as to which of them would get a seat on the Seventh Circuit. Parkinson, according to several judges, desperately wanted the job and believed he needed to speak ill of Swygert. It was Parkinson's wife who, as Swygert puts it, did the knife work when, as part of the contest between the two district judges, she embarked on a smear campaign against Swygert, using his mental health problems against him. She claimed he was unstable, that he had been hospitalized, and that his problems kept him from even doing his own work on the district bench and that Parkinson had to help out. Swygert's mental health issues—what he described as black moods and what we now would describe as manic-depressive behavior—was known to many. It was using the information to suggest that Swygert was unfit

---

[266] Luther Merritt Swygert, "The Oral History of Judge Luther M. Swygert," Circuit Library, U.S. Court of Appeals for the Seventh Circuit (1985), p. 284.

for his position—no one believed it—that so marked Parkinson's attack on him, carried out by his wife.[267]

Swygert, for his part, was remarkably candid about his condition in his oral history.

> I think each person has his own mental make-up, and some people are prone to be sort of a manic-depressive type. I don't think that it is something to be ashamed about. Unfortunately, I have it. It is a very unpleasant thing to have. I wasn't aware that other people ever had it when I was going through some of my experiences in that kind of situation, but as you probably know, Lincoln had some very severe depressive experiences, depression, i.e., which Churchill called black moods, and so I am not trying to compare myself with those two luminaries, but it is not an uncommon situation. Fortunately, they are not fatal ordinarily.

But to hear Swygert report, there was more than enough tension to go around. District Judges Evans and Barnes did not get along—and made something of a spectacle of it. Swygert recalls,

> Evans and Barnes didn't get along at all. It was very embarrassing at the judicial conferences when just a handful of judges, twenty maybe, and of the district and court of appeals judges, twenty-five at the most. All of them didn't attend. Baltzell attended hardly at all. Barnes usually sat in the back up at 1212 in the conference room, and he would, to put it rather bluntly, sort of bait Evans. Barnes, himself, was a very hard-bitten guy in a way, although again, very personable on a one-to-one basis. I never practiced before him, but he was very dictatorial and had kind of a mean disposition, really, from the bench, and of course, Evans had the same kind of disposition in a way on the bench, but there was always sort of a "back-biting" situation at our conferences between him and Barnes for some reason. I don't know what generated it. Evans and Sparks were very close friends. I think he got along well with the other judges, too.[268]

There were other personality clashes involving Parkinson. "Judge Knoch was one of the easiest men that I knew of to get along with," Swygert explains.

---

[267] *Ibid.* at 283.
[268] *Ibid.* at 239.

Judge Knoch told me this story himself. That Parkinson had a sadistic streak in him. And he liked to go out of his way to be critical with the district judges if he reversed them. So he took off on Judge Igoe in some case, wrote an opinion, very critical of Judge Igoe and Knoch couldn't go along on the panel. And Parkinson insisted that his version be maintained. Igoe was a Democrat, very prominent for his appointment. Knoch was a Republican, so there was no partisanship there. But Knoch was a kind man to start with and never said anything. I'm sure he said hardly any kind of words that would be critical of anything or anybody. So he was not, he didn't want to go along with Parkinson. So he told him—he gave an ultimatum to Parkinson. He said, "If you insist, I'm not going along with that opinion, no matter what," which was rather unusual for Knoch to take that kind of a stand, and so Parkinson finally deleted it.[269]

Later, Parkinson's tenure ended prematurely when he, by most accounts, took his own life by walking into Lake Michigan.

Swygert as the circuit's chief judge had tension of his own with district judge James Foreman (N.D. Ill. 1972–present). Swygert wanted Foreman to move closer to his chambers, but Foreman refused. As Swygert recalls it,

Judge Foreman was very affable and not an antagonistic type of person, but he lived in Metropolis, close to Cairo, and he would have liked to have his posted duty in Cairo and then come to East St. Louis where almost all of the business was located. I tried to persuade him, and in fact, the director of the administrative office, Bill Foley, talked to him too at my insistence, I guess about it, and we thought Judge Foreman was going to move to East St. Louis. In fact, I think he indicated that he would at the time of his appointment or shortly thereafter, but time went on and he didn't and it became a source of some concern on my part. We had various discussions. In fact, I went to East St. Louis and talked to Judge Foreman about it. Finally, it came to sort of a head and we brought it to the council. We became acquainted with the problem, and as I recall, finally through the administrative office, we cut off his per diem. So, it was one of the unhappy situations.[270]

---

[269] *Ibid.* at 284.
[270] *Ibid.* at 226.

The conflict took its toll on Foreman. In describing his career on the bench, he says,

> It would have been a lot more enjoyable if I had been closer to my work all the time. That sounds funny and you can say, why didn't you move closer? Well, number one, nobody is going to move to East St. Louis. I'd always pointed to coming to Benton anyway, so if I'd moved there, or to that area, I would have had a second move probably down here. I'd say, on the whole, I've enjoyed it, but I would've enjoyed it more had I lived in the same town where the court is located.[271]

William Campbell (N.D. Ill. 1940–88), in his position as chief judge of the Northern District of Illinois, sometimes struggled with the chief judge of the circuit. In explaining how he solved one particular problem, Campbell explains that he arranged to have the chief judge come to the district so that the judges there would hear the chief judge's side of the issue. This was particularly effective, Campbell explains in a surprising aside, because the court of appeals judges did not like to associate with the district judges. The issue was a new rule regarding jurors.

> I'd bring [Judge Schnackenberg] to a meeting where we were discussing procedure in the district court and let them get it straight from the horse's mouth that all we are trying to do is follow the rules of civil procedure and to save the expense of the administration. And it was a salutary method of dealing with him face to face rather than on paper, and he more or less felt that he was in a superior position as he was and that he wasn't going to associate with district judges. In fact, I had that problem when I tried to build the judges' dining room in the new courthouse. He didn't want to associate with district judges at lunch.[272]

The problem of circuit judges not wanting to associate with district judges came to the fore in the most remarkable display of a conflict on the Seventh Circuit upon the occasion of a dinner and dance, as recalled by Gene Brooks (S.D. Ind. 1979–96).

---

[271] Foreman, James L., "The Oral History of Judge James L. Foreman," Circuit Library, U.S. Court of Appeals for the Seventh Circuit (1985), p. 32.

[272] William Joseph Campbell, "Oral History of the Honorable William J. Campbell," Federal Judiciary History Office, Federal Judicial Center (1982), p. 43.

There had been a prelude to the conflict—tension between the district judges and the newly created position of United States bankruptcy judge, a non-Article III judicial position. Chief Justice Warren Burger had been dismissive of the new positions and let his near contempt for bankruptcy judges be known. Not surprisingly, some district judges felt the same way.

At conferences, some district judges, according to Brooks, also a former bankruptcy judge, refused to sit in the same room as the bankruptcy judges.

> I used to talk to [Judge] Noland about it. He would kind of kid about it even though he was serious. I could tell he was serious. Their thoughts were there were so many federal judges up here and when you expand that, you dilute the whole thing, the prestige of it. The more you make—he is right to a certain extent. If you get thousands, it is not nearly as prestigious as if you have three hundred. His deal was once bankruptcy judges get in, then magistrates, everybody was going to get in this circle which is probably right. He thinks you have to separate them, just like we did at the dance. We had to separate them [laughter].[273]

The dance to which Brooks refers was an annual dinner dance to which the circuit's chief judge had summoned all of the district and bankruptcy judges. "We clearly had Article III judges mad at the interlopers," he continues, "and we had some of the magistrate judges and bankruptcy judges upset at being asked because they thought it was a command performance that they attend. So we managed to irritate both sides. They had insisted we come. 'Absences are decried,' the letter read when I said I did not plan to attend."[274]

---

[273] Gene Brooks, "The Oral History of Retired Judge Gene E. Brooks," Circuit Library, U.S. Court of Appeals for the Seventh Circuit (1994), p. 38.
[274] Id.

CHAPTER SEVEN

JUDICIAL OPINIONS

A distinguishing trait of the federal court system—and the American legal system generally—is its commitment to judicial opinions explaining not just the result but the reasoning behind the result for issues presented to the court.

The courts of appeal are charged with the task of reviewing the decisions of the lower district courts and use the judicial opinion as the exclusive tool of setting precedent, although only a small percentage of cases actually set precedent, with the rest having only marginal utility. The stubborn issue that the courts of appeal struggle with is exactly which of their opinions they should publish. There is not enough room for all to be published, even though each case is decided by way of a written opinion, leaving the judges of each circuit to declare which of the opinions are to be published and to be relied on as precedent. They could learn something from their lower court colleagues.

To better understand judicial opinions from the federal courts, the publication issue is only the threshold issue. There are also the issues of style and the process of composition. And for district judges, there is also the issue of how they feel when they get reversed by the circuit court of appeals.

Publication

In the oral histories, district judges rather than circuit judges struggle with the matter of publication. The issue is highlighted at the district court level because district court opinions, by their very nature, do not carry precedential weight.

In the opinion of Seventh Circuit hard-liner Luther Swygert (N.D. Ind. 1943–61 and C.A.7 1961–88), who had himself been a district judge, district court opinions should not be published separately at all. They should be published only as an addendum to a court of appeals opinion when the district court opinion is sufficiently worthy.

> In fact, I tried to sell the idea to one of the judicial conference committees to do away with *Federal Supplement* and to have the court of appeals adopt, if they felt that should be done, the district court opinion and publish it as an appendix even though the district judge had not sent it in for publication. I felt that this would dignify or reward the district judge, giving him an incentive to write a good opinion, and secondly it saved a lot of time on our part. Sometimes it was embellished or we would say that there would be some introductory comments about his opinion or whether we disagreed with all of it or not and so on. It saved a lot of duplication.[275]

Judges who publish only when their opinions break new ground despair at what other judges think should end up in between hard covers. Richard Mills (C.D. Ill. 1985–present), for example, takes a hard line on what his fellow district court judges publish. He says,

> I have a very strong feeling about some of these cases that are filed in *Federal Supplement.* It is just absolute trash, it is garbage to put in orders and motions and other things that are clearly not precedential. It is all a rehash of old settled law. It is nothing more than an ego trip to have your name in print. I find it very offensive because I believe printed opinions ought to be for that which adds to the body of law and not just reiterated. But there's too much unprecedential opinion writing that goes into the hard volumes. These attorneys have to pay tremendous amounts of money for all those books. *Federal Supplement* itself, what are we talking about? Every year you're talking about eight, ten volumes, and there's not twenty-five percent of it that is really of value, is really worth something.

He has harsh words for the opinions from the circuit court level as well, saying, "You get to the regular courts of appeals around the country, you've got a lot of just crap in there. Law review items that as opinions you don't need. There is so much redundancy."[276]

[275] Luther Merritt Swygert, "The Oral History of Judge Luther M. Swygert," Circuit Library, U.S. Court of Appeals for the Seventh Circuit (1985), p. 72.

[276] Richard Henry Mills, "The Oral History of Judge Richard H. Mills," Circuit Library, U.S. Court of Appeals for the Seventh Circuit (2000), pp. 62–63.

Other judges had fully worked out positions on publication. District judge Fred Taylor (D. Id. 1954–88) explains,

I don't always send my opinions to West unless it is a unique decision. When I first went on the bench, I had several first impression cases, but I can't remember what they were, and I sent those into West. But not anymore. What I do, after reading the briefs and hearing the arguments and maybe getting a memo from my law clerk, I decide which way I'm going and then sit down and try to write it.[277]

William Gray (C.D. Cal. 1966–92), from the Central District of California, would publish only if he thought the opinion would be useful to others. "I'm reluctant to publish opinions," he says,

because every time one of those opinions is published, it appears in every copy of the *Federal Supplement,* whether it has any value or not. And people have to buy those volumes, and I think that's a shame. So I will only publish a case where I think it might be of some value to another judge, or if it's of some other potential value. For example, years ago we were greatly concerned about whether or not we should accept the results of a lie detector test. And I took three days to let the records show what happens when you have one of those polygraph machines. And we came to the conclusion that it just isn't worth a candle. And it was published, and a lot of judges followed it. But otherwise, I do not like to publish unless it has some potential value.[278]

Carolyn Dimmick (W.D. Wa. 1985–present) takes the same position, saying that

I will only publish when it is a case of first impression and I think I've done enough research so it would be helpful for some other district court judge, well knowing that it's not authority that anybody can rely on. That's got to be from the court of appeals. When I first came on, I talked to Judge Eugene Wright, and I said, "Well, there's one judge who publishes everything he writes." And he said, "Oh, such a waste of paper, such a waste of paper," and I got that through

277 Frederick Monroe Taylor, "Oral History Interview with Hon. Frederick Monroe Taylor," Ninth Circuit Library, Boise, Idaho (1987), p. 29.
278 William Percival Gray, "Oral History Interview with Hon. William P. Gray," Ninth Judicial Circuit Historical Society (1994), p. 19.

my head. And so even though I come from the Supreme Court where we published everything, I've been very selective in publishing.[279]

Milton Schwartz (E.D. Cal. 1979–2005) came out the same way, and in describing the issue gives us some behind-the-scenes information.

I was so ignorant when I came over here that I thought that if I wrote an opinion and it was published in Federal Supp. that that was a determination of something. First of all I thought everything was published in the *Federal Supplement* and that they sort of emphasized some sort of philosophy over it or whatever, because they're phony too. They phone you—I didn't know any of this stuff—they phoned me and said, "There has been a request made to us to publish this decision." And I said, "I wonder why? It's absolutely fact oriented from the day it was born until the end. There are no precedents that I believe will have any—that would be helpful to anybody. Do you mind telling me why you think it's worthy of publication?" And he said, "Oh, as a courtesy to the judge who has authored the opinion, we always call and ask." And I said, "What if I said no, it's a waste of paper and money and everything else because it has no value. What would you do?" And he said, "Well, then that would go to the top Board of Editors, blah, blah, blah." You know, double talk. And I said, "Well, you have the right to publish anything you want to publish and it's there. And even if you don't publish it some other service might pick it up on its own that doesn't even ask the judge for his thoughts. So do what you want to do. But if you'd ask me, I can't imagine any value that it would possibly have to anybody."

And I forget what—But then I learned kind of how this game is played, and so they—they will tell you that—I forget what words they use because it doesn't really mean anything. It means we would like to publish it because we will sell more books, so we would love to publish it but we're at last consulting you as a courtesy. They don't say, "We won't publish it if you say 'No.'"

And I went down and I talked to Larry Karlton then, and I said, "What do you do about publishing?" And he said, "I publish for two reasons only. One if there are a number of cases on point

[279] Carolyn R. Dimmick, "Oral History Interview with Judge Carolyn R. Dimmick," Ninth Judicial Circuit Historical Society (1991), p. 20.

and they're all here in the Ninth Circuit and some of them in our court, and they all decide the same way on the same issue, on the same important issues, and I don't agree with that. If I'm going to come up with a different result, I think I owe a duty to my colleagues to let them know that it isn't all in one direction, there's at least one jackass that has published an opinion in this court that disagrees with that. Because otherwise it's too easy for them to think, 'All of the literature I can find is all the same way."

And so I think that if you are different from a great majority of decisions, and there's nothing authoritative from the Ninth or from the Supreme Court, I think you owe a duty because we get a lot of help from district judges' opinions. They're at least trying to be impartial. And you can't read lawyers' briefs to help you analyze their case, and I get a lot of help and I think I owe the bank some money. The other reason I do it is if I feel that there is nothing in the area that is of any value. Then I think I owe a duty to contribute to the bank also and let people see what at least one district judge thought about it and how he got there and then he can make up his own mind. Because otherwise, I'm not that interested in seeing my name in print which I know some judges would like to do and then at the end of the year you get a bound volume of all your own opinions that you published that year.[280]

How Written

The judges in their oral histories acknowledge what has long been suspected and sometimes reported—that law clerks are chiefly responsible for the opinions that come from both the circuit court of appeals and the district court.

Thomas Fairchild (C.A.7 1966–present) explains,

I think Chief Justice Rehnquist, a long time ago, commented that the work of judging was getting to be more a matter of judges editing the work of law clerks. My clerk writes the first draft in most cases, and then—I don't just edit it in the sense of shoving a few

---

[280] Milton L. Schwartz, "Hon. Milton L. Schwartz Oral History," Historical Society for the United States District Court for Eastern District of California (n.d.), pp. 119–120.

words or sentences around. I often carve them up or send it back to my law clerk with a lot of notes on different approaches that ought to be taken. So it isn't just a matter of editing. But there's less personal input than when I came. I think that's true with any judge who spanned that period of time.[281]

Robert Bork (C.A.D.C. 1981–88) explains his process this way:

Depending on the case, the clerk whose case it was would do a first draft. Sometimes I did the first draft. And the ones I regarded as kind of rich intellectually and where it made a big difference, I'd do the first draft and then send it around to the clerks. And the clerks varied. One set of clerks that I had, every time I discussed a case with one clerk, the other two would come in, sort of seminar. Other clerks didn't do that. I would call them in because we were really stumped and we wanted to hear [what they thought].[282]

On a more cynical note, he observes, "And I'm sure nobody ever reads those opinions, ever. Maybe the parties, maybe the counsel does. But by way of compensation, I think we have more constitutional law cases than other circuits do. Those were interesting." [283]

Alfred Goodwin (D. Or. 1969–71 and C.A.9 1971–present) explains his roles as writer and editor. "Occasionally I write an opinion all by myself, but most of the time for the last few years I've [been] reworking material prepared by law clerks, and it isn't really original writing. It's editorial. It's more like working on the rim of the copy desk, editorial doctoring."[284]

William Justice (E.D. Tex. 1968–present) is also an active editor.

I had a succession of brilliant law clerks. I can talk with them. They'd submit me drafts of things. Some of them were just extraordinarily good and I'd publish those. I was, however, I think noted as a pretty strict editor [laughter]. I changed a lot of things in the drafts they would submit to me. All of them thought it was rather odd that I was so conscious of the commas or the lack thereof [laughter]. I did

[281] Thomas E. Fairchild, "The Oral History of Judge Thomas E. Fairchild," Circuit Library, U.S. Court of Appeals for the Seventh Circuit (1999), p. 85.
[282] Robert Heron Bork, "Honorable Robert H. Bork," Historical Society of the District of Columbia (1992), pp. 12, 16.
[283] *Ibid.* at 6.
[284] Alfred T. Goodwin, "Oral History Interview with Alfred T. Goodwin," U.S. District Court Collection, Oregon Historical Society (1986), p. 594.

a lot of editing, but some of the clerks I had I didn't have to edit. They were just that good.[285]

James Buckley (C.A.D.C. 1985–present) at times can be forced to rewrite.

They work on the first draft, and then how it goes from there depends on a lot of things, including the clerk. Clerks come in different varieties. In terms of writing, there are those who write and frame an argument the way I do, and those who don't. In those relatively few instances where I have had a very close fit, I have had relatively little reworking to do. In other instances, even when I am presented with a draft that is competently written, I find the style and approach so foreign to mine that I end up completely rewriting the opinion. In only a few instances have I signed off on an opinion without having made significant revisions in both the style and substance.

As a rule, I do a major rewrite that will involve a half dozen or more drafts to get things just right. When I find that the clerk has simply missed things or that some additional research is required, I will return the draft with a number of notes listing all the things that need to be done or redone, and I will discuss them with the clerk and ask for a second draft, which I may well end up rewriting. I'm a heavy editor and very conscious of the fact that the opinions will appear over my signature.

One thing I strive for is what I call "reader friendly" opinions. That is one of the reasons I have banished footnotes. I tell my clerks that a reader should never have to read a sentence a second time, or flip though the pages, or look up a case or statute in order to understand what is being said. I am aware, however, that the quality of my writing can be uneven. Polishing takes time.

Luther Swygert (N.D. Ind. 1943–61 and C.A.7 1961–88), who started on the district bench before moving to the Seventh Circuit Court of Appeals, has over his career moved to relying on clerks to write his opinions, something about which he has no reservations.

---

[285] William Wayne Justice, "Oral History Interview with Judge William Wayne Justice," Fifth Circuit Court of Appeals Library, New Orleans, LA (2002), p. 55.

A lot of times, we discuss the case at length before oral argument. After argument, again it depends on the law clerk. At first, when I came on the court I was writing a lot more myself individually. I had more time. Then pressure came on and I depended more on the law clerks for first drafts. There was a time when I would say you write a draft and I will write a draft to the law clerk. After awhile I felt that was a waste of time. Also I felt that you can't mesh two kinds of writing very well. I either adopted his or hers or else I took it over. I felt that was a waste of time and also not very good opinion writing. It depends on the law clerks. There are sometimes that a law clerk will write a draft that I will approve. There were times when many of my law clerks were much better writers than I am. I certainly don't think that I am abdicating my role as a judge.[286]

Abner Mikva (C.A.D.C. 1979–94) squarely takes on the issue of clerks writing opinions.

I think that is one of the great silly arguments that go on in the discussion of appellate jurisprudence, the notion that the judge must be responsible for initially writing every word of the opinion. In the first place, if the judge insists on writing the first draft all the time, in many ways it is the easiest way to lose control of the opinion. If you've written the first draft and it's gone through eight or nine or ten drafts, and the clerks are constantly giving *this* suggestion and that suggestion—by the time it reaches its final stage, the judge is so tired of it and has so lost his or her perspective, that control frequently is lost.

I always found that I didn't care who did the first draft. Some of the time I had the clerks do the first draft. Sometimes I'd write the first draft. But I wanted to make sure that I still felt enthusiastic about the opinion and fresh enough by the time it got to the final draft. That's where my work counted. There were never questions, when push came to shove, about whose opinion it was. There were occasions when I would have to tease a clerk, saying, "You remember, the commission runs to me; it doesn't say 'or his clerks.'" The judge should be able to feel that strongly about an opinion and

---

[286] Luther Merritt Swygert, "The Oral History of Judge Luther M. Swygert," Circuit Library, U.S. Court of Appeals for the Seventh Circuit (1985), p. 83.

what's in it at the end of the day and not feel so bored and jaded about it that he's not in control.[287]

Mikva always reserves the opening of an opinion for himself, he tells us. For him, clerks, coming right out of school, simply did not have the skills to write a good opening. The writing they learned in law school, Mikva notes, narrows their ability.

There is such a premium on a word meaning a single thing, on using the word precisely or exactly, that it squeezes all the juice out of writing style. The result is that legal writing is very dull. When I got to legal opinion writing and legal opinions later on, I used to insist that no matter how many different variations and [permutations] a draft went through between the clerks, I would write the peroration, and I insisted that people who came out of those good law schools couldn't possibly know how to write a good opening to an opinion.[288]

Wilbur Pell (C.A.7 1970–2000) for his part recognized the dangers inherent in the dynamic of law clerks writing opinions. For him it goes to the heart of the decision-making process.

I think they are going to be too influential on the judge. I think the judge will more and more let them make suggestions on how the cases should be decided. I never discussed cases in advance of sitting on them. I read the briefs. I had the clerks do a lot of drafting work on opinions, but when I voted I voted my own convictions after reading the briefs. I read all the briefs in advance of argument and then voted on them. I then went back and told the clerks what cases had been assigned to me and how they were to be written. I think I wrote all of my dissents from scratch. In fact, I dissented quite a few times. I never felt that I was having any problem with a clerk not being able to write or do research and come up with an opinion supporting the position I had taken.[289]

---

[287] Abner J. Mikva, "Honorable Abner J. Mikva Oral History," Historical Society of the District of Columbia (1996, 1999), pp. 222–223.

[288] *Ibid.* at 68.

[289] Wilbur Frank Pell Jr, "The Oral History of Judge Wilbur F. Pell, Jr.," Circuit Library, U.S. Court of Appeals for the Seventh Circuit (1998), p. 51.

Procter Hug (C.A.9 1977–present) explains his procedure following the post-argument conference.

I draft, from that conference, kind of an outline of what I want to do and usually the clerk does the first draft and then I work from that. Sometimes I can use it and sometimes I can't. And sometimes I use quite a bit of it and sometimes I use just a little bit of it and write a lot of it myself. On the difficult cases, I find myself writing several, quite a few drafts. I work in longhand and also dictation. Sometimes I'll write out an outline of those things I want to say and then dictate it. And then from that draft—that will be a rough draft that will have to come back to me first—and then I'll smooth that out and rearrange it and so forth. I'm sure that I probably will be like those who have gone to the computer, but I find the dictating works pretty well for me if I outline my thoughts and dictate it, and then I get a draft back and they can type faster than I can.[290]

Otto Skopil (D. Or. 1972–79 and C.A.9 1979–present) gives some historical perspective on the law clerk's role.

The importance of a law clerk has increased so tremendously in the last thirty years that it is almost unbelievable. When I first went on the circuit court, and that was in 1979, I prepared all of the original drafts of the opinion, every one of them. As the workload increased I couldn't do that anymore. So the law clerks prepared the initial draft and I worked off of it. I modified the initial draft to have it fit what my thinking and what my writing style are. The big principle is writing style. That's the big educational part as far as the law clerk is concerned. So their importance has just increased tremendously. I don't see any other solution unless you just keep appointing more judges.

See, when I went on the court we never heard any more than four cases a month, principally arguments all in one week. Generally, we were supposed to sit only ten months out of the year. I can't remember ever taking any time off vacation-wise while I was an active judge. So you can see over a period of what, four cases a month, that wasn't too many. That was only forty cases. Now they take no less, well it will average thirty-five cases a month. And you see? I think they

[290] Procter Ralph Hug Jr., "Oral History Interview with Hon. Procter Hug, Jr.," Ninth Judicial Circuit Historical Society (1995), p. 161.

probably sit the same way we did before. Maybe they can't, because there's certain times I just think that a judge gets behind and it's not fair to him or her to go on without getting caught up. But now they're involved in about, this is almost unbelievable, between 350 and 400 cases a year, each judge. Now, that's not just the argument cases. That's what we call "the screening calendar." They may hear a hundred cases in a week. Now, most of those are very simple cases, and maybe do not demand the time that—but it's so very hard to go ahead and find that out until you've gone through everything.[291]

Malcolm Marsh (D. Or. 1987–present) explains that what he knows about the important issue of salmon fisheries and the opinions they spawned, he learned from his clerk. In a world in which clerkships last for one or perhaps two years, Marsh had his salmon expert at his side for fourteen years.

I had this one clerk, Kelly Zusman, who was with me for fourteen years. She was my clerk on all the salmon cases. And she really, I think of all the human beings walking the earth, she probably knows more about that issue than anybody because she really dove into it and made great big charts for me, and we would sit down and she would go through these kind of comical charts, and kind of walk me through the different things that I would have to be dealing with just to get it organized. It was such a massive issue with so many internal issues. So I learned in doing that, that I would sit down in any case and start just discussing and see where they were.

More generally, on the opinions from his chambers and the work of his law clerks, Marsh says,

I work very closely with my clerks and I think they're very important to judges. I would hate to see any tinkering with the clerk system because there's just too much volume for one person to keep track of. One time, I said, "Well why don't you give me an opinion this way and this way and this way?" Three different opinions. And so they went off and they wrote three different drafts and came back, and I looked at them. In the meantime, I'd been thinking about it and working on it myself so that I could pick one or the other. But my order to

---

[291] Otto Richard Skopil, "Oral History Interview with Judge Otto Skopil," U.S. District Court Collection, Oregon Historical Society (2006), pp. 39–40.

them is you read the briefs carefully and you check all the citations in the briefs and then you do your own independent research. In other words, you don't just stop with what they give you. You go in then like a new advocate and decide what really is the law here. And I find that's very productive. And of course they all rejoice when they find some miscitation or something and can bounce that back.

Anyway, I work very closely with my clerks, and I think they're very important to judges. I would hate to see any tinkering with the clerk system because there's just too much volume for one person to keep track of.[292]

Milton Schwartz (E.D. Cal. 1979–2005) had thought about the very idea of putting his name to an opinion written by someone else.

I thought it was going to be very difficult to sign things that would go out for publication that somebody else had written that didn't sound like me. And I thought, "How do I correct or change writing that a law clerk does without saying 'I don't know why I'm telling you this, but this is just me,' or 'This is the way I like to say it, or like it to be phrased,' or whatever, and 'I'm not really criticizing your work, it's just probably styling. And you can't really learn what's in my mind as style.'"

And then I realized that over the years I had acquired four or five law clerks who were real stars. There are some very good ones. All certainly entirely acceptable and good, but certainly there are a very few, in my opinion, real stars. And I had several of those and they wrote just quite the opposite style, if there is such a thing, as any of the other stars, and yet they all wrote beautifully. And so, I decided that it's not stylistic. What I'm looking for is clarity and brevity, and I'm looking for something that flows well, and easily. And I can live with all kinds of styles if it's good writing. And that made me feel better, that I didn't have an idiosyncratic style that somebody had to try to copy. And when I realized those kinds of things it was easier. But then I had the reverse thing. I used to reach a point where I'd say, "Write something that I can change, and correct, because otherwise you're going to feel that I am a lazy lout who rubber stamps everything so I can go out and play tennis."

---

[292] Malcolm Francis Marsh, "Oral History Interview with Malcolm Marsh," U.S. District Court Collection, Oregon Historical Society (2005), pp. 109–110.

And there were times, a number of times, when several of my law clerks wrote more like me than I do, and I not only could not improve it any, but if I changed it, it wouldn't be as good. And I had to keep explaining to them that I had read it all.[293]

William Gray (C.D. Cal. 1966–92) explains that he is more of a reader than a writer.

I use my law clerks—they spend a lot of time preparing memoranda of motions, summary judgments, injunctions, and all that sort of thing, and at the end of the day they have prepared a memorandum in a three-hole binder. And at the end of the week, I will take the binders, and I will take the files themselves, but I will read the memoranda that the law clerks have made. They will show the contentions of the motion—what the parties are contending—and then, they will also set out the opposing memoranda. And sometimes they will summarize some of the major cases.[294]

Mary Lou Robinson (N.D. Tex. 1979–present), who had been a court of appeals judge in the Texas system, employes a process built on candor.

Well, of course obviously the law clerks do intensive briefing for me, write memos, or even write draft opinions and bring them to me. I will read the significant cases. I will talk to them about it. I may talk to them about a proposed draft and see if they have a different reaction. Law clerks are really the only people that judges can try ideas out on and can see if their thought processes are going along the right track. And so I am very receptive to their comments; nobody has to be careful what they say to the judge. And I had a law clerk who was in the court of appeals with me; he came to visit here the other day. I remember something he said to me one time. He says, you know, he says you can say anything in the world you want to you; it just doesn't make a damn. But that's not true. I do listen, but I make the decision.[295]

---

[293] Milton L. Schwartz, "Hon. Milton L. Schwartz Oral History," Historical Society for the United States District Court for Eastern District of California (n.d.), p. 73.

[294] William Percival Gray, "Oral History Interview with Hon. William P. Gray," Ninth Judicial Circuit Historical Society (1994), pp. 19–20.

[295] Mary Lou Robinson, "The Oral History of Judge Mary Lou Robinson," Library, U.S. Court of Appeals for the Fifth Circuit (2006), p. 58.

Style

Alfred Goodwin (D. Or. 1969–71 and C.A.9 1971–present) had extensive writing experience before going onto the bench—he had been a journalist—which influenced his style.

> I've always been grateful for my journalistic experience because I think it did help me. I always said the two most valuable courses I took in high school were Latin and typing, and I think that carried on through. Because I could type I worked as a newspaper reporter and learned how to boil facts down and put them in a sentence. Writing wasn't the agonizing work for me that I think it is for some judges. So to that extent it was a useful background.[296]

Andrew Hauk (C.D. Cal. 1966–2004) wanted his opinions vigorous, active, and, invoking a version of the parsimony rule—no longer than they needed to be. He points proudly to the training that made him the writer he became.

> I learned to write when I was at Catholic U and Yale, and when I worked at the Library of Congress. Vladamir Gsovski, who was head of the foreign language department of the Library of Congress, I worked under him. He was a Russian émigré. And he's the one that taught me how to write. I have a great feeling that thoughts should be connected. For instance, you can say first, second, third, fourth, or you can say moreover, in addition. I'm a great believer in writing so it can be understood and saying what you mean and meaning what you say. I always say that. I mean what I say and I say what I mean. And if you do that you can't go far wrong, and if you're at all articulate that's no problem. So they just have to mean what I say and say what I mean and be articulate so people can read them and understand them. Not too long. Just long enough to cover.[297]

Other judges consider excessive length to be the principal enemy of a good opinion. In surveying the landscape of opinion writing, Wilbur Pell

---

[296] Alfred T. Goodwin, "Oral History Interview with Alfred T. Goodwin," U.S. District Court Collection, Oregon Historical Society (1986), pp. 269–270.

[297] A. Andrew Hauk, "Oral History Interview with Hon. A. Andrew Hauk," Ninth Judicial Circuit Historical Society (1990), pp. 76–77.

(C.A.7 1970–2000) of the Seventh Circuit notes,

> Many of our opinions are too long. I think they are repetitious and they treat it as though the subject had never been discussed before and point by point by point. There surely is so little difference that you do not have to dwell on it. This is substantially the same case as so and so. I think there is a reluctance to do it, and I think it is up to the judge to take the time to do it. If you are willing, as I had been in recent years anyway, to accept the writing of the law clerk and work from that, and I blame myself for that, then I should do the thing that I am saying should be done. After they have written it, point out that this issue is disposed of by these cases and just say that without analyzing or repeating what those cases hold.[298]

For Abner Mikva (C.A.D.C. 1979–94), if the nature of the opinion is understood properly, the opinion runs little risk of being excessively long. Opinions narrowing their issues, ideally to one issue, are both shorter and more useful for pedagogical purposes. Mikva says that

> [the opinion] should as much as possible be limited to a single issue. It should recite enough facts to make it understandable and make the issue that you're deciding applicable for future cases; but, on the other hand, it should not recite so many facts that it makes the opinion intolerably long and, more important, so many facts that it makes it too easy to distinguish as a future precedent. A good precedent is one that can apply to a lot of cases. If you put too many facts in there that future advocates can distinguish it by saying, that was a blue card, this is a yellow card, as a precedent it's not as useful. It should be short.
>
> I think nothing has done more to harm appellate jurisprudence and law school teaching than the length of opinions. The reason why the Holmes opinion is still such a great teaching tool is that it is one issue, and it is short, and law school teachers can put the whole opinion in their casebooks; they can assign it as an assignment, and the issue can be discussed and exemplified.
>
> Those are the kinds of things that Langdell had in mind when he first started advocating using opinions as a means of teaching law rather than teaching by the black letter rules. But when you start

---

[298] Wilbur Frank Pell Jr., "The Oral History of Judge Wilbur F. Pell, Jr.," Circuit Library, U.S. Court of Appeals for the Seventh Circuit (1998), p. 64.

out with today's opinions, which sometimes have their own indices they are so long, by the time a law school textbook writer is through cutting it up, you might as well go back to a black letter rule as a way of teaching. So, therefore, legal opinions are just nowhere near as useful as teaching tools as they were during the Holmesian era. But, secondly, they are not as useful in settling the law, in establishing a precedent. If there are ten issues, who knows what issue is really the *ratio decidendi* of the case.[299]

Dorothy Nelson (C.A.9 1979–present) thinks that by necessity opinions should be shorter.

I think we have a responsibility as judges to administer our chambers so that cases don't become that old, and I am very happy to say that in recent years our court has really basically caught up to date. I do think it is a responsibility to the litigants; and if we have to make our opinions shorter to keep up to date, then I think we have to make our opinions shorter. If we are able to tell the litigants what we are ruling and why we are ruling, that's the first thing we should do. And then if we want to embellish our opinions and make them learned, so to speak, I think that's fine. I don't think we have the luxury of writing the opinions of a Learned Hand, of a Cardozo, of a Frankfurter, except in the most unusual case. Not that we have the ability to write those opinions, mind you, but what I'm talking about is the extra time it takes to try to make your opinions a little bit more literate, so to speak.[300]

The fullest complaint against excessive length comes from Ruggero Aldisert (C.A.3 1968–present). He testily notes,

You will have opinions written that will occupy twenty pages in the *Federal Reporter*, with citation after citation after citation, with incomprehensible sections. I think that the serious problem in the federal courts of appeal today is that too many opinions are being written by law clerks, too many law clerks fresh from law reviews, where the art of writing a law review article or editing

---

[299] Abner J. Mikva, "Honorable Abner J. Mikva Oral History," Historical Society of the District of Columbia (1996, 1999), pp. 210–212.
[300] Dorothy Wright Nelson, "Oral History Interview with Hon. Dorothy W. Nelson," Ninth Judicial Circuit Historical Society (1988), p. 60.

a law review article is light years away from writing an opinion or editing an opinion. The law review is a very tentative instrument, very tentative, because the writer is not confident, is not sure, so it's sprinkled with a lot of citations and a lot of footnotes.

The purpose of a judicial opinion is not to be tentative, but to give direction to the litigants and indirectly to those people who are similarly situated. And an opinion should be expressed in language that the layman can understand. When you get esoteric, pseudo-intellectual, you've missed the whole point of why we have published opinions.

If I may, I would criticize many of the opinions of the U.S. courts of appeals because the writers are following the format of the United States Supreme Court. And we've had too many statements, which are probably true, from justices of the Supreme Court admitting that they are not writing the opinions but that law clerks are writing the opinions. And again, we see that tentativeness. We're seeing essays coming out of the Supreme Court. We are seeing a multitude of concurring and dissenting opinions that are absolutely not necessary. They do not help the lawyer in that law office giving advice to the client.[301]

For some, though, footnotes are the great enemy. Myron Gordon (E.D. Wis. 1967–present) pithily notes that "footnotes are for the birds in legal opinions."[302]

It is Abner Mikva (C.A.D.C. 1979–94), though, who most decries footnotes. For him, using footnotes is related to loose opinions.

I resent the criticism that is made that law clerks seem too influential in the judicial process. I think the influence they have is a needed and useful influence, except when they are allowed to ramble on all the issues that are covered in the opinion. That's one of my objections to the use of footnotes. One of the ways we end up in all of these unnecessary pastures is that footnotes frequently project issues into the case that don't have to be there. What happens when

---

301 Ruggero John Aldisert, "Judicial Interview of Judge Ruggero J. Aldisert," Historical Society of the United States Court of Appeals for the Third Circuit (1998), pp. 55–56.
302 Myron L. Gordon, "The Oral History of Judge Myron L. Gordon," Circuit Library, U.S. Court of Appeals for the Seventh Circuit (1999), p. 67.

the opinion has been crafted and there's an argument going on within the judge or between the judge and the clerks as to whether or not *this* issue needs to be covered or not, it's too easy to say, "Well, let's put it in the footnote." That's how footnote four in *Carolene Products* got in and ended up creating a whole piece of jurisprudence about disparate impact; that issue shouldn't have been decided in that case and probably, not probably, definitely, shouldn't have been decided in a footnote.

So I used to resist footnotes on the theory that it was a way of keeping the opinions shorter and cleaner. And I used to talk to my law clerks about it because they're so used to footnotes. [Writing without footnotes] forced me, and my clerks, to consider whether we were off on some kind of a tangent or whether this was really essential to deciding this case. If it was essential to deciding *this* case, then it should go in the text. And, when it was one of those borderline forays, I cut them out completely.[303]

Effect of Writing

Those who do write their opinions subject themselves to the transformative effects of writing, as detailed by a few of the judges. Mary Lou Robinson (N.D. Tex. 1979–present), for example, notes that an opinion is geared to the audience, but it has another function, too.

> It does something for the writer, because if it didn't sound right when it's written down, you need to go back and look at it again. So the writing of opinions is an intellectual discipline for the judge who's actually writing it. And sometimes—I can remember one very significant case, and I probably shouldn't say what it is, but we completely wrote the opinion and when we got through, I said, you know, that doesn't fly. And we went back and actually reached a different result. So it is an intellectual discipline. There are many aspects to the effect of it. It's a good idea to put things on paper.[304]

---

[303] Abner J. Mikva, "Honorable Abner J. Mikva Oral History," Historical Society of the District of Columbia (1996, 1999), pp. 221–222.

[304] Mary Lou Robinson, "The Oral History of Judge Mary Lou Robinson," Circuit Library, U.S. Court of Appeals for the Fifth Circuit (2006), pp. 48–49.

Luther Swygert (N.D. Ind. 1943–61 and C.A.7 1961–88) addresses the matter well:

> Generally speaking you have an outline in your mind. I think the briefs help. In fact, to write an opinion you have to refer a lot to the briefs and the issues and development. Many times, with a good argument and a good brief, you don't feel that there is too much need for outside research in the first place. I have never had much time for outside research. My law clerks at times go and do independent research, of course. One thing, of course, that happens, and I know it has happened to me and I am sure has happened to a lot of other appeals judges, is that once you start to write and get into it you change your mind. I think that for the possibility of the writer of the opinion to change his mind, the ratio is high. Much higher than the other two people if they are in agreement. They tend not to get into the depth as the writer of the opinion does.[305]

Reversed

The oral histories provide the first accounts of how judges react to being reversed. The accounts here are, of course, from district judges but also from court of appeals judges remembering their time as district judges. The reactions range broadly from indifference to resentment.

District judge Prentice Marshall (N.D. Ill. 1973–96) was, he says, indifferent to being reversed, and then, in an interesting aside, observes that he was troubled by judges who were not and who devised strategies to avoid reversal.[306]

Paul Rosenblatt (D. Ariz. 1984–present) takes the philosophical approach:

> As a trial judge, you do your best and then you forget about it and let the court of appeals worry about it. Sometimes they reverse you and sometimes they don't, and sometimes they reverse you for the

---

[305] Luther Merritt Swygert, "The Oral History of Judge Luther M. Swygert," Circuit Library, U.S. Court of Appeals for the Seventh Circuit (1985), p. 82.
[306] Prentice H. Marshall, "The Oral History of Retired Judge Prentice H. Marshall," Circuit Library, U.S. Court of Appeals for the Seventh Circuit (1999), p. 97.

wrong reasons. The only way you can survive is to just make your call and let the system work the way it's supposed to work.[307]

Otto Skopil (D. Or. 1972–79 and C.A.9 1979–present), a court of appeals judge who has also served as a district judge, says that being reversed never bothered him at all.

It didn't make any difference to me. I figured, I'm going to do the best job that I can possibly do and I'm going to apply the law as I think the law should be applied. If that's wrong, they have the responsibility of telling me that it's wrong. So I couldn't tell you how many times I've been reversed. The only one that I do remember is when I did come back and try a case after I went on the circuit court and got reversed by Ted Goodwin, my very good friend. But that's the only case that I could tell you I was reversed on. I don't think I got reversed a lot of times, but I couldn't tell you how many. I know that bothered some people. That didn't really bother me.[308]

Some judges say they did not mind being reversed, but they qualify their responses to leave a bit of doubt. Bruce Thompson (D. Nev. 1963–92) says,

I have never been offended by any of their decisions in cases which were appealed from my court that were either reversed or modified. Most of the time I thought that their decision was probably correct. In some instances, I thought the misdirection of their appellate review was the result of a misunderstanding of the situation that confronted the trial court. I think they are too inclined to ignore the practicalities of the situations that arise resulting from historical mistakes which are not easily correctable and to seek a theoretically sound solution which does little to solve the problem presented. I think that attitude among the judges is more a current attitude than it was in the early 1960s when I first became familiar with the court and how it operated.[309]

Paul G. Rosenblatt, "Oral History Interview with Judge Paul G. Rosenblatt," Ninth Judicial Circuit Historical Society (1998), p. 87.

Otto Richard Skopil, "Oral History Interview with Judge Otto Skopil," U.S. District Court Collection, Oregon Historical Society (2006), p. 18.

Bruce Rutherford Thompson, "Oral History Interview with Hon. Bruce R. Thompson," Ninth Judicial Circuit Historical Society (1988), pp. 96–97.

Andrew Hauk (C.D. Cal. 1966–2004) qualifies his feelings about being reversed to the extent of implying that, if he had tried harder, the result would have been different. He says he did not mind being reversed,

> because on most every occasion I have been reversed I deserved it. It was a fast decision I had to make on the spur of the moment when you're in trial don't have time for big research, or the law clerks didn't do a good job in research, or I didn't do a good job. And I think most of the time if I didn't deserve it, at least it was arguable.[310]

Those who did mind being reversed generally remained defiant. Gene Brooks (S.D. Ind. 1979–96), who had been an athlete, says that he was "very, very competitive in sports" and that he resented being reversed.[311]

Luther Swygert (N.D. Ind. 1943–61 and C.A.7 1961–88) says, "I never felt good about it and I still don't."[312]

Fred Taylor (D. Id. 1954–88) boasts that his record was pretty good on the court of appeals but that he was like an older colleague who said one time at a conference, "I don't care what the court of appeals says, I'm still right."[313]

In the opinion of William Gray (C.D. Cal. 1966–92),

> Nobody likes to be reversed. Sometimes I recognized that I was wrong, but usually I concluded it was the court of appeals that was wrong. But on the other hand, my attitude is this: I want to make my decision as best I can. And I want it to be right, because it's expensive to have to reverse a case and go through all the appellate process, so I want to be right as best I can. And then, if the court of appeals has a different view, well, that's their prerogative.[314]

---

310 A. Andrew Hauk, "Oral History Interview with Hon. A. Andrew Hauk," Ninth Judicial Circuit Historical Society (1990), pp. 41–42.

311 Gene E. Brooks, "The Oral History of Retired Judge Gene E. Brooks," Circuit Library, U.S. Court of Appeals for the Seventh Circuit (1994), p. 52.

312 Luther Merritt Swygert, "The Oral History of Judge Luther M. Swygert," Circuit Library, U.S. Court of Appeals for the Seventh Circuit (1985), p. 149.

313 Frederick Monroe Taylor, "Oral History Interview with Hon. Frederick Monroe Taylor," Ninth Circuit Library, Boise, Idaho (1987), p. 36

314 William Percival Gray, "Oral History Interview with Hon. William P. Gray," Ninth Judicial Circuit Historical Society (1994), p. 27.

Raul Ramirez (E.D. Cal. 1979–89) expresses his own version of defiance. He did not mind being reversed, he says,

> not as long as they told me why. The only time I got reversed—I didn't get reversed that often—the only time I got reversed and I was very sensitive about it was on a case—and I don't even remember the case or what it was about. I thought it was a commercial transaction. Nah, it wasn't that. It was some kind of a statutory problem and I read that opinion at least four times and I finally threw it in the trash. I just couldn't understand it. I swear I couldn't understand what they were trying to say. It was that complex and difficult and confusing. That kind of bothered me. But otherwise no. It didn't happen that often.
>
> I imagine I had a pretty good nonreversal rate. And we keep track of them. Not that you count. But you know, they send you all of these figures at the end of every quarter, year or whatever. I think Judge Schwartz had the best, but you know, if you don't get reversed that means you're doing something wrong. You know, my attitude is that gets into politics with liberal or conservative views. A couple of times I got reversed, I asked for it because there was no law and I wanted to know. I wanted to know why. I wanted an answer from the Ninth Circuit or from the Supreme Court.[315]

Malcolm Marsh (D. Or. 1987–present) once took an "I told you so" position and does not mind being reversed,

> if I thought they were wrong. But no, as I said, I really feel that the right of review of the appellate court and the Supreme Court is a very important element within our system and I'm not infallible. I think that there were times, and in fact it would take us too long, but I could take you through a case where they reversed me on something and only about two cases later said, whoops, we were wrong, and kind of backed off from what they had said. And so you get vindicated sometimes [laughs].[316]

---

[315] Raul Ramirez, "Oral History Interview with Hon. Raul Ramirez," Ninth Judicial Circuit Historical Society (1990), p. 41.
[316] Malcolm Francis Marsh, "Oral History Interview with Malcolm Marsh," U.S. District Court Collection, Oregon Historical Society (2005), p. 100.

Aubrey Robinson (D.D.C. 1966–2000), gives some insight into the way his colleagues reacted to being reversed as part of his own response. He suspects that some of his colleagues resented being reversed, he says,

> by the way they react to reversal. Some of them go apoplectic when they're reversed. I never felt that that was necessary. I tried to learn from every reversal that I got and see what the mistake was and try not to repeat it. They have the right to, an obligation to, review the cases. There have been times when they reviewed my work and the case has gone on to the Supreme Court and the Supreme Court has sustained my position. That's happened I think twice during my tenure. That, of course, is very satisfying.[317]

Oliver Gasch (D.D.C. 1965–99) summed up the dominant position this way.

> We don't look with favor upon a reversal. Judge Thomas Goldsborough's famous comment when Joe Weiss, his law clerk, told him that he had been reversed by the court of appeals, was, "I still think I was right." It's rare that a trial judge likes to be reversed. Sometimes you recognize that you should be reversed, and that, of course, makes it a little easier. But, generally speaking, the trial judge thinks he's right, and he's sore as hell when he's reversed and wants to see something done about it. Well, ordinarily there's not much you can do about it.[318]

At least one judge just won't take no for an answer. Stanley Harris (D.D.C. 1983–2001) astoundingly declares in his oral history that there have been times that the court of appeals was wrong in reversing him and that he felt compelled to write an even stronger opinion when the case returned to him explaining why the appellate court was wrong. It does not seem to bother Harris at all that the court of appeals serves a different function from the trial court. Nor is he concerned that the law is absolutely clear that the lower courts are to follow the appellate courts.

To Harris, his belief "in the need for the law to be sound as an institution" allows him to defy the appellate court. What matters for him is whether the district judge is acting in good faith. He says, "If a trial judge

---

[317] Aubrey E. Robinson Jr., "Honorable Aubrey E. Robinson, Jr. Oral History," Historical Society of the District of Columbia (1992), p. 68.

[318] Oliver Gasch, "Honorable Oliver Gasch," Historical Society of the District of Columbia (1991, 1992), pp. 70–71.

is asked to do things or directed to do things which he believes in good faith to be the result of an error by the court of appeals, then the trial judge must challenge the court, lest a faulty opinion stands in the reporter system forever . . . and becomes established law."

He does acknowledge that he has "earned a little enmity from some of the judges on that court for having the presumptiveness to challenge the validity of their thinking."[319]

As Stanley Harris's comments indicate, there can be a charged dynamic between the trial judge and the appellate court. Joyce Hens Green (D.D.C. 1979–present) explores this dynamic from the personal side.

> While several of the appellate judges are friends, I never, ever, discuss cases; I just won't discuss a case with them which they may review some day, or on a case which they have concluded. It makes our conversation a little sterile, but friendships can endure this way. I firmly believe that, but it is disconcerting to read an appellate opinion which says "X" was not in the record, or the district judge must have overlooked this sentence, when, in fact, the district judge did examine the record, did not overlook a sentence, and this is patently obvious when the district judge's opinion is read. It makes a district judge wonder if her opinion is read in the appellate court. There is no way we can defend ourselves by saying not so, not so, appellate judge. The circuit's opinion has issued, been sent out for publication, and distributed. It's over. All you can do is gnash your teeth and say, well, better day tomorrow. The district judges certainly talk about such things among themselves, as we know that what I've described is not a rare occurrence. But I think in most instances appellate judges do try to get the record straight.

But then, moving on to her own experiences sitting by designation on the court of appeals, Green pulls the curtain back and lets us in.

> I have sat on courts of appeal, by invitation, numerous times (both on the local D.C. Court of Appeals and the U.S. Court of Appeals for the D.C. Circuit). Later, in conscience, I chose not to sit again on the appellate court. There are a couple of reasons [for this]. One is I was asked to sit on the cases of my fellow district judges, and I

---

[319] Stanley S. Harris, "Honorable Stanley S. Harris," Historical Society of the District of Columbia (2002), pp. 169–170.

found that difficult. If I could have affirmed them all at the time, not so difficult. But I found it very difficult to sit on cases of people I know so well, and am so very fond of, but I knew so much about them that really, it became to me a conflict. Were I to review agency cases or something neutral, no problem.

That was one concern. She moves to her second reason and makes a startling revelation.

The other concern was with some panels'—certainly only some, not all—casualness, even mockery, with which they view the district judges' labors. We are asked to write opinions, we are asked to provide findings of fact in our written opinions, we are asked to set it out so the court of appeals can truly review this.

Astonishingly, some judges on some panels I joined made it strikingly clear, unhesitatingly, right in my presence, that they had never read the opinion of the district judge whose case they reviewed, or, if read, some laughed about style, the judge's family life, as well as the legal conclusion. All they had to know, they said, was whether the district judge granted or denied relief, and what that relief was. They just ran roughshod over the trial judge's opinion. It was clearly a matter a judge had worked on for days or weeks, for months sometimes, and had tried to make as clear as possible.

When I would defend the opinion, one or more circuit judge would cough and claim they don't read those opinions. Even if I agreed with the panel's legal decision, I just could not accept that attitude and the personal criticism of my fellow judges. There were other cases, of course, most, where the panel judges were extraordinary, brilliant, who knew the case intimately, considered each case thoroughly, who earnestly strived to give the fairest understanding of the law to that particular case they were reviewing. And when they revised, they did not cast snide remarks. You had to respect and honor those judges.[320]

---

[320] Joyce Hens Green, "Honorable Joyce Hens Green Oral History," Historical Society of the District of Columbia (1999, 2001), pp. 242–246.

CHAPTER EIGHT

JUDGES ON LAWYERS AND
OTHER JUDGES

Article III judges are in perhaps the best position to assess both lawyers and other judges. After all, they had practiced law before going onto the bench and learned the ways of lawyers and lawyering. On the bench, they saw even more lawyering, only from a different perspective. The same is true with their ability to assess other judges. As lawyers, their own experiences with judges helped them form opinions about good and bad judges and about good and bad traits in judges. On the bench, they form judgments based on their own experiences and on what they learn about other judges when they invariably compare and contrast particular judges with what they know more generally about judges.

Judges on Lawyers

With the emphasis expressed by so many judges to move things along, it is not surprising that the judges find preparation to be the most important quality that a good lawyer possesses.

Raul Ramirez (E.D. Cal. 1979–89) looks for what he thinks every judge looks for from a lawyer: preparation.

> Consider the audience and its level of expertise and recognize that the judge is to be persuaded, not impressed. Got to be prepared. Don't try and fake it. I'm not impressed with string citations. I'm not impressed with case law that you're just flipping off the top of your head for propositions that are true if you read the headnotes, but when you read the substance it isn't there. That doesn't impress me. I'm looking for attorneys who will make it short and to the

point because I don't have the time to play with it, and if it's a unique, one-of-a-kind issue, I'm not going to rule for you right there anyway. I'm going to research the hell out of it. So why try and impress me?

As for oral arguments, he advises,

Be prepared, highlight. Highlight, emphasize. But still at the same time admit the weak point. The best lawyers are the kind that'll come in front of me and say, "Judge, that oral argument, there's a new case that just came down yesterday. I'm sure you probably have it"—that makes the judge feel good—"it does go against our position. But we wanted to bring it to your attention. We felt absolutely bound to do so, but it is distinguishable and here's why." You know, points are just flowing out all over the place where the clown on the other side didn't even find it, let alone bring it to my attention, and tell me it was in his position or somehow will say something because he hasn't even read the case that will just blow him right out of the water in any event. So be prepared. Use a lot of common sense. And if you're going to be a jury trial attorney, don't be arrogant. Fifty percent of my cases were decided on personality of the lawyer.[321]

Bruce Thompson (D. Nev. 1963–92) looks to preparation, knowledge of the law, the ability to organize facts, and good writing skills.

The basic quality of a good lawyer is knowledge of the law and preparation. Those are the two most important things. I don't know that he has to have a memory or intellectual resource like Dean Pound, who reputedly remembered everything he read and recited verbatim, but he has to know enough law to recognize the real issues in the case and to know where to go to find the answer. He has to be willing to spend the time on the case to assemble the basic facts that are going to determine the course of the law suit and to analyze them with respect to the law. A sound knowledge of the English language and written and oral communication are important. I am not persuaded that oratorical ability is very important any more. Any good lawyer has to have a basic understanding of the ethics of the profession and a willingness to comply with them. I think that

---

[321] Raul Ramirez, "Oral History Interview with Hon. Raul Ramirez," Ninth Judicial Circuit Historical Society (1990), p. 8.

is generally true of the bar here in northern Nevada. I think most of them are very good.[322]

Fred Taylor (D. Id. 1954–88) goes farther and believes lawyers with purer motives have the advantage.

I think a good lawyer has got to be open-minded, so to speak; I think he has to approach the law business as a duty, serving the public and his clients, and not try to slicker someone. He should be honest with himself and his clients, and use the best judgment he can and do the best job he can within the law. But I think we have some lawyers that look to the law business strictly as a money maker, and I don't think that's right. I think they have a duty. I can remember when I was in law school, the old dean looked down at us and said—sure, you have to make a living, but you owe a duty to the public. And the more I'm in the business, the more I believe that. We're almost in the same capacity as a minister, because people depend on lawyers, they believe they ought to know the law. But sometimes they're mistaken, and I'm beginning to wonder if any of us know the law.[323]

Aubrey Robinson (D.D.C. 1966–2000) looks to what the lawyers do with people.

A good trial lawyer knows his or her case. They have developed the facts. They marshal the evidence to sustain their theory of the case or their theory of the prosecution or defense of a claim. They know courtroom procedure. Basic courtroom procedure—which is the cart and which is the horse?—which comes first? A good trial lawyer has also the ability to understand people that he has to deal with in the context of a particular case. Then, a good trial lawyer ought to know something about the judge before whom the case is being tried. What are the judge's "no, no's," idiosyncracies, level of patience, if you will. What is the judge's judicial temper in fact in a court-room situation. How does it change? What makes it change? How can you eliminate changes that adversely affect you and obviously your client?

---

[322] Bruce Rutherford Thompson, "Oral History Interview with Hon. Bruce R. Thompson," Ninth Judicial Circuit Historical Society (1988), pp. 87–88.
[323] Frederick Monroe Taylor, "Oral History Interview with Hon. Frederick Monroe Taylor," Ninth Circuit Library, Boise, Idaho (1987), pp. 31–32.

A good trial lawyer knows and has some sense of understanding of what makes jurors tick; especially when they are randomly selected from a very diverse population. How to be clear. How to be direct without being condescending. How to walk that chalk line between establishing a record in the fashion that the trial judge understands so that the applications of the legal principles are made more easily and at the same time, establish a record that the jury understands. The development of the case. What you're really contending. So a good trial lawyer is really a person who understands people and knows how to deal with people in the context of adversarial litigation.[324]

It is not much different for Mary Lou Robinson (N.D. Tex. 1979–present).

Preparation, preparation, preparation. It's the difference between a good lawyer and an excellent lawyer. There are lawyers, of course, that seem to have a natural aptitude for the courtroom. They are just good in the courtroom. They can communicate with the jury well. But that's not enough. It's being totally prepared, not only for the law, but for what those facts are going to be and what may be unfavorable to you.[325]

Andrew Hauk (C.D. Cal. 1966–2004) finds the bar generally woefully unprepared, which makes preparation for him even more pressing.

Preparation, preparation, preparation, and preparation *ad infinitum*. And why do I say that? Because ninety-nine percent, I wouldn't say that, it's a little heavy, ninety percent come in totally unprepared, five more percent come in partially unprepared, and only five percent come in ready and prepared, and they're top-notch lawyers. That's the first thing, fundamental. Secondly, be respectful to the court and to your opposing counsel, because if you don't do that you'll get nowhere.[326]

---

[324] Aubrey E. Robinson, "Honorable Aubrey E. Robinson, Jr. Oral History," Historical Society of the District of Columbia (1992), pp. 77–78.

[325] Mary Lou Robinson, "The Oral History of Judge Mary Lou Robinson," Circuit Library, U.S. Court of Appeals for the Fifth Circuit (2006), pp. 40–41.

[326] A. Andrew Hauk, "Oral History Interview with Hon. A. Andrew Hauk," Ninth Judicial Circuit Historical Society (1990), pp. 100–101.

Paul Rosenblatt (D. Ariz. 1984–present) has also seen ill-prepared lawyers.

> In federal court generally the stakes are usually bigger and the lawyers are usually better and better-prepared, although every now and then you see a lawyer who comes in federal court who you wish hadn't. And a lot of lawyers won't come to federal court because they don't want to have to learn a new set of local rules and they don't like the formality. But the good lawyers love to come there for the same reasons. So usually you have good lawyers and good tough legal issues. It makes a very challenging job of it, and I guess that's why I'm still pulling in the harness rather than thinking of something more relaxing.[327]

Judges, ever in the best seat in the house, become acute critics of the lawyers appearing before them and are, sometimes at least, keen to report on high-quality lawyering.

Harold Ryan (D. Id. 1981–95) does just this and deepens our appreciation of lawyering with his description.

> One guy comes to mind; a guy named Scott Reed in Coeur d'Alene who has come in with some cases which are very tough. He came in with a securities case one time in my court, and had some top-notch Boise law firms up against him, and multi-defendant suits where they'd sued this securities firm. There was Scott from a one-man law office giving me just excellent briefs and doing an excellent job of trying this case. He never seemed to get rattled, and he was going uphill in spades all the time because they were good attorneys on the other side and conceded nothing to him. He came out with a very nice verdict for his client in the end. I love to sit there and see good lawyering like that, that you see going on before you, and I marvel at how bright Scott is, that he can do that with the very limited resources that he was using—just himself, and how he was getting all this written work product out and revising jury instructions and suggested jury instructions and everything as the trial went on. The trial went on for several weeks. I just sat there and marveled at him, at what a good job he was doing.[328]

---

[327] Paul G. Rosenblatt, "Oral History Interview with Judge Paul G. Rosenblatt," Ninth Judicial Circuit Historical Society (1998), p. 99.

[328] Harold L. Ryan, "District Judge Harold Ryan," Ninth Circuit Library, Boise, Idaho (1990), pp. 70–71.

Perhaps because they were themselves lawyers before going onto the bench, judges are rarely fooled and can appreciate the interactions between lawyers in ways that would escape most other observers.

Milton Schwartz (E.D. Cal. 1979–2005) describes the games lawyers play.

> You certainly know it's coming because they don't hide it that well. I mean you can see things right off the bat darting back and forth. They cover them—I hate it when they do this—they'll say "I would like very much to accommodate my opponent. We have a very good relationship, we're working well together, we're getting a lot of discovery that we would ordinarily have to demand and we're getting it." And they tell you what a wonderful—they volunteer this wonderful relationship which is at least half the time an outright lie. They don't even speak to each other if they can avoid it. But that's part of the schtick they use to show the court that they are working very hard in trying to accommodate each other. And I usually feel I can spot it right while—the first time they're in the courtroom and they're saying these lovely, lovely things to each other and about each other. I'd rather have a kind that are out and out ugly. I mean, you know what to expect and you just say "Stop it, you're not going to do that in my courtroom," because it just impacts my time and I get mad, and all that.

Schwartz knows as well why lawyers sometimes turn in shoddy pleadings. He says,

> The reason I get mad at very sloppy pleadings is that they are indicative of something much worse. And that is you're not reading your own pleadings. You are too busy. A busy, busy lawyer who thinks, "Well, it doesn't matter because the judge will find these things and correct them for me. That's what he's paid for." But I'm not getting any money, really, out of this case, and I haven't got time to read. And you know I usually will say it's an insult. The reason I get angry is you expect me to listen to every single thing you say where I think there is any credence and be absolutely fair, and yet you don't give me the same return courtesy of giving me your best product in your pleadings. Because those pleadings help me enormously figure out what your case is. And that's why I get angry. And if you're not going to practice carefully you're going to be in deep trouble the entire

time you're here. You might as well get out of my court because it'll be miserable for you.[329]

Judges on Particular Traits

Oral history interviewers often asked their subjects about the traits that make up a good judge. Sometimes the responses are stock and trite, but on other occasions the responses surprise. For example, Andrew Hauk (C.D. Cal. 1966–2004), on what makes a good judge, says,

> Love God above all things, love your neighbor as yourself. If you do that you can't go very far wrong. Do to others what you would have them do unto you. That's number one. To make a good judge you've got to be a good person, man, good human being. You do that, then you are a good person and you'd make a good judge. But to be more specific I would say that number one is if you want to look good have some good law clerks and secondly enjoy your work. If you don't enjoy it, get the hell off the bench, get out of the profession. You've got to enjoy your work, have fun doing it, or else you can never handle it with that detachment that a judge should have.

He elaborates,

> That's the first thing, you have to enjoy your work. The second thing, when you go out there and you're a judge you've got to be prepared. That's with the help of good law clerks of course on research and you learn all you can know about a case before you go out there and sit on it, the file and the law so far as you have time to know it, which isn't an awful lot sometimes. And then I think be decisive because that's what a judge has to do. A judge has to make decisions and sometimes very difficult decisions, and one side or the other is going to be terribly unhappy, and the other side is going to be terribly elated. And so a district court judge is a judge who can go out there and decide as soon as the case is finished, the facts are all in, and the law looked at. Be ready and make your decision right

---

[329] *Ibid.* at 112–113.

from the bench and don't take things under submission because you haven't got time to do that as a trial judge.[330]

Fred Taylor (D. Id. 1954–88) warmed to the question and had a ready response. "I'll tell you that the qualities of a good judge is a man who has good judgment, works hard, is fair regardless of his personal opinions, and tries to do the best he can and what he figures is the right thing to do. It takes personal character and integrity and all of that."[331]

Joyce Hens Green (D.D.C. 1979–present) provides a surprising answer. For her it is a combination of brains and courage.

> Everyone will say, and rightfully so, that a judge has to have wisdom. It's better yet if a judge has great intellectual powers. It's wonderful if a judge is fair in temperament, in approach, in expression. But a judge must have courage. There are so many situations trial judges, in particular, encounter, where a judge's very life is in peril from those of the public who vehemently disagree with us. Look at the record where judges have been murdered in the courtroom, in the home, or attempts at murder have been made. A judge has to have courage and express the way it is in her opinions, whether oral or written, not to just ride with the waves of the time, economically, politically, emotionally. You have to do what you verily believe as an independent thinker, appointed to exercise judicial independence, but also to follow, if appropriate and if possible, precedent. A judge has to exercise responsibilities in a way and manner that will bring justice. That is our duty. That is our responsibility. That is our privilege and that is our joy if we succeed.[332]

An aggressive, clear thinker if ever there was one, Milton Schwartz (E.D. Cal. 1979–2005) thinks little of the commonly understood meaning of judicial temperament and believes that a judge has to have some scrappiness about him or her.

> There are so many platitudes that have to do with this that bother me. Like, I'm not so sure about Judge So-and-So, who's been named

---

[330] A. Andrew Hauk, "Oral History Interview with Hon. A. Andrew Hauk," Ninth Judicial Circuit Historical Society (1990), pp. 91–92.

[331] Frederick Monroe Taylor, "Oral History Interview with Hon. Frederick Monroe Taylor," Ninth Circuit Library, Boise, Idaho (1987), p. 31.

[332] Joyce Hens Green, "Honorable Joyce Hens Green Oral History," Historical Society of the District of Columbia (1999, 2001), pp. 299–300.

as a judge. I don't think he has the temperament—the judicial temperament. Which translated means nice, deliberative, kind, thoughtful, popular because of the way he behaves. To me most of that means "weak." If you don't generate anything more than that he's a really nice guy and he's honest, and that sort of thing, I think most of that translates out to weakness. And some of the best judges I've known were fierce. Fiercely competitive. And they'd say he doesn't have temperament. He has the temperament for the job he's got now, which is to fight. I just think that is such a weak analysis because for most of the lawyers that fit the category of fine temperament it usually mean weakness or kinds of wimps—wimpish.[333]

Examples of Bad

The judges were not at a loss to provides examples of bad judicial traits and bad judges. How well the judges treated the lawyers was at the center of many observations.

Paul Rosenblatt (D. Ariz. 1984–present) recalls one judge he knew well and notes. "He was a judge whose reputation was of no nonsense, and he was very tough on lawyers, and in particular, on young lawyers. I tried not to be that kind of a judge."[334]

James Moran (N.D. Ill. 1979–present) complains about judicial tyranny. He tells a story about Julius Hoffman (N.D. Ill. 1953–83) from his own days of practice. The story concludes with Moran in the courtroom being verbally abused and lighting on the essential question regarding such judicial behavior.

> We were representing Ralston and Company on a case that was going to [become part of multi-district litigation] in Oklahoma. So we got an extension of thirty days to file an answer or otherwise plead. Well, the MDL panel hadn't ruled yet. I was off in New York taking depositions the day before the answer was due to go in on a motion for another thirty days. Frank Higgins, who was my compatriot, was going to do that but he was sick that day.

---

[333] Milton L. Schwartz, "Hon. Milton L. Schwartz Oral History," Historical Society for the United States District Court for Eastern District of California (n.d.), p. 124.

[334] Paul G. Rosenblatt, "Oral History Interview with Judge Paul G. Rosenblatt," Ninth Judicial Circuit Historical Society (1998), p. 59.

So Carol Childs, who was a young associate, went in and the next thing I heard was Carol hysterically sobbing over the telephone that Julius not only denied the motion for thirty more days, he had entered *sua sponte* a $25 million judgment against Ralston, and I wasn't quite sure whether it was because I was the lawyer or because he thought Carol was a secretary or what.

Anyway, I said, "Carol, I'll get on the next plane. You get a certified copy of the order showing the motion and that the answer wasn't even due until tomorrow. Put together just a general denial and I'll go in tomorrow morning and we'll straighten it out." Well, he had to vacate the judgment, but not before he had spent half an hour ripping me up one side and down the other in front of a crowded courtroom, where the only thing I could say was, "Yes, sir" or "No, sir"—stressful. The only thing I could really think of was, "You arrogant little bastard. What makes you tick? I haven't got the the vaguest idea."[335]

Luther Swygert (N.D. Ind. 1943–61 and C.A.7 1961–88), who had been our guide in understanding the tensions and conflicts in the Seventh Circuit, felt sufficiently comfortable with his oral history interviewers to give them his candid assessments of judges he had known. He etches judicial personalities and, through his assessments, allows us to more forcefully ask questions about why judges act as they sometimes do. Some judges he had practiced before. Others he had served with on either the district or circuit bench. He knew Cale Holder (S.D. Ind. 1954–83) as a fellow judge.

Holder was a different type of person. He was pretty crusty on the bench, but he was a pretty nice person off the bench. Agreeable person, but on the bench he was very sharp with lawyers and in some ways he was sort of unorthodox. He cut corners in the sense that he, well, he wouldn't make findings sometimes when he should and various short cuts that diminished his trials, and I think he was reversed a great deal.[336]

---

[335] James B. Moran, "The Oral History of James B. Moran, Senior District Court Judge of the United States District Court for the Northern District of Illinois," Circuit Library, U.S. Court of Appeals for the Seventh Circuit (1994), p. 99.
[336] *Ibid.* at 331.

Albert Anderson (D. Ind. 1902–25 and C.A.7 1925–38), Swygert continues, "had a good mind. He struck terror in lawyers and was very mean to them, and took very drastic verbal actions, or had verbal bouts, and made derogatory statements to lawyers. He had a very imperial attitude on the bench. I don't know what his attitude off the bench was and whether he was very social. But he generated a number of stories and anecdotes."[337]

About the circuit's former chief judge, Swygert says,

> I had many impressions about Judge [Elmer Schnackenberg (C.A.7 1953–68)]. He had a lot of good qualities, and he had some that were not particularly admirable. On the good side, I think he tried to be fair in his judicial work and in looking at cases, and also fair in his personal relationships. On the other hand he could be quite arbitrary and be quite abrupt and sometimes, I would say, even abrasive. For example, he was pretty stubborn. In any event he had I think good intelligence.[338]
>
> He was a martinet on the bench. For example, he had little cards made up which would show minutes and even seconds, and so he would have those in front of him and you would have forty-five minutes or thirty minutes, and he would keep very strict account of the time, and when the time was up he would say to the lawyers, "Your time is up!" And the lawyer could be right in the middle of a sentence and he wouldn't let him finish a sentence.
>
> And then he had a sort of a sadistic type of practice, I thought. He would, if he was presiding, maybe sometimes if he wasn't, he would say to the lawyer, "Just repeat what you said, just repeat what you said, just what did you say just then?" Of course the lawyer was nervous to start with, and of course he would go blank. He couldn't remember the exact words he said just before. The poor man, the poor lawyer would stumble around. He would say, "Just tell me just exactly what you said," and this would go on. Well I don't know what happened and finally it would drift off. Then he would say, "Where is that in the record?" And of course the lawyer wouldn't know what page, you know, "Well," he would say, "Where is it, what happened to the record where that fact is or where you

---

[337] *Ibid.* at 308.
[338] *Ibid.* at 255.

made that statement, where is it in the record?" And it was some-times very embarrassing. I was very upset sometimes by the way he had handled things like that.[339]

Examples of Good

Swygert had in the 1930s tried cases in the courtroom of Walter Lindley (E.D. Ill. 1922–49 and C.A.7 1949–58) and thought highly of him, prais-ing his incisive mind.

> I tried some cases in front of Lindley, a few. He was a fast, fast worker and intelligent. He was really a very smart person and had a good mind, very incisive. I think that is the most characteris-tic word that I can think of, an incisive type of mind. He was quick and to the point, just like a knife, a sharp knife. And his opinions I think indicate that too. They have a very, very direct kind of approach. He got his opinions out in a hurry, and he made good friends.[340]

He also sat with Robert Sprecher (C.A.7 1971–82) and admired pretty much everything about him.

> He was so quiet and subdued in a way; humble, I guess that's what you would say. But he was a hard worker and he read the briefs and make voluminous notes before he'd hear the arguments. He'd have a whole sheet of fine-written, small letters—he wrote in a small handwriting. And he'd have this whole sheet full of notes that he'd made for preparation of the hearing, but he'd hardly ever ask any questions. He'd be very quiet on the bench. Very quiet, and he wouldn't go after lawyers, like I did, or some of the other judges [laughter]. And he never was abrasive. I never heard him say one word that you would say was abrasive. Humility I would say was his trait; that was my feeling. He didn't have any vanity. He had a certain kind of feeling that he was capable. He didn't feel that he was incapable. But he didn't try to demonstrate it.

---

[339] *Ibid.* at 259.
[340] *Ibid.* at 293.

About Sprecher's opinions, Swygert says, "You never read ten pages and wondered what the case was about. I mean you knew right away, and it was always well written. He had a craftsmanship, there was no question about that. He didn't sparkle, but it was well done. Well structured."[341]

Other judges in the oral histories venture illustrations of good judges. Bruce Thompson (D. Nev. 1963–92) points to Fred Taylor (D. Id. 1954–88) for the way he acted on the bench. "There was a judge who recently died at the age of 88, up in Boise, Idaho, named Fred Taylor, who had an excellent conception of proper judicial decorum and behavior and the handling of trials and lawyers."[342]

Procter Hug (C.A.9 1977–present) thought that Charles Merrill was "pretty much an ideal judge."

> If I were to model myself after one he'd be a very good model. He was extremely fair. He was very polite to counsel. He had a very pleasant manner in presiding over oral argument and a very pleasant manner in presiding at conference with the judges. He was an extremely bright person who thought through things very well but had virtually no prejudices that I could discern. He approached each case openmindedly and reasoned his way through, and then he had this beautiful resonant voice and he just looked like a judge and then with this resonant voice was kind of a commanding appearance, I thought. Actually, I replaced him. He was the Nevada judge that I was appointed to replace. He had been on the Nevada Supreme Court, too. I'd tried cases there in front of him.[343]

Alfred Goodwin (D. Or. 1969–71 and C.A.9 1971–present) has two examples. The first, Otto Skopil (D. Or. 1972–79 and C.A.9 1979–present), gets unreserved praise.

> I always thought Judge Skopil probably was pretty close to a model of temperament. He didn't lose his cool, but he was dignified. He ran an orderly courtroom. He was expeditious in his handling of matters. He dealt with problem attorneys firmly, but he didn't

---

341 *Ibid.* at 306.

342 Bruce Rutherford Thompson, "Oral History Interview with Hon. Bruce R. Thompson," Ninth Judicial Circuit Historical Society (1988), pp. 95–96.

343 Procter Ralph Hug Jr., "Oral History Interview with Hon. Procter Hug, Jr.," Ninth Judicial Circuit Historical Society (1993), pp. 162–163.

terrify anybody. There was no reign of terror or no sense of concern or trembling with fear on the part of young lawyers going before Skopil. It's a matter of style. He's retired now from active service as an appellate judge, but during the years he was a trial judge, I think he enjoyed a very good reputation with the bar as far as temperament is concerned.[344]

With Goodwin's second example, Gus Solomon (D. Or. 1949–87), we come to our conclusion and are properly presented with the tension between demeanor and performance and with the fundamental question of when bad manners should be tolerated. Solomon might have been a product of his martinet times. He could be churlish, but he also could earn high marks for his performance.

Oh, he scared hell out of me when I first appeared before him. But I knew he was conscientious. He was running a good courtroom. He was a no-nonsense judge, and he'd get mad. I mean he'd either get mad or feign anger at ill-prepared, bumbling lawyers. If you were planning to be ill prepared and bumbling, you could expect trouble in Judge Solomon's courtroom. The two or three times I appeared before him I was always well prepared. I spent very little time sleeping a couple of days before an appearance before Judge Solomon. All the young lawyers in the state who were sapient were aware of Judge Solomon's quick gavel and quick putdown, and he didn't suffer fools gladly, and he didn't stand for time wasting. But even as a young lawyer who was conscious of that and apprehensive of it, I still admired him because I knew that his results were good.[345]

---

[344] Alfred T. Goodwin, "Oral History Interview with Alfred T. Goodwin," U.S. District Court Collection, Oregon Historical Society (1986), p. 445.
[345] *Ibid.* at 442–443.

LIST OF QUOTED ORAL HISTORIES

Alarcon, Arthur Lawrence, "Oral History Interview with Judge Arthur L. Alarcon," Ninth Judicial Circuit Historical Society (1991).

Aldisert, Ruggero John, "Judicial Interview of Judge Ruggero J. Aldisert," Historical Society of the United States Court of Appeals for the Third Circuit (1998).

Beatty, William Louis, "The Oral History of William L. Beatty, Senior District Court Judge of the United States District Court for the Southern District of Illinois," Circuit Library, U.S. Court of Appeals for the Seventh Circuit (1999).

Bell, Griffin Boyette, "Diversifying the Federal Judiciary: Interview with Judge Griffin Bell," Federal Judicial Center (1995).

Bork, Robert Heron, "Honorable Robert L. Bork," Historical Society of the District of Columbia (1992).

Brooks, Gene, "The Oral History of Retired Judge Gene E. Brooks," Circuit Library, U.S. Court of Appeals for the Seventh Circuit (1994).

Buckley, James Lane, "Honorable James L. Buckley," Historical Society of the District of Columbia (1995, 1996).

Burns, Ellen Bree, "Diversifying the Federal Judiciary: Interview with Judge Ellen Burns," Federal Judicial Center (1995).

Campbell, William Joseph, "Oral History of the Honorable William J. Campbell," Federal Judiciary History Office, Federal Judicial Center (1982).

Choy, Herbert Young Cho, "Oral History Interview with Hon. Herbert Y.C. Choy," Ninth Judicial Circuit Historical Society (1990).

Crabb, Barbara Brandriff, "Diversifying the Federal Judiciary: Interview with Judge Barbara Crabb," Federal Judicial Center (1995).

Curtis, Jesse William, Jr., "Oral History Interview with Hon. Jesse Curtis," Ninth Judicial Circuit Historical Society (1989).

Dillin, S. Hugh, "The Oral History of Judge S. Hugh Dillin," Circuit Library, U.S. Court of Appeals for the Seventh Circuit (1994).

Dimmick, Carolyn R., "Oral History Interview with Judge Carolyn R. Dimmick," Ninth Judicial Circuit Historical Society (1991).

Fairchild, Thomas E., "The Oral History of Judge Thomas E. Fairchild," Circuit Library, U.S. Court of Appeals for the Seventh Circuit (1999).

Flannery, Thomas Aquinas, "Honorable Thomas A. Flannery Oral History," Historical Society of the District of Columbia (1992).

Foreman, James L., "The Oral History of Judge James L. Foreman," Circuit Library, U.S. Court of Appeals for the Seventh Circuit (1985).

Gasch, Oliver, "Honorable Oliver Gasch," Historical Society of the District of Columbia (1991, 1992).

Gessell, Gerhardt Alden, "Honorable Gerhardt A. Gessell," Historical Society of the District of Columbia (1999, 2001).

Goodwin, Alfred T., "Oral History Interview with Alfred T. Goodwin," U.S. District Court Collection, Oregon Historical Society (1986).

Gordon, Myron, "The Oral History of Judge Myron L. Gordon," Circuit Library, U.S. Court of Appeals for the Seventh Circuit (1999).

Grant, Robert A., "The Oral History of Judge Robert A. Grant," Circuit Library, U.S. Court of Appeals for the Seventh Circuit (1988).

Gray, William Percival, "Oral History Interview with Hon. William P. Gray," Ninth Judicial Circuit Historical Society (1994).

Green, Joyce Hens, "Honorable Joyce Hens Green Oral History," Historical Society of the District of Columbia (1999, 2001).

Green, June L., "Honorable June L. Green Oral History," Historical Society of the District of Columbia (1998, 1999).

Greene, Harold H., "Honorable Harold H. Greene," Historical Society of the District of Columbia (1992).

Hall, Cynthia Holcomb, "Diversifying the Federal Judiciary: Interview with Cynthia H. Hall," United States Court of Appeals for the Ninth Circuit (1995).

Harris, Stanley S., "Honorable Stanley S. Harris," Historical Society of the District of Columbia (2002).

Hauk, A. Andrew, "Oral History Interview with Hon. A. Andrew Hauk," Ninth Judicial Circuit Historical Society (1990).

Higginbotham, Aloyisus Leon Jr., "Interview With The Honorable A. Leon Higginbotham," Historical Society of the United States Court of Appeals for the Third Circuit (n.d.).

Hufstedler, Shirley Ann Mount, "Diversifying the Federal Judiciary: Interview with Judge Shirley A. Hufstedler," Federal Judicial Center (1995).

Hug, Procter Ralph Jr., "Oral History Interview with Hon. Procter Hug, Jr.," Ninth Judicial Circuit Historical Society (1995).

Jones, Robert Edward, "Oral History Interview with Robert F. Jones," U.S. District Court Collection, Oregon Historical Society (2005).

Justice, William Wayne, "Oral History Interview with Judge William Wayne Justice," Fifth Circuit Court of Appeals Library, New Orleans, LA (2002).

Kelleher, Robert Joseph, "Oral History Interview with Judge Robert J. Kelleher," Ninth Judicial Circuit Historical Society (1990).

King, Samuel Pailthorpe, "Oral History Interview with Judge Samuel P. King," Ninth Judicial Circuit Historical Society (1991).

MacKinnon, George Edward, "Honorable George E. MacKinnon Oral History," Historical Society of the District of Columbia (1994).

Marsh, Malcolm Francis, "Oral History Interview with Malcolm Marsh," U.S. District Court Collection, Oregon Historical Society (2005).

Marshall, Prentice H., "The Oral History of Retired Judge Prentice H. Marshall," Circuit Library, U.S. Court of Appeals for the Seventh Circuit (1999).

Merrill, Charles Merton, "Oral History Interview with Judge Charles M. Merrill," Ninth Judicial Circuit Historical Society (1989).

Mikva, Abner, "Honorable Abner J. Mikva Oral History," Historical Society of the District of Columbia (1996, 1999).

Mills, Richard Henry, "The Oral History of Judge Richard H. Mills," Circuit Library, U.S. Court of Appeals for the Seventh Circuit (2000).

Moran, James B., "The Oral History of James B. Moran, Senior District Court Judge of the United States District Court for the Northern District of Illinois," Circuit Library, U.S. Court of Appeals for the Seventh Circuit (1994).

Nielsen, Leland Chris, "Oral History Memoir of Leland C. Nielsen," Ninth Judicial Circuit Historical Society (1998).

Nelson, Dorothy Wright, "Oral History Interview with Hon. Dorothy W. Nelson," Ninth Judicial Circuit Historical Society (1988).

Parsons, James Benton, "The Unfinished Oral History of Judge James B. Parsons," Circuit Library, U.S. Court of Appeals for the Seventh Circuit (1996).

Pell, Wilbur Frank Jr., "The Oral History of Judge Wilbur F. Pell, Jr.," Circuit Library, U.S. Court of Appeals for the Seventh Circuit (1998).

Ramirez, Raul, "Oral History Interview with Hon. Raul Ramirez," Ninth Judicial Circuit Historical Society (1990).

Reinhardt, Stephen Roy, "Oral History Interview with Judge Stephen Reinhardt," Ninth Judicial Circuit Historical Society (1993).

Reynolds, John W., "The Oral History of Judge John W. Reynolds," Circuit Library, U.S. Court of Appeals for the Seventh Circuit (1997).

Robinson, Aubrey, "Honorable Aubrey E. Robinson, Jr. Oral History," Historical Society of the District of Columbia (1992).

Robinson, Mary Lou, "The Oral History of Judge Mary Lou Robinson," Circuit Library, U.S. Court of Appeals for the Fifth Circuit (2006).

Rosenblatt, Paul G., "Oral History Interview with Judge Paul G. Rosenblatt," Ninth Judicial Circuit Historical Society (1998).

Rothstein, Barbara Jacobs, "Diversifying the Federal Judiciary: Interview with Judge Barbara J. Rothstein," Federal Judicial Center (1995).

Ryan, Harold L., "District Judge Harold Ryan," Ninth Circuit Library, Boise, Idaho (1990).

Schwartz, Milton L., "Hon. Milton L. Schwartz Oral History," Historical Society for the United States District Court for Eastern District of California (n.d.).

Schwarzer, William W., "William W. Schwarzer, Litigator, Federal District Judge, Director of the Federal Judicial Center, and Professor, 1952–1997," Northern California U.S. District Court Oral History Series, Regional Oral History Office, The Bancroft Library, University of California, Berkeley (1997).

Seitz, Collins Jacques, "Interview with the Honorable Collins Jacques Seitz," Historical Society of the United States Court of Appeals for the Third Circuit (1993).

Skopil, Otto Richard, "Oral History Interview with Judge Otto Skopil," U.S. District Court Collection, Oregon Historical Society (2006).

Sneed, Joseph T. III, "Oral History Interview with Hon. Joseph T. Sneed III," Ninth Judicial Circuit Historical Society (1994).

Steckler, William Elwood, "The Oral History of Judge William E. Steckler," Circuit Library, U.S. Court of Appeals for the Seventh Circuit (1987).

Swygert, Luther Merritt, "The Oral History of Judge Luther M. Swygert," Circuit Library, U.S. Court of Appeals for the Seventh Circuit (1985).

Tang, Thomas, "Oral History Interview with Hon. Thomas Tang," Ninth Judicial Circuit Historical Society (1998).

Taylor, Frederick Monroe, "Oral History Interview with Hon. Frederick Monroe Taylor," Ninth Circuit Library, Boise, Idaho (1987).

Thompson, Bruce Rutherford, "Oral History Interview with Hon. Bruce R. Thompson," Ninth Judicial Circuit Historical Society (1988).

Waters, Laughlin E., "Oral History Interview with Judge Laughlin E. Waters," Ninth Judicial Circuit Historical Society (1989).

Weigel, Stanley Alexander, "Stanley Weigel, Litigator and Federal Judge," Northern California U.S. District Court Oral History Series, Regional Oral History Office, The Bancroft Library, University of California, Berkeley (1988).

Will, Hubert L., "The Unfinished Oral History of Judge Hubert L. Will," Circuit Library, U.S. Court of Appeals for the Seventh Circuit (2001).

Williams, David W., "Oral History Interview with Hon. David W. Williams," Ninth Judicial Circuit Historical Society (1998).

Williams, Spencer Mortimer, "Law, Politics, and the Judiciary: The Honorable Spencer M. Williams," Northern California U.S. District Court Oral History Series, Regional Oral History Office, The Bancroft Library, University of California, Berkeley (1992, 1998, 2000, 2001).

Wollenberg, Albert Charles, "To Do the Job Well: A Life in Legislative, Judicial, and Community Service: Interviews," Northern California U.S. District Court Oral History Series, Regional Oral History Office, The Bancroft Library, University of California, Berkeley (1997).

Wood, Harlington Jr., "The Oral History of Judge Harlington Wood, Jr.," Circuit Library, U.S. Court of Appeals for the Seventh Circuit (1997).

Wright, Eugene Allen, "Oral History Interview with Judge Eugene A. Wright," Ninth Judicial Circuit Historical Society (1987).

Zirpoli, Alfonso Joseph, "Faith in Justice: Alfonso J. Zirpoli and the United States District Court for the Northern District of California," Northern California U.S. District Court Oral History Series, Regional Oral History Office, The Bancroft Library, University of California, Berkeley (1982–1983).

Zobel, Rya Weickert, "Diversifying the Federal Judiciary: Interview with Judge Rya Zobel," Federal Judicial Center (1995).

INDEX

Gray, William, on, 32
Nelson, Dorothy, on, 35
preparation
 judges and, 211
 lawyers and, 205–208
pretrial conferences, 158–160
procedure of federal courts, 136
Proxmire, William
 Fairchild, Thomas, and, 99

Q
quotas in appointments, 117–118

R
Ramirez, Raul
 appointment, 118
 on being reversed, 200
 college experience, 22–23
 criminal defense work, 62–63
 on qualities of good lawyers, 205–206
reading, amount required, 131–132
Reed, Scott, 209
Reed, Stanley Forman, 48
Reinhardt, Stephen
 appointment, 110
 clerk of Luther Youngdahl, 45
 law practice, 70–72
Reynolds, John
 appointment, 84
 on district judge job, 143–144
 military service, racism during, 24–25
 on USSG, 154
Ribicoff, Abraham, 125–126
Richardson, Elliott, 92
Robinson, Aubrey
 on being reversed, 201
 law practice, 59
 law school, 31
 on making decisions as district judge, 144
 on qualities of good lawyers, 207–208
 transition to the job, 130
Robinson, Mary Lou
 appointment, 85
 early choice of the legal profession, 18
 on isolation, 147
 law practice, 54–55
 on qualities of good lawyers, 208
 on transformative effect of writing an
  opinion, 196

on work of her law clerks, 191
Roosevelt, Franklin, 89–90
Rose, Jonathan, 95–96
Rosenblatt, Paul
 appointment, 120
 on bad judges, 213
 on being reversed, 197–198
 government lawyer, 68
 on ill-prepared lawyers, 209
 on isolation, 147
 law practice, 54
 on range of subjects and issues, 145
 transition to the job, 130
Rothstein, Barbara
 appointment, 125
 on getting a job, 62
Ryan, Harold
 appointment, 114–115
 bar examination, 51
 childhood, 13
 college experience, 23–24
 on getting the job done, 157–158
 on high-quality lawyering, 209
 law practice, 75–81
 transition to the job, 129–130
 on USSG, 155

S
Sacks, Al, 32
Salinger, Pierre, 93–94
Schaefer, Walter, 73
 Fairchild, Thomas, and, 99–100
Schmults, Ed, 96
Schnacke, Bob, 135
Schnackenberg, Elmer, 215–216
school, 16–19
 Catholic, 17
Schwartz, Milton
 appointment, 127–128
 at Boalt Hall School of Law
  (U.C. Berkeley), 36
 isolation, 139–140
 on judges
  qualities of a good judge, 212–213
  weak judges, 166–167, 213
 law practice, 54
 on lawyers in the courtroom, 165–167, 210
  sloppy pleadings, 210–211
 motions, 161–162